Building & Flying
RADIO CONTROLLED MODEL AIRCRAFT

Given that I can't get
you to read 'proper'
books — I thought you
might manage this!
Although how we can
discuss 'airbus' — I
am not sure!

Ray

Building & Flying
RADIO CONTROLLED MODEL AIRCRAFT

David Boddington

Nexus Special Interests

Nexus Special Interests Ltd.
Nexus House
Boundary Way
Hemel Hempstead
Hertfordshire HP2 7ST
England

First published by Argus Books 1978
Second edition 1982
Reprinted 1985, 1986, 1987, 1989, 1990, 1993
Third edition published by Nexus Special Interests Ltd. 1996

ISBN 1-85486-135-2

Phototypesetting by The Studio, Exeter
Printed and bound in Great Britain by Bookcraft (Bath) Limited

Contents

Preface

It is nearly twenty years since I first wrote *Building and Flying Radio Controlled Model Aircraft* and during that time there has been a minor revolution in the design and manufacture of radio control equipment and, to a lesser extent, with the model aircraft. Certainly, with R/C (the common abbreviation of radio control) helicopters, the advances have been dramatic. From a time when to fly a model helicopter was achievement enough, now the models are highly aerobatic to a point where their performance far outstrips the abilities of the full size 'choppers'.

The book has been revised from time to time and reprinted on numerous occasions but it has now been rewritten to bring into it the latest developments of designs, equipment, materials, techniques and operation. The aims of the book remain the same − to assist and inform potential modellers and beginners in the hobby. Some of the text will remain, but will include any R/C model introductions since the first writing and consequent revisions.

As ever, I have to thank many people in helping with the preparation of the book and I hope they will forgive me in not mentioning them all personally. Manufacturers, distributors, retailers and publishers have all been most helpful in supplying information, photographs and line drawings and individuals with advice − sometimes taken. The proprietors of the Hostal Fornells, in Menorca, have been most kind in supplying the ambience and sustenance necessary for writing the text. Lastly, I could never have been able to indulge my hobby over so many years and extended these interests into writing, without the total support of my wife, Jill. To her I give my very special thanks.

CHAPTER 1

Introduction

Before leading you into a hobby world that is fascinating and rewarding and represents, in my opinion, one of the most intriguing and satisfying of hobbies, I should perhaps point out what the book is *not* about.

It is not a book about electronics — the days of the electronic experimenter has all but passed, not completely thankfully, because the experimenter will always add new ideas and introduce items that the mainstream manufacturer, for production and economic reasons, cannot consider. You will not, therefore, find theoretical circuits and wiring diagrams or details of integrated circuits and micro-processors. They will certainly be mentioned and their uses explained, but the discussions will stop there. Design of radio control equipment is now so far advanced that it is difficult for the modeller to contemplate commencing from basics and constructing a complete radio control outfit. For the same reasons, the servicing of today's radio equipment should be left to the experts; the untrained electronics enthusiast is more likely to cause damage to the equipment, than to achieve a repair.

Whether the change from do-it-yourself radio equipment to off-the-shelf completed outfits, which only require installation, is to be regretted or welcomed, depends on your interest in the workings of the radio control equipment and your particular skills in wielding a soldering iron. For those of us without a good grasp of electronics and viewing the wiring of a set of plugs with sheer horror, the days of completely pre-wired, ready to go, R/C outfits couldn't come soon enough. What is indisputable is the fact that the reliability of radio equipment has improved immeasurably over the years. Radio control cars and boats are also specialised subjects in their own rights and have their own publications both magazines and books. Helicopters are not easy to cope with in a book dealing with the general subject of R/C aero-

modelling, but it is an essential part of the hobby — rotary wing model aircraft are certainly here to stay. The chapter on helicopters will deal with the types available, how they operate and the specialist radio systems for them. It will not include how to set them up and how to fly them. This, again, deserves a separate publication.

That is the negative side, but what of the positive aims. Radio control magazines can, from time to time, present articles dealing with the building, radio installations, engine operation, learning to fly and repair and maintenance of models. Articles will be included on the design of models, new types and styles, aerodynamics, safety, floatplanes and all the other diverse aspects of R/C model aircraft. They cannot, however, continuously repeat these articles and there is an obvious requirement for the gathering together of this information and producing it into a digestible and understandable form, hence the book.

There are, in essence, three elements for R/C model flying — the radio equipment, the model and you, the operator. The first two elements I can deal with, hopefully sensibly and logically, but what about the operator. Will you fit the bill? The requirements to become a successful flyer of an R/C aeroplane are not so great, if they were a lot of us wouldn't have made it there already. The main requirement is a reasonable eye/brain/hand co-ordination so that the model can be seen to be in a certain attitude. The brain recognises this and sends signals to the hands and the hands take the necessary action by moving the control sticks. Naturally, that complete reaction time should be as short and accurate as possible; the radio equipment will do its part if you can give it the information. From this description you will realise that your eyesight will have to be reasonable — model aeroplanes have a habit of getting away and looking small very quickly. If your eyesight is not at its best then you will have to be satisfied with

Early radio equipment was bulky, unreliable and involved a lot of wiring, soldering and constant adjustments on the flying field.

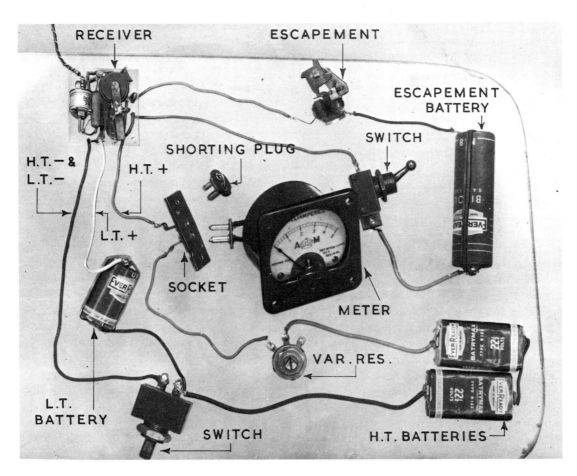

building and flying large, slower flying models. Many of the 'more advanced' (in age) citizens enjoy flying this type of model anyway, they have gone past the tear around the sky, let's go faster flying. Brain power also, so my children constantly tell me, diminishes with age, but not to the extent that it is sufficient a deterioration to stop people from safely flying most types of model aeroplanes. Hand control is more dependent on innate skills than age. Some of the best models I have seen have been made by modellers past the flush of youth — and Rembrandt wasn't painting too badly in his seventies. In other words, age is not a bar to taking a full part in this hobby, although it has to be said that the older the learner, the longer it will probably take to teach him the flying skills.

Just as important as the basic physical requirements for the hobby are other attributes. A sense of humour is certainly needed, otherwise there will be times when we could finish up crying! A sense of proportion is another definite benefit, remembering, when all around you is falling apart, that *it is* only a hobby. There will be the days of frustration when you seriously question the reason for taking up this so-and-so hobby and models will inevitably be crashed, it is all part of the learning curve — and ever onwards. To this extent it will help if you have an understanding spouse or friend, a sympathetic ear (rather than a "why do you bother to play with toy aeroplanes") can be very soothing in moments of despair. Incidentally, people accusing me of infantile pursuits and not growing up, worries me not one jot. My answer usually is that I hope never to grow up if that means ceasing my association with aeromodelling. You will probably find that such critics have a boring life, have no real interests outside work and are probably jealous of your pursuits.

Note that, when talking about attributes and physical requirements I have been referring to model aeroplanes i.e. fixed wing types. A helicopter is technically an aircraft but when it comes to flying it is definitely a different animal. For success with helicopters you do need good eyesight, sharp reactions and agile hand movements; the co-ordination must be of a high order. If not exactly a young person's game, I doubt that, in the future, you will find any world champions in R/C helicopters over the age of thirty or thirty-five.

Note, also, that I have tried very hard so far not to be sexist and avoid the use of 'he' or 'him'. There is, of course, no reason why the ladies should not be just as good — or even better — than men at building and flying radio control model aircraft. There is no great physical effort that would make men superior and the remainder of the requirements are there in full measure. Why more ladies are not actively engaged in the hobby I don't know but we certainly do not encourage them to the flying field by providing them with excellent facilities — in the UK at least. There are, however, a few lady flyers throughout the world. Inevitably, during the passage of this book I shall refer to 'him' or 'he' instead of including both sexes — I apologise in advance and hope the feminists will forgive me. If there is any way that we can encourage more females into the male-dominated hobby (it is also a recognised sport in many countries) I would be pleased to hear about it.

Cynics consider R/C model aircraft flying as a substitute for the full-size activity. This is not true and we have many modellers who are, or have been, full-size pilots — I am one myself. They do not attempt to differentiate on the grounds of superiority or inferiority, they enjoy the challenges of both disciplines and are only too happy to be involved in both types of aviation interest. There is a term 'TAP' — total aviation person, they are probably the most fulfilled of all. Denigration probably results from the same reasons as the 'boys with toys' criticism, a great big inferiority complex.

When starting into R/C model aircraft you will probably have some idea of what you eventually want to do in the hobby; it is often to build and fly a 'Spitfire' or a fast jet, or a helicopter. You may, or may not, reach that aim but it does not mean that failure to achieve the goals will result in you having no success, enjoyment or satisfaction. More likely it will mean that, having got into the hobby, your aims have changed and your pleasures come from different aspects than those you first considered. Finding your own niche in the hobby will come — it may be at a conservative level, or it may be at a high level of competition — the vital thing is that it is the area that gives *you* satisfaction. If it is not too contradictory, after the last statement, I would suggest that you aim to progress as far as possible, but not to the extent that takes away the enjoyment from the hobby.

The one they all want to model when they start! Beautiful it may be, but it is no training subject − start with the simple models.

Ignore remarks about model flying being a substitute for the real thing. Many aviation enthusiasts do both and rate them equally highly.

Whatever our initial thoughts and aims, we all have to start at the beginning and learn our trade at the basic level. There is no way round this, you cannot start by building and hoping to fly a Boeing B-17 Flying Fortress, or hovering a helicopter within the first couple of days of flying. The simple (or relatively simple) tasks of learning to fly trainer models must come first. Far from being disappointing, the training period is one of the most rewarding and the 'first solo' is an achievement you will never forget. I still envy the new modeller coming into the hobby and progressing through those first faltering steps to the time that

he is in charge of the model − for most of the time at least.

During the various chapters there may be mention of a particular manufacturer's equipment. This is not intended as a personal endorsement of the product but it is given as an example of a type or piece of equipment. Indeed, making this a 'buyer's guide book' is not intended − the changes of equipment happen so rapidly that the listed equipment would probably be obsolescent by the time that the book was published. It is unlikely, however, that the principles of operation and installation would change and the illustrations will remain

Modern radio control equipment is reliable, easy to install and, in real terms, less costly than it has ever been. Think before purchasing and obtain what you need − not what you desire.

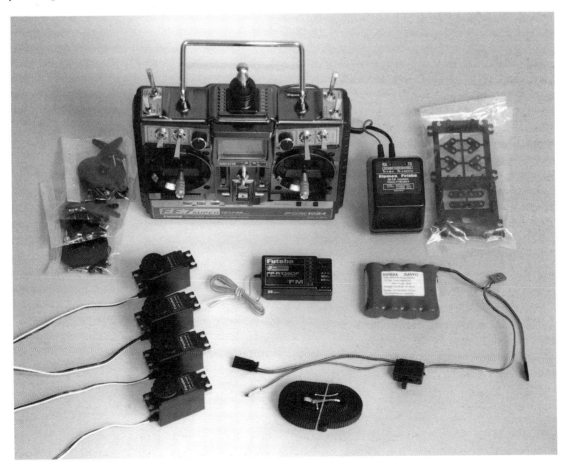

good for the purpose of description. For up-to-date analysis and reports of radio control equipment, engines and ancillary products you should read the model magazines

It is interesting to see that in my previous book I stated that (in the mid-1970s) the systems of imperial and metric measurements were still in a state of flux and I opted to remain with imperial measurements – with a suggestion that they may be changed to metric in future revisions. Well, we are still in a state of flux and measurements will be metric with, where appropriate, imperial alternatives.

I hope that you will take the trouble to read the book in its entirety, and then use it as a reference book – unless you have borrowed it from a library. Good luck with your participation in our hobby, whatever the level and style it may take. Don't be put off by the traditionalist who believes that the only true aeromodeller is the one that builds all his own models, preferably also using traditional methods. If you find that building models is not for you and that it is the flying aspects that give you all the satisfaction, so be it, follow that line. But please be tolerant to others who do not follow your own inclinations and bear in mind that you will only get out of a hobby as much as you put in it i.e. the modeller who involves himself in all aspects of the hobby and all types of models will probably obtain the maximum return.

Good luck, good flying and happy landings.

CHAPTER 2

Radio Control Equipment

It is always tempting at this stage to relate the problems associated with the early days of radio control flying. By the early days I do not mean during the first quarter of the century when some progress was made towards successful flying with near full-size aircraft, nor the second quarter when the Americans had started to commercially produce simple, but bulky and heavy outfits. The batteries alone for these R/C systems weighed more than the full installation complement of modern equipment. No, the struggle usually referred to is the development from single channel non-proportional equipment onwards. Suffice it to say (and still the "all my goodness here we go again" types) that the progress from the single and multi-function radio equipment could be exciting, utterly frustrating, challenging and expensive in terms of the equipment and the crashes – and I wouldn't have missed a moment of it.

With the advent of proportional radio control, where the control surface movements are directly related to the control stick movements, the R/C flying bonanza started – once the costs were put in bounds. It affected R/C boats less, because they were generally slower and could use 'cascaded' systems of control off one channel, but allowed the introduction and tremendous growth of radio controlled cars, first with track racing and then to off-road machines which could be operated almost anywhere. Proportional radio with the introduction of the transistor, produced a revolution and it is now accepted as standard equipment and expected to work with precision and reliability, which thankfully, it does.

This is not to suggest that there has not been any advancements within proportional radio outfits since they were first introduced. There have been enormous improvements; increases of facilities and functions, improved reliability and, in real terms, better value for money. Perhaps the two most important developments relate to the introduction of the integrated circuit and the micro-processor. The former allowed for simple circuit, less component count, lower weights and more efficiency and reliability at lower costs. What the micro-processor has given us, through the designers

Proportional radio control equipment has come a long way since the days of simple, no-frills four-function outfits. Now the up-market systems are highly sophisticated, computer controlled and have almost unlimited programming facilities – at a price.

and manufacturers, is the ability to programme the functions on our transmitters and store this as a memory for one or more models.

Before continuing to describe the various components in a radio control outfit I would like to clarify the use of two terms – channel and function. In the days of non-proportional multifunction equipment the transmitter would be described as, say, having eight channels. This would equate to four basic functions – aileron, elevator, rudder and engine throttle control – because it needed one channel to move the control in one direction and a second channel to move it in the opposite direction. When proportional equipment was introduced initially it was always referred to as four or five function radio i.e. the four function radio would give the same number of controls as the eight channel gear – plus trims. In recent times the proportional equipment has started to be termed, once again, as channels, BUT, this time a channel is the equivalent of a full function. Confused? Don't be, because whether it states function or channel it is the same thing, each one controlling a basic function such as aileron, elevator etc., or an ancillary function.

In two areas of describing radio control modelling there is the risk of over simplification, or overlong and unnecessary explanations. Aerodynamics is one, the technical operation of radio control equipment is the other. I have no doubt that some R/C modellers would love to have detailed explanations of exactly how the equipment works, complete with circuit diagrams, component values etc.! On the other hand, the vast majority of model flyers have not the slightest interest in what ICs are fitted in the transmitter and receiver or that the latter has a sensitivity of five micro seconds minimum. It might be different if we could actually service and maintain (apart from the common sense cleaning and checking) the equipment but it is far too complex for us to contemplate such action, even on the electro/mechanical devices like servos.

In previous books I have included a general description of how an FM (Frequency Modulated) signal is sent from the transmitter, accepted by the receiver, passed onto the servos and for these to amplify the signal and translate it to mechanical energy. But, there are now three methods of transmitting the signal: AM (Amplitude Modulation),

FM (which is also known as PPM – Pulse Proportional Modulation) and PCM (Pulse Code Modulation) and it would become quite a theoretical exercise to include explanations of all these systems. I think, therefore, that we will leave it with a basic description of the transmitter, through its coder sending signals (in sets, or frames of information) for the receiver to pick up and extract. The decoder in the receiver separates the individual signals and directs them to the respective servos. The servo compares the length of the incoming signal with an internally produced, standard, signal and moves the servo until the two signals are equal – this relates to the position of the transmitter stick or control function. There are, no doubt, many technical books dealing with the design theory of radio control electronics for those wishing to enquire further into the operation of the equipment.

For the average modeller, it is more important to understand the limitations of the systems and why these limitations exist. The Radio Regulatory bodies have strong demands from many organisations, both military and civil, for allocations from the favourable VHF (Very High Frequency) wave bands. As our hobby is not the most important, as far as the authorities are concerned, our allocations are relatively small and we have to make the best use of it by using very precise frequency control for our transmitters and receivers. Our first allocation, when the equipment became superhet (super heterodyne) and could be better controlled, was on the 27MHz band. Initially this band was separated into 50MHz frequency 'spots' and, as the equipment improved, these spots were further subdivided into 25MHz spots. The frequency allocation was to serve for all radio control models, boats, vehicles and aeroplanes. All was well, apart from a few minor altercations between factions with closely located sites, until unauthorised CB (Citizen's Band) transmissions began. These were eventually legalised and even then we could probably have lived with the situation (by avoiding the frequencies that absolutely coincided with our own) if some of the CB'ers had not amplified their transmitters, again illegally, and literally blasted us out of the skies.

This intolerable situation was eventually resolved by having further modelling allocations on VHF. In the UK and many European countries the allocation is on the 35MHz band and this is strictly for aircraft, surface vehicles have an allocation on 40MHz. Not all countries have these same allocations − some operate in the 50, 60 and 70MHz areas − you should always check the authorised frequencies before flying in another country. In the UK we have a further allocation for aircraft on the UHF (Ultra High Frequency) band between 458.5 and 459.5MHz. This is a very 'safe' frequency, but has the disadvantage of being more complex and with a much higher component count, making it also more expensive to manufacture and buy. At present there are no UK manufacturers of UHF radio control equipment and probably none in the world making specifically for hobby purposes. Should other countries licence the use of this UHF band and then some of the major manufacturers produce the equipment in quantity, the price could be reduced considerably.

Now that the CB craze has all but passed (the latest Yuppie toy seems to be the portable telephone − they don't give us a problem) the use of 27MHz

is again reasonably safe, particularly if your flying site is well away from main roads. It would be sensible to avoid the blue frequency (27.245), this is the only spot frequency that coincides with a CB frequency, the others are at least 10KHz away. In any case, the supposed interference from CB was mostly imagination and a darned good excuse for pilot error. A legal CB, using its maximum permitted output, would have to be very close to cause interference. I am not suggesting that you use 27MHz when flying at public events, or on a strange site, but for small and sports models, with a frequency monitor in operation, I would consider it reasonable to use the waveband.

If your club or group's flying site does suffer from radio interference on 35MHz and the cause cannot be traced (you could call in the BT boffins with a detector van) there is a temptation to use a frequency that is only legal in another country i.e. 53MHz or 72MHz. The answer to this temptation is to resist it completely. For one thing you may interfere with some important user of that frequency

27MHz equipment may be used for surface vehicles and aircraft. It offers an inexpensive way of getting started in R/C flying, but you must ensure that your flying site will not suffer from interference by other 27MHz users. Two channel equipment will get you flying with a glider or powered glider.

e.g. a hospital or ambulance service, and the fine for illegally operating on an unauthorised frequency can be very high and your equipment confiscated. Any insurance would be invalidated immediately and if you did have an accident while operating on an illegal frequency you would be personally liable.

We have strict output power limitations for our transmitters and what might seem to be an imposition is, if you consider the alternatives, a benefit. Imagine that we could increase the output and hence the range, of our transmitters ten-fold. It would mean that either the flying sites would have to be separated by ten to fifteen miles, or there would have to be some very complicated system of subdividing our spot frequencies into geographical areas — surely an unworkable system. With a present airborne range of at least a mile in good operating conditions and with the equipment in proper order, we are likely to run out of visual range, or have orientation problems before we lose radio range. Only the largest of models would be flyable at maximum range and even that would be stretching the pilot's ability to the limit, something he is unlikely to do with an expensive model.

At present we operate our 'spot' frequency system at 10KHz separation and this is fine with modern equipment which is serviced regularly, if only to check that there is no frequency drift and that the battery is in good condition. If there is some older equipment being operated it is a wise precaution to keep to a 20KHz separation. There are more than twenty frequencies to select from and you do not really want more than six models flying at a time, through the risk of collision, so 20KHz spacing should not be too much of a limitation. Spot frequencies are accurate because they are controlled by crystals, cut to oscillate only at that specific frequency and, of course, used in matched pairs, one for the transmitter and one for the receiver. There are a number of factors regarding crystals (frequently written as Xtals) that are important. First, the crystals must be for the correct modulation method i.e. AM, FM or PCM and the FM (PPM) will require a different type of crystal if the receiver is 'dual conversion'. Crystals from one waveband i.e. 35MHz, cannot be used in equipment designed for another waveband i.e. 40MHz. More expensive

outfits have a removable transmitter module which will allow you to remove one waveband module and replace with another waveband module. However, they are not inexpensive and you will have to purchase a separate receiver. Secondly, the receiver and transmitter crystals are not interchangeable. It always pays to buy the manufacturer's recommended crystals. You may find some less costly crystals being offered for sale — they may be OK or they may cause your model to crash. Thirdly, because the transmitter is of a different modulation type does not mean that you can fly on the same spot frequency as the other i.e. AM radio on frequency 75 must not be flown if a PCM or FM radio is being operated on that frequency.

List of Frequencies and Pennants

27MHz frequencies	Pennant colour
26.995MHz	Brown
27.020MHz	Brown/Red
27.045MHz	Red
27.070MHz	Red/Orange
27.095MHz	Orange
27.120MHz	Orange/Yellow
27.145MHz	Yellow
27.170MHz	Yellow/Green
27.195MHz	Green
27.245MHz	Green/Blue
27.245MHz	Blue

Pennant colour Orange

35MHz frequencies:	Pennant Number
35.000MHz	60
35.010MHz	61
35.020MHz	62
35.030MHz	63
35.040MHz	64
35.050MHz	65
35.060MHz	66
etc. to	
35.250MHz	85

Note, from the above lists, that there is a pennant of specific colour and number for each of the spot frequencies. This should always be displayed on the transmitter and if the frequency is changed, say from 62 to 74, then the frequency pennant must also be changed. 'Flying' the pennant gives

Many R/C outfits are designed with a 'buddy-box' training system, allowing control to be passed to the pupil with a 'slave' transmitter. Note the use of a number 74 pennant (signifying frequency 35.140MHz) on the main transmitter.

an immediate check on the frequencies in use and this should tie up with the pegs on the frequency pegboard — more of that later.

THE SYSTEM

Irrespective of how costly, sophisticated or simple the radio control outfit is, it basically comprises of two parts:

1. The ground-based equipment ie. the transmitter.
2. The airborne package i.e. the receiver/decoder, servos, battery and switch.

There are, of course, additional items such as battery chargers, but these are the basic components in the system. Radio equipment, in the initial phases at least, is normally bought as an outfit and this will consist of:

Transmitter and frequency pennant
Receiver
Servos

Battery pack (or battery holder)
Switch harness
Charger (if rechargeable batteries are included)
Servo accessories, including mounting tray
Instruction book, or owner's manual

In keeping with modern selling methods, these outfits are most attractively packaged and presented, to catch the eye and seduce you into purchasing the goods. It should be remembered at all times when buying R/C equipment, or other modelling goods, that the purchases should be based on actual requirements and not impulse buying. The more that you can evaluate your needs and keep to those aims, the better the value of the goods and their usefulness. It would be nice to be able to say that there are no retailing 'sharks' whose intention is to sell you as much as possible without consideration for the future, regrettably there are a few. Hopefully, this book will help you to make some of the right decisions before committing yourself to hand over your hard earned money, do take the trouble to read it through before making a list of your needs. Purchasing the R/C outfit is probably the largest sum we will invest in our hobby and we want to get it as near right as possible from the beginning, so the more *useful* information that can be gathered, the more informed the selection. To this end it will pay you to visit the local model flying club, see what equipment they use and ask how satisfied they are with the operation, reliability and servicing of the equipment they use. Assuming that you are going to join a club to learn to fly — and it is highly recommended — it would be sensible to join before you start buying the radio equipment, engine and model etc, it could save you money and heartaches. However, there will be prospective R/C modellers who do not have a club, or group of flyers, nearby so I will do all possible for you to come up with some educated guesses on the goods to buy.

Crystal balls are highly expensive and mine is only second-hand, so you will forgive the fact that I will not be able to predict the type of model you will be flying initially and in the future. Quite possibly you won't have a clear picture yourself, or you may change your mind along the way. Perhaps you will find that R/C modelling is not for you — and you don't want to have spent

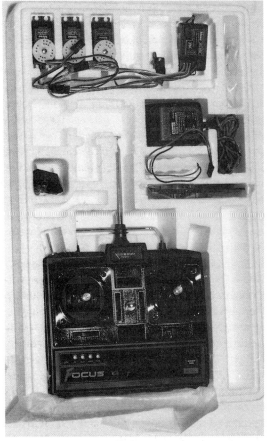

Outfits are supplied complete, for the beginner a four to six channel system with three or four servos is adequate. Rechargeable nicad batteries are highly recommended.

hundreds of pounds in coming to this conclusion. Again, the more information you can assimilate and the more experience you can gather the more chance there will be of coming to the right conclusions. You will find most modellers are very approachable and most retailers honest and ready to help — don't be afraid to ask.

Your eventual aims in the building and flying of R/C model aeroplanes should affect your initial choice of equipment. For instance, if you are certain that your goal is R/C helicopters then you would certainly be advised to go for a helicopter version of an R/C outfit right from the beginning. The initial cost may be higher — you will need good specification equipment to fly the rotor wing aircraft — but it will be cost effective in the long run. Be warned, though, read the chapter on helicopters first (and specialist books on the subject), it is not the easiest form of R/C flying. Few of us will have such positive aims in the first place, but will only know, or think, that the hobby is one that will give pleasure and satisfaction and that you will decide to which branches of the hobby you will move after you have learned to fly. Later in the book I explain how some of the clubs have a fully co-ordinated training scheme, although there are all too few of them I'm afraid. If this is the case, make use of it before you make any other commitment.

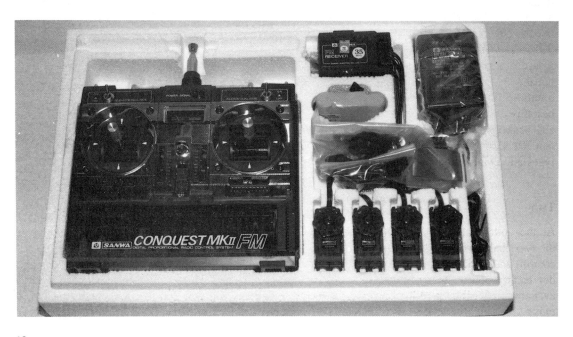

2, 4, 6, 8 – which will we appreciate

Go into your local model shop and, if it is well stocked, you will find a bewildering selection of radio control outfits with costs ranging from well under £100 to over £1000. They are, apparently, all designed to perform the same functions so how can you decide which one will be suitable for you? Actually, quite a few of them will be suitable for you but, in the end, we have to button it down to one specific outfit.

Because this is not a 'buyer's guide' type publication I do not mention specific manufacturers as a general rule. Most of the manufacturers names will be well known to modellers and if you keep to one of the better known names, who has been in existence for a few years, you won't go far wrong. In the list of contents for an R/C outfit there was an option, often given in the 'economy' outfits of having 'dry' batteries or rechargeable, nickel cadmium, batteries. If you are at all serious about the hobby I would strongly recommend having the rechargeable cells right from the start. 'Dry' alkaline batteries certainly have a longer life these days, and are less likely to leak and spread acid over the equipment, but they are a false economy. The complement for the transmitter and airborne pack will be 12 size A batteries (not supplied) – quite costly in the first place. If you are a cautious person, and you need to be when flying R/C model aeroplanes, you will probably discard the batteries well before they actually need to be changed and then there is the problem of access to the battery box tucked away in the innards of the model fuselage. Battery boxes are not the best of products as far as electrical continuity and reliability are concerned and they are best thrown away. Buying an outfit with rechargeable batteries, is, in my opinion, a must. Following is a selection of typical outfits – there are many types and combinations.

Two-channel systems

At the bottom end of the outfit range there is the two channel (normal for rudder and elevator control) with two servos – and usually the dreaded dry battery power. Many of the outfits are only available on 27MHz and 40MHz (surface vehicles only) although a few may be available on 35MHz (for aircraft only). Extremely reasonably priced, but with few features included, the simple two function (channel) should not be dismissed out of hand. If your means are strictly limited you can buy one of these systems, fit it into a powered glider-style model and be flying for a little over £100. Obviously, two functions limits the potential for future model types but, because it is inexpensive, it can always be used as a second system when a further and more comprehensive outfit is purchased. Even the most elementary two-channel outfit will have servo reversing facilities and some with EPA (end point adjustment) for the servos.

Four-channel outfit

Four channels, providing control of elevator, ailerons, rudder and engine throttle, can be considered as the 'basic' outfit. It is suitable for trainers, most sports models, but not helicopters where a fifth function is required. These outfits are, if only modellers would admit the fact, suitable for well over half of the models and modellers. It is only when we get into the realms of more sophisticated R/C aircraft that we need more facilities and functions. They are mostly produced as economy outfits and will feature a modest number of facilities:

Four-channel outfits will be adequate for many aeromodellers in their first years in the hobby. It can be retained for general flying when more sophisticated equipment is purchased.

Transmitter Four channel (functions) FM (PPM) transmission, servo reversing on all channels, end point adjustment (also known as adjustable travel volume) control trims and frequency crystal change facility. A training socket and switch, for 'buddy-box' system may be included.

Receiver Narrow band (FM/PPM) of moderate dimensions and weight (typically 45g) and quoted air range of 3000ft (900 metres).

Servos Three or four may be supplied. These will be of the manufacturer's 'standard' type of moderate size, weight and output torque and quite adequate for training and sports models generally.

Batteries 600mAh nicads (nickel cadmium cells) for the transmitter (9.6 volts − 8 cells) and receiver (4.8 volts − 4 cells). On/Off switch, with charging socket and battery charger.

Accessories and instruction book Economy four-function outfits may not have the facilities for converting the mode 1 stick arrangement to mode 2 and vice versa, so you will have to make the mode selection (more on that later in the chapter) when you purchase the equipment. You may also find 5 and 6 channel economy outfits with similar specification.

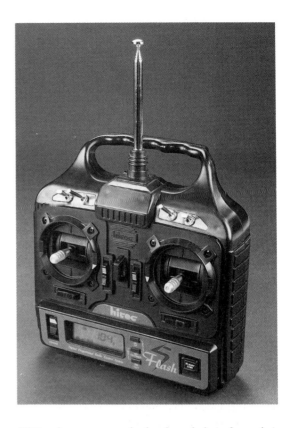

PCM radios are now to be found regularly in five and six channel systems. They allow you to programme, transmit, mix functions, servo travel etc. for a number of models.

Six-channel FM computer outfit (also available on 5 channel) At one time computer was synonymous with PCM (pulse code modulation) and reserved for the higher specification − and cost − radios. Now it is possible to buy entry level (i.e. for beginners to R/C) FM/PPM outfits with computer technology and programming. Some experienced modellers actually prefer the FM computer systems because of the lack of a fail-safe system − they can then incorporate their own methods of fail-safe, should they wish. A two or three model memory, for storing the positions of trims, servo directions, mixing arrangements etc, is typical for these outfits; some will be suitable for fixed wing and helicopter flying, others are specific to one type.

The fifth and sixth functions may be used for, say, retracting undercarriage and flaps, although there are numerous other controls for which they may be used. Additional to the standard servo reversing and EPA facilities the transmitter may include:

Dual rates (switchable to reduce control surface total movements). Mixing facilities (rudder moving to a predetermined degree when aileron control is given, for instance, but not the reverse). Exponential servo movements (where the servo movement, or rate, increases as the stick moves i.e. little movement of the servo when the control stick is first moved, gradually increasing in response). Variable travel response ('soft stick centres'). Subtrims (allowing the trims fed into the model during flight to be programmed in the transmitter after flight). Differential (to give more control movement in one direction from neutral, than in the other direction), low transmitter battery alarm (audible or visual warning when the transmitter battery is getting low) and a 'buddy-box' trainer facility.

Three or four servos will be included in the outfit as will be a miniature FM/PPM receiver, nicad batteries, servo accessories and operating manual. In common with all new R/C outfits there will be warranty for a three or six month period. Please remember that any modifications or alterations to the equipment will make this warranty null and void. For helicopter versions of the outfit the transmitter will provide numerous mixes plus throttle and pitch curves.

Eight-channel PCM/FM selectable with eight model memory for aeroplanes, gliders or helicopters

PCM operation, as explained, gives the system the added function of fail-safe, however, there will also be many other features and facilities not available on the lower specification outfits. These may include exponential rates, electrical trims, programmed subtrims, additional timer functions, snap roll buttons, and landing attitude programming. For gliders there will be butterfly mixing, dual flap trim and wing camber switching and, for helicopters, stunt trims, swash adjusters and inverted flight switch. These are just typical examples and the options and features will vary from one outfit to another. Because the transmitters and receivers have an increased number of channels and functions it does not follow that there will be a corresponding number of servos

388, in this instance, stands for three classes of flying (glider, power and helicopters), eight channels for eight different models.

supplied with the outfit, four servos being the normal complement. Also, some helicopter sets will be supplied with more expensive, ball raced servos. This should be borne in mind when considering the overall costs.

Nine- or ten-channel PCM system designed for separate use on aeroplanes (powered and gliders) and helicopters

The outfit may be supplied as a transmitter/receiver combo, or as a complete outfit with servos, batteries etc. With this number of functions the programming facilities and features available to the modeller is vast. Each of the manufacturers will have their own ideas of the precise list of features to be included and it is tempting to sometimes think that they are inventing uses for the transmitter rather than programming the transmitter to serve model users. Be that as it may, there is a constant battle between manufacturers to provide the modeller with more and more facilities and features. Here is a typical description of the 'top-of-the-range' system.

Transmitter – general features.
Large, clear LCD, 'soft touch' panel display. Plug-in large capacity nicad battery to give long

Everything an R/C flyer could want − until the manufacturers think of something else! Top-of-the-range transmitters have a truly phenomenal amount of programming facilities and will cope with the most complex of model aircraft. For sport, scale, competition, helicopters and all types of R/C models.

safe operation (three hours plus) adjustable control stick length and tension. Central processing unit (CPU) will allow compatibility with the maximum variation of receiver types. Memory will store the setting of up to ten models, long-life lithium back-up battery will prevent the loss of memory if the transmitter nicad fails or goes flat.

Receiver
High specification dual conversion PCM receiver with CPU to provide maximum resistance to electro-mechanical noise interference and high signal selectivity for rejecting cross modulation.

Servos (where included)
Dual ball race outputs with good resistance to high vibration levels (suitable for IC powered cars) high resolution, precise neutral positioning, virtual zero deadband, high torque coreless motor, indirect drive, dust and moisture resistant and low current drain.

Special features − fixed-wing aeroplanes

Touch panel operation
As for standard computer touch panel inputs, bleeping sound confirms input.

Back-up battery
The lithium battery with a five year life, as previously mentioned. Transmitter must be returned to the servicing agent when battery fails or is damaged.

Direct servo control
DSC enables you to make adjustments to your model without transmitting any radio frequency by using a direct wire (from Tx to Rx) system.

Battery alarm
When the transmitter battery drops to a pre-determined voltage a visual and/or audible warning is given.

Data input
Transmitters may have the facility to enter data by two methods, direct and by code number. The latter method is a shorthand way of accessing a specific function without the need to scroll through the menu of functions and adjustments. You will need to know, or refer to, the code number e.g. variable pitch propeller mixing might be Code 72.

Switch position warning
Visual or audible indication that an important switch, for example flaps down, is in the 'on' position.

Reversing switches
Electronic means of reversing the rotation of the servo. Fine for a computer outfit where each model is separately programmed and the settings retained in the memory, but potentially a little more dangerous with transmitters that require resetting for each model. Changing the rudder and elevator rotations gives obvious results on the model, less so on the ailerons − you must always double check that the ailerons really are moving in the correct direction i.e. the right-hand aileron is going *down* for a left-hand turn.

EPA or ATV
To limit the movement of the servo in each direction from the neutral position. This prevents the servo from 'stalling' (when the linkage meets with a stop).

Throttle ALT

Allows the throttle trim to be active only in the bottom half of the throttle stick movement. Provides accurate idle setting without affecting the full throttle settings.

Dual rate

May be available on aileron and elevator, or on rudder also. Dual rate switches from high to low control movement positions so that the control movements are reduced with the switch 'in'. The amount is variable, it is a useful control for using 'out' for acrobatics, landing etc. and 'in' for smooth general flying.

Exponential

Exponential control reduces the sensitivity around the neutral, progressively increasing the control effectiveness as the stick is moved to its full extent. It is also possible to have adjustments to combine the effects of exponential and dual rate, the rate change coming in at a predetermined position of the servo movement. How necessary, or useful, this latter control adjustment really is I cannot determine − you would certainly need to know your model extremely well to use it effectively.

Sub-trim adjustment

This feature allows you to set electronically the servo centres required by the model, with the trim levers on the transmitter in the central positions. The same result can, of course, be achieved by adjusting the linkages on the model.

Cross-trim

Transmitter trim levers are positioned adjacent to the respective control e.g. if the elevator stick is on the left-hand side the elevator trim will be on the inside immediately adjacent to the stick. It may be more convenient, when constant elevator changes are required and the finger and thumb constantly on the elevator stick, to have the trim on the other hand (normally throttle trim). With some Tx's it is possible to transpose these trims.

Flap

When the flap lever is operated it will lower all flaps in unison to a pre-set or adjustable deflection. A similar control may be used to droop or raise the whole of the trailing edge in a glider.

Crow mixing

Known also as 'butterfly' mixing, it is used by sailplane pilots to move the flaps in the opposite direction to the ailerons. A useful adjustment for accurate spot landings in contests. Another mix allows for one flap to be raised and the other lowered to create an aileron, banking effect.

Flaperons

Normally programmed to move the ailerons down so that in addition to working as ailerons they will also give some flap effect.

Elevons

For delta or flying wing designs the aileron/elevator functions are combined to provide rolling and pitch controls. Travel volumes, dual rates and differential movements are options with elevon mixing, as it is with flaperons.

Quad flaps

A strictly glider option, the four flaps (essentially the ailerons and flaps) can be adjusted together to vary the camber of the wing for maximum efficiency in a specific contest task.

Ruddervator

Used for 'V' tail configuration where the effects of yaw (rudder) and pitch (elevators) are combined. To prevent excessive movement of one side of the ruddervator (when the pitch and yaw movements combine in the same direction) the individual movements have to be limited.

Snap roll

To achieve an instantaneous snap (or flick) roll the aileron, elevator and rudder surfaces have to be moved in unison to a selected position (towards the maximum end of the movement). These movements are programmed so that, on depressing the snap roll button on the transmitter, they move to the required settings and the model automatically performs the snap roll − providing the entry speed is correct.

Variable pitch propeller mix

Variable pitch propellers can be used on large-scale models to advantage but, unless we are flying with the assistance of a co-pilot, we are unlikely to be able to spare a hand, or finger, to operate the propeller pitch control lever. For this reason the pitch changes are linked with the throttle control, either on a fully variable setting or with pitch changes occurring at pre-set throttle positions. This function can be switched in or out during flight.

Elevator to flap mixing
Smaller radius turns, in pitch, can be achieved with some models (usually aerobatic types) if the movements of the flaps and elevators are linked so that the flap is depressed as the elevator moves up. Switchable in flight.

Landing systems – sailplanes
With high lift and low drag the modern sailplane (glider) needs drag application to give consistent landing approaches. Elevator trim, flap position and spoilers (air brakes on the wing) are programmed to give the required degree of lift and drag.

Landing attitude system – powered aeroplanes
Flap extensions are programmed to occur as the engines are throttled back and any pitch change is taken care of by a re-adjustment of elevator trim. If leading edge wing slots, or spoilers, are incorporated these can also be programmed to deploy at a specific throttle setting. Note, this programming relates to throttle settings, not aeroplane speeds, and the facility to switch out the system could be important.

Undercarriage retract speed variation
To adjust the retraction, or lowering, of the undercarriage to give a scale-like speed. This system only slows down the servo movement, so you must ensure that the servo is suitable for slow operation and that the retracts are of mechanical operation.

Servo testing
Programmed to cycle slowly through their full movement range, it will give you the chance to observe whether there is any irregular movement or 'jittering'.

Fail-safe
As previously described. It is really a misnomer as, properly programmed, it will not save the aeroplane.

Trim offset adjustments
During test flights it will be necessary to feed in trim adjustments and when these are satisfactory the positions can be programmed into the model memory and the transmitter trims reset to neutral.

Trim rate adjustment
If a small movement of a trim lever is giving too much effect the rate of movement can be halved.

Timers
Integrated timers will provide the accumulated time reading for each model in the memory bank. Count-down timers are a stop-watch style timing device used during a single flight, increasing the audible warning 'bleeps' as the zero point is approached.

Data transfer
To allow the data stored in one transmitter to be transferred to a second transmitter.

Modulation selection
To select, on a PCM transmitter, whether PCM or PPM (FM) modulation transmission is to be used.

Model selection
For storing the model settings in the transmitter memory and also for copying the settings of one model to a similar model (for competition models where you are trying to achieve as near identical flying characteristics with the reserve model).

Keyboard lock
By inserting – and remembering – a multi-digit code it provides a safeguard against 'unauthorised' adjustments to the transmitter settings. Unless the key-code is first inserted in the transmitter there is no access to the controls.

Expandable systems
An alternative to buying an outfit with a specific number of functions is to buy a basic outfit and to add channels and functions as they are required. This sounds like an ideal solution to an ever-

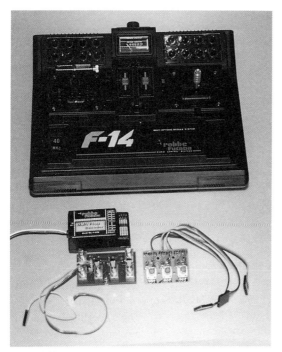

Expandable systems allow the adding of further functions (channels, mixers, exponential, decoders etc.) as and when required.

present problem, but it is a system that has never found great favour in the UK. The only country where it has been commonly used by modellers is Germany − the USA, Australia, Japan and South Africa, for instance, not seeming to take to the extendible system idea. Perhaps cost has been one reason for its unpopularity, or the fear that, when the additional transmitter mixes, rates, switches etc. are needed, they will no longer be in production. The problem then becomes a 'chicken and egg' situation, retailers won't stock the items because there is insufficient demand and the modeller is disinclined to go for the system because the additional transmitter and receiver components are not readily available.

Transmitters
I said earlier that it was not intended to go into technical detail on the methods of transmission i.e. AM, FM (PPM) and PCM. However, a little more must be explained to enable choices to be made of outfits. With AM there are few problems because this method, where the signal amplitude (loudness) is proportionally adjusted, is now only used on a few of the two-function economy outfits

− and probably only on the 27MHz band. Theoretically more prone to interference in the 'quiet' passages, it served well enough for a number of years.

Frequency Modulated, or Pulse Proportional Modulation as it is more commonly called these days (by the Japanese manufacturers at least), is a series of channel pulses, carried in a frame of information with a pause at the end of the frame to prepare for the next series of pulses. Because the pulses, of varied duration, are all transmitted at the same strength the risk of interference is lower than with AM transmission. Pulse Code Modulation (PCM) makes use of micro-processors and the receiver not only accepts the signals, but compares them with the foregoing sets of pulses. With minor variations, due to interference, the PCM receiver/decoder can interpolate the signals and produce an acceptable control signal. When the interference becomes too bad to be able to 'manufacture' any logical signals it locks-out i.e. it goes into fail-safe. Now, fail-safe is, as mentioned, a misnomer because all the receiver can do is to set the servos to pre-programmed positions, or to hold them at their positions immediate to the fail-safe coming into operation. PCM computer transmitters, in the top range, offer more facilities than any other types.

Which mode?

I seem to have been writing about the supposed advantages of the various modes (control stick arrangements) of transmitters for about 50 years! For all the arguments in favour − and against − the various modes it does not seem to have made the slightest difference. There is as much disparity of thought, and use, as there ever has been. For instance, the World Aerobatic Champion uses a transmitter tray and flies with a mode 2 transmitter arrangement. In complete contrast the World Helicopter Champion flies on mode 3, the almost unheard of (these days) 'cuddle box'. There is no unanimity between individuals with regard to mode types, but there probably is in geographical terms. Assuming that you will be learning to fly at your local model club, it would be sensible to learn to fly on the mode that the majority of their experienced pilots use. There will be the further advantage that, with the same

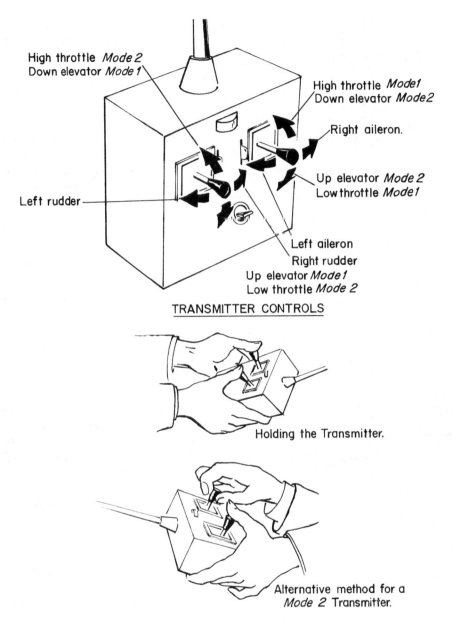

High throttle *Mode 2*
Down elevator *Mode 1*

High throttle *Mode 1*
Down elevator *Mode 2*

Right aileron.

Up elevator *Mode 2*
Low throttle *Mode 1*

Left rudder

Left aileron
Right rudder
Up elevator *Mode 1*
Low throttle *Mode 2*

TRANSMITTER CONTROLS

Holding the Transmitter.

Alternative method for a
Mode 2 Transmitter.

mode and the same type of equipment you are more likely to be able to use a 'buddy-box' trainer lead joining the transmitters.

Of the modes illustrated, mode 1 and mode 2 are used by well over 90% of all modellers, with mode 2 possibly having the lion's share. If you are having real difficulties in learning to fly, say, on mode 1 by all means try mode 2. If you can't manage with either mode 1 or 2 you could try the obscure mode 3 (if you can find the equipment) or mode 4 but these would be slim chances indeed. The reason people have learned on these obscure

arrangements is more likely to be because their mentor used that system.

Computer programming

To young modellers, brought up in the computer age, programming of the computer transmitters will hold no terrors. Certainly some of the very sophisticated transmitters (eight and more channels) have a very wide range of functions and facilities, evinced by the 100-page owner's manual! However, the manufacturers have learned a few lessons

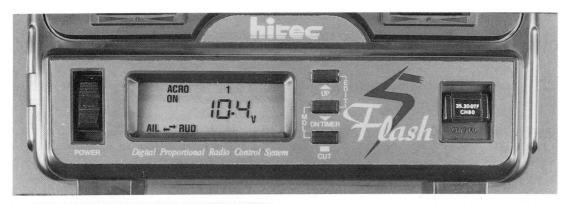

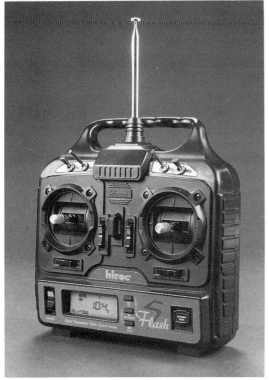

'Entry level' computer transmitters do have user friendly programming that can be understood in the owner's manual.

in the past years and systems once described as 'user friendly' are actually understandable and logical. But what of the computer illiterate? Well, I consider myself as having been in that group and I can honestly say that the 'entry level' computer outfits (FM and PCM) have instructions (in the owner's manual) which are written in understandable English, are easy to follow and once the basic methods of putting the instructions into the computer are learned, there is nothing more to worry about. First follow the instructions with the equipment installed and the model in front of you, then you will find you can make adjustments on the flying field without recourse to the manual.

With the more sophisticated PCM computer systems the problems could be two-fold. In the hands of the poseur − and we have to face that some people buy the equipment not because they need it, but to display their wealth and possessions − he could come unstuck because he will not have the time and inclination to understand the programming of the transmitter and will, therefore be unable to show it off to his fellow enthusiasts. They are systems for the serious modeller and those that are likely to be able to make full use of the unparalleled range of functions i.e. the advanced R/C model pilot. Even the most advanced of flyers may find difficulty, with variable rates (combined exponential and linear) and full ranges of mixing and differentials, programming them and then sensibly judging the effects. It would take a long time − virtually a full-time occupation − to experiment with all the variations and to properly assess the results. You would, I think, be lucky to be flying the same model at the end of testing all of the options and variations.

Receiver

Supplied as a matching unit to the transmitter in the outfit, it will not be the only receiver that can be used with the transmitter.

FM (PPM) receivers can be of the single or dual conversion types (the latter less suspect to interference, especially from the 'harmonics' of transmitters within the same waveband). As stated previously, PCM transmitters can also be programmed to operate FM receivers, which are considerably cheaper than the PCM receivers.

Plug-in crystals allow frequency changes for the receiver and transmitter.

variety of servos is much greater. They come in sub-micro, micro, mini, standard, large and giant sizes, with plain (oilite) or ball race bearings, with plastic or metal gear trains, direct or indirect potentiometer connections, core or coreless motors – just in the normal operation servos. Then you have low-profile servos and retract servos, where the output movement is over 180 degrees rather than the nominal 90 degrees. Most of the major manufacturers will have in excess of a dozen servo types for aircraft.

Most modellers will build up to having a number of airborne R/C packs as it is far more convenient to have the equipment fixed in a model and not have to move it around. It may be that a PCM receiver, with fail-safe facility, is required for a large-scale model, but a four or five channel FM (PPM) receiver would be quite adequate for a sports model. Miniature receivers, with weights down to 12g are also available for indoor or very small models. Remember that you must have the correct frequency crystal for the receiver, not just the actual frequency (i.e. 35.020) but the trans-mission type (i.e. PCM or FM) and whether it is single or dual conversion.

Servos

The final link in the chain, the servo converts the signal from the servo/decoder into a mechanical servo output movement corresponding with the position of the transmitter control. Gone are the days when servos were available in rotary and linear (rack and pinion) outputs. Now there are just rotary output servos, operating in one direction – reverse directions are catered for by the trans-mitter reversing switches. In other respects the

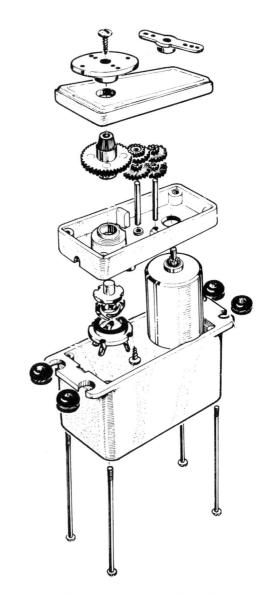

Construction of a rotary servo showing the mechanical parts only.

How do you select from such a bewildering array? The original R/C outfit, unless it is a high specification outfit for helicopters, is likely to have the manufacturer's 'standard' servos supplied with the set. These will be of average size, output torque and speed, probably plain bearing, plastic gears and an indirect 'pot'. Will these servos be adequate for your model? Let me give two examples. Many years ago, before the standard of servos was as good as it is now, my colleagues and I took part in a WW1 television series with models of BE2cs, Avro 504s, Albatros C1s and Fokker Eindekkers etc. After the filming, where they were used extensively, they were displayed at the Imperial War Museum where the transmitters were direct wired to the models so that the public — mostly young lads — could operate the model controls. For over two months, for seven days a week, for eight hours a day, those transmitter sticks were going to all corners of the boxes. If I remember correctly, three servos failed (through worn 'pot' tracks) during that period.

Of course, the models were not suffering from one of equipment's chief enemies, vibration. But the record was still pretty good. More recently a member of the MPA built two trainer models to be used at MPA events and, in particular, at the training weeks at the beginning and end of the flying season. They are now in their fourth year of operation, looking a bit the worse for wear, still going strong after many, many hours of dual and solo flying. These models were all fitted with the standard, inexpensive, oilite bearing servos and in the case of the two MPA (Model Pilots Association) trainers there was one servo that went slow and was replaced. It should also be said that the equipment for the two trainers was the economy 'basic' outfit, but with nicads of course. All the original equipment and batteries — and engines — are fitted in the models, which should say something for the quality and reliability of modern equipment.

Selection of other types of servos does become fairly obvious after you have gained some experience with models. Sub-micro, micro and mini servos are obviously going to be used in small models, although the latter types, usually fitted with metal gears to cope with the fairly hard usage, may be fitted in wings for aileron servo operation in gliders. Ball raced servos are used

Servos are supplied with rubber grommet mounts, fixing components and alternative output discs and arms.

where the loads of the servo outputs are high (closed loop controls, for instance) or they are going to perform a lot of work at high resolution standards e.g. helicopters. Large and giant servos will be used in the biggest and heaviest of models — and they are getting bigger all the time. Plastic gears are perfectly satisfactory for most installations, it is only when they have to cope with extraordinary and 'rough' treatment that metal gear trains are necessary. Naturally, metal gears are more expensive to make and buy, plastic gears are not too costly to replace — and models aren't built to crash!

Some of the latest servos have extremely high qualities of resolution, speed and torque — they also cost upwards of £100 each. Take five of these super-servos (nil deadband) plus a PCM computer 10-channel transmitter and receiver, a gyro and a battery, charger and a few more items and you can say goodbye to the best part of £2,000. Is it worth it and do you need it? If you are up to world championship standards in any of the competition disciplines — and particularly if you have some sponsorship from the manufacturer or agent — then it is both worthwhile and necessary. At those levels every bit of extra response, speed and accuracy is important. For lesser mortals, you probably won't notice the technical improvements, except on the work bench.

Batteries and chargers

Batteries also come in all shapes and sizes. The 'standard' transmitter battery complement is eight 600mAh pen cells giving a working voltage of 9.6 volts (at least 10.4 volts when initially charged). Some of the advanced transmitters use larger capacity cells, to give a good safe operating time, but this, together with the fair amount of hard and software in the circuitry, can result in the transmitter becoming quite heavy. No problem for short, ten minute flights, but not so good if you are holding it for an hour or so with a glider. Time to think about fitting a neck strap or using a transmitter tray.

Battery capacities for the airborne packs range from tiny 50mAh packs, for indoor work, through 80, 100, 150, 280, 600, 1,400 − right up to 4,000 (4Ah) capacities. In larger models the receiver and servos use separate battery packs, the current drain from numerous large servos can be considerable. With the larger servos − and powerful 'standard' size servos − there are advantages in going to a 6 volt pack as the motors and electronics are designed to take this voltage. If there is any voltage drop due to long leads it will have less effect. However, if a common battery pack is being used for the receiver/servos, albeit a larger capacity nicad, check to see whether it is safe to supply the receiver at 6 volts. Some receivers are safe to operate at the higher voltage, others may suffer (especially during the initial high voltage surge after charging). Manufacturers will have their own range of batteries, but it is possible to buy pre-wired and pre-plugged battery packs from separate sources. I have used these packs regularly and without any problems.

More batteries are now coming onto the modelling market with nickel hydride cells instead of the nickel cadmium types used for so many years. These have the advantage of being acceptably 'green' and more environmentally friendly, also they are more efficient and the size of the packs are about two-thirds of the nicad units for a similar capacity. On the down side is that they are not, at present, suitable for electric motors with high current requirements e.g. power motors for electric flight, and they are also more expensive.

There are two types of charger, standard rate and rapid charge. Transmitter and airborne pack batteries are nearly always charged at the standard 'overnight' rate (actually 14−16 hours), the only need for a rapid charger is if you forget to put your equipment on charge, or you leave the equipment switched 'ON'! Obviously, you will need a different charger for different capacity batteries; for the airborne packs and multi-capacity, multi-pack chargers are available. It is also possible to buy battery cyclers. These discharge the batteries to a safe level of 1.1 volt per cell, and then charge them to peak capacity at the 'overnight' rate. Manufacturers do recommend cycling the batteries from time to time and you can do this without using a cycler simply by operating the equipment until it reaches a measured (volt-meter) of 1.1 volt per cell e.g. 4.4 volts for the airborne pack and 8.8 volts for the transmitter. You then recharge in the normal way. I have had battery packs that have lasted for six to eight years without having any special treatment − just sensible charging and a little TLC.

Nicad batteries are very tolerant and take a lot of abuse without failing. Providing you charge at the standard rate it is impossible to over-charge them. Modellers tend to get worried about the length of charge they should give a battery if, say, they charged it the previous week but didn't operate the equipment again. The very simple answer is to give it a full charge again, it won't come to any harm and it won't shorten the life of the battery.

Now for one fallacy and one fact. Rumours abound of nicad batteries having built-in memories i.e. they do not always give up the full charge of

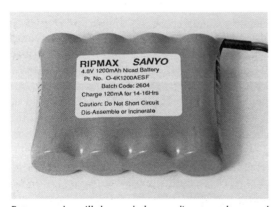

Battery packs will be marked according to voltage and capacity. They are available in a wide variety of cells, capacities and shapes. Nickel hydride, more environmentally friendy than nickel cadmium, are increasing in popularity.

A standard rate transmitter (9.6 volt) and receiver (4.8 volt) charger are normally supplied with an outfit. Multi-chargers and quick chargers are available as optional extras.

the battery. I have yet to see any proof of the phenomenon, or meet any modeller with verifiable experiences of nicad 'memory'. Best to forget that it was ever mentioned. Not so easily dismissed is the 'black wire corrosion' condition. This happens on the negative lead (usually with a black plastic coating — but may also be grey) between the battery and the switch, usually when the equipment has been left standing for any length of time. The precise reason for this happening is not known, but you had better believe it can happen. When a model is not being used for a month or more unplug the battery — this will prevent the corrosion occurring, but make a visual check

every six months. If corrosion is present it will be obvious on the soldered joint to the switch and if the insulating sleeve is removed the negative wire will be seen to be dull and affected. It must be replaced.

Servo accessories, labels and pennant

A variety of servo output, in the form of discs, unequal crosses and arms will be supplied. An adjustable arm is particularly useful for 'basic' outfits for fine adjustments for the throttle control. Also in the little servo accessory bags will be the rubber grommets or pads, screws and brass eyelets for mounting the servos — use them! Self-adhesive labels printed with 'elevator', 'aileron' etc. are useful for sticking to the servo plugs and for the extension lead, normally used for the aileron extension lead where the servo is fitted in the wing. Using these labels can avoid continuous plugging in of different leads to find the correct socket.

Flying a pennant on your transmitter to notify the frequency in operation is, as discussed elsewhere, a very important safety feature. Remember to fit the pennant to your transmitter, with the correct frequency number displayed, and also remember to change the number if you change the crystal. If I am using the same transmitter for a number of different models, but on different frequencies, I usually write the frequency of the model on the fuselage, in the wing seating area, as a reminder of the frequency to use.

Instructions or owner's manual

Owner's manual is just a 'posh' way of describing the instruction book, although with the number of pages in some of the outfit instructions the term manual is fully justified.

Read, learn and inwardly digest!

DIY radio equipment

I once wrote that I could not see why modellers bothered to build their own radio equipment because it cost almost as much as the commercially finished product. Modellers' rightly chastised me over this sin, I had overlooked the 'satisfaction factor' in building the equipment from a kit of pc boards, components, wire leads and plugs and sockets. Kits for transmitters, receivers, speed controllers and a few other items are still available and, if not totally state-of-the-art, are up to date in the non-computerised specifications. Costs are lower than the finished commercial product and where additional receivers are required for models this is a legitimate way of obtaining them at a modest cost. Just ensure that the design is compatible with your transmitter and the sockets are the right type for the servo plugs.

Second-hand equipment

There is a fair throughput of modellers in the hobby for a whole lot of different reasons. Perhaps time didn't permit them to indulge their dreams, perhaps the interest was just not there, or perhaps they kept crashing. Whatever the reasons there will, at any given time, be quite a lot of second-hand equipment on sale, either privately (the small 'ads' in the local papers will have these under 'hobbies' titles) or at retailers. If I were to buy second-hand equipment I would want either a bench demonstration and a guarantee of money back if the equipment did not operate properly on the field or a flying demonstration. You can see some particularly enticing 'bargains' at 'swop meets' for modellers. However, there is no come-back with these purchases, the equipment may be faulty or completely out of date − even though it may look 'nearly new'.

On the subject of obsolete equipment, providing it is doing the job you want and that spares and servicing is available it is, as far as I am concerned, operational and not obsolete. You might be tempted to buy an 'economy' outfit which looks in very good condition with a view to having it sent away for checking and servicing. The problem here is that, for the servicing agent to do a thorough job, he will have to spend quite a time checking it all through and this charge, plus the initial purchase cost, will probably exceed the price of a new outfit. The buy and have serviced scheme is better used for the more expensive equipment bought at a 'bargain' price.

Ancillary equipment

Life is not so simple that, when you have bought your R/C outfit you won't want, or need, any

other equipment.

Purchasing the top-of-the-range outfit will give you access to the vast majority of facilities, but not quite all. It is, however, the lower cost and specification outfits which will benefit most from the ancillary items. We have learned that the PCM outfits incorporate fail-safes, but the FM (PPM) systems don't have this feature. Fail-safes are available as separate items, for one or four channels, for operation with FM/PPM outfits.

Servo slowers, slowing down the output speed of a retract servo for instance, are on the market, as are servo testers. What about long leads for servos? Well, you can buy 'boosted' leads to compensate for any potential drop in voltage and leads with 'chokes' to prevent any signal return in

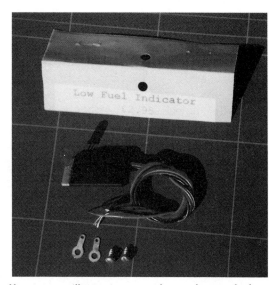

Numerous ancillary units, servo slowers, battery checkers, fuel level indicators etc. are designed to operate from auxiliary outputs on the receiver.

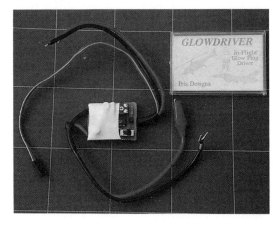

a long lead. 'Y' leads, for ganging up two servos are a standard accessory.

For airborne installations there are specialist products such a 'low fuel warning' and low battery level (usually indicated by the use of green, amber and red pilot lights). Multi-engine models have been a source of concern to modellers with the thought of one engine producing more power than the other, or failing all together. Standards of engine reliability and the introduction of spark ignition engines on larger models, have reduced the risk of an engine stopping, but it makes flying easier if the two, or more, engines are operating at the same speed. There are electronic products on the market to achieve this situation. To further reduce the risk of an in-flight engine failure, with a glo engine you can fit a glo plug energiser which switches in an on-board battery (1.2 volt) to the plug at low idle settings to prevent the plug from going 'cold'.

Large models need to be treated with particular care and consideration, and here the more 'twinning' or back-up systems that can be included the potentially safer will be the flying of the aeroplane.

A battery backer, cutting in the reserve battery if the initial source fails is an obvious advantage. 'Twinning' of receivers, servos and switches, allowing at least one side of a model to operate in the event of failure of one receiver or one servo, is another way of improving safety and equipment is available for these facilities to be included.

Gyros, autopilots and horizontal auto leveller

Virtually all helicopters are fitted with gyros to assist in keeping the tail end from yawing with changes of torque from the main rotors. Early helicopters were flown without the benefit of gyros, or collective pitch control and although they will never be easy aircraft to fly, these two controls have made it a more practical proposition than it ever was. Gyros have been little used in fixed-wing models, probably the fact that they were banned from competition flight prevented serious development of gyros in this type of aeroplane. We may not wish to enter competitions, or even like them, but there is little doubt that they result in advances in equipment and model design.

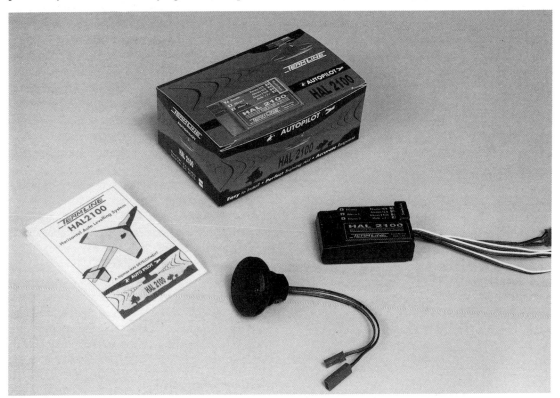

One of the most useful add-ons to be introduced recently is the HAL 2100, an autopilot system to assist the trainee.

Perhaps gyros will be used more in fixed-wing models in future − in scale models they are capable of smoothing out the flight considerably.

Autopilots make use of gyros and the R/C model versions have two, one for pitch and one in the roll plane. Developed from RPV (Remote Piloted Velude) technology the model autopilot is plugged in between the receiver and servos and corrects any unwanted changes of pitch or roll. The advantage of the gyro instrument is that it senses changes and reacts immediately. We are poor substitutes because we have to watch, analyse and react − a much slower action than you will get with an autopilot fitted. Indeed, it is uncanny to watch the speed and precision with which the autopilot regains straight and level flight of the model. It cannot, incidentally, maintain a heading or specific height, those features only come in the military versions which are much larger and more expensive.

A low-cost alternative to the autopilot, now on the market at the time of writing, is the horizontal auto leveller (HAL). This system works on the basis of measuring light intensities from four photo electric cells mounted externally on the top of the fuselage and comparing them. The micro-computer compares the readings (dark for ground, light for sky) and gives corrections to maintain the model on a level course. Both of the foregoing systems have uses during the training programmes

Dual frequency systems will help to make the flying of large models safer.

and may well have important applications in respect of tying-in with the fail-safe feature. If the autopilot, or HAL, can put the model in a gentle descending turn and maintain it in that attitude, it may be a safer method than the ones we now employ.

A further new development is the solid state gyro, i.e. with no gyros or working parts to wear out. This piezo electric gyro system has a small vibrating prism which detects any change of angular velocity by using the Coriolis effect (not a lot of people know that!). The technicalities to overcome were considerable, not least the prob-lems of temperature drift and vibration isolation, but the result was demonstrated in an electric R/C model bicycle which was driven very slowly around the floor.

Electric flight has spawned its own batch of electronic devices, from the humble ON/OFF switch for the electric motor to the 'soft' start versions to prevent a sudden surge of power from the motor. Electronic speed controllers have been substantially reduced in size and increased in faci-lities. Taking the place of the carburettor throttle on an IC engine, the speed controller may include progressive forward and reverse speeds, brake, thermal overload and BEC facilities. The BEC (battery eliminator circuitry) measures the voltage of the common motor/receiver battery pack and on reaching a pre-determined low-voltage level will give priority to the receiver only. R/C model car requirements have also resulted in great im-provements in equipment relating to electric power. It is worthwhile keeping an eye on their developments.

On-board measuring systems, capable of relaying speeds, engine rpm, headings and heights to the ground controller are feasible. They are also banned in some countries as they are considered as a risk to security. It is not the model infor-mation that they are concerned about but the surveillance type operations using video cameras transmitting back 'sensitive' pictures. Even with a simple system, using cameras and technology used in Formula 1 racing cars, the results were very good. The dangers can also be appreciated.

And more to come

You may think that the R/C equipment designers

and manufacturers will have run out of ideas for developing and advancing the equipment. Not a bit of it! Synthesized frequency is on its way — providing we can ensure a foolproof system of the operator both checking the frequencies in use first and putting on the transmitter the appropriate frequency pennant. There may be an alternative one day soon where the transmitter, before sending out any RF signal, will scan the users on the site and lock onto an unused spot frequency. If all systems were of this type it would theoretically be impossible for any clash of frequencies — or even to know the frequency on which we were transmitting. These ideas will not be put into fruition for a while yet.

Giant models, weighing 20kg (44lb) or more would certainly benefit from a dual frequency radio system whereby the transmitter *automatically* switches over to a reserve frequency and the receiver does the same. Again, it has proved to be practical but, in the UK and some other countries, we don't have a second frequency band suitable for this type of equipment. 27MHz is not a suitable back-up frequency as this may well be used for toys or other surface vehicles at displays and demonstrations. However, it will surely come and we will start to have a genuine 'fail-safe' system.

There is a danger that we will have so many aids and automatic controls that the pilot almost becomes redundant. It would, now, be possible to design an automatic landing system only requiring human intervention in the sense of programming the transmitter. This would be fascinating, but also counter-productive. The whole reason in the first place was to have radio control so that *we* could control the models. It would be rather ironic if electronics started to take it all back again. Whatever the developments, we know that we can always go back to basics.

CHAPTER 3

The Trainer

Learning to fly an R/C model aeroplane is the most rewarding and the most challenging of all phases of the hobby. Some modellers find the whole procedure too daunting and never make the stage of competently flying solo. This is a pity as there is no reason why, given a sensible approach, the correct selection of model equipment and a little assistance, that nine out of ten potential R/C aeromodellers should not learn to fly most types of models. The tenth person? Well, it does take a degree of hand and eye co-ordination, reasonable eyesight and reactions, but you certainly don't have to be Superman.

Let us rid ourselves of some fallacies. First, there is no such thing as an ideal trainer. Any model design, the way it is constructed and powered, is the result of a series of compromises. It has to

be designed to fly in a variety of conditions, be within reasonable cost restraints and based on assumptions on how the person will learn to fly e.g. on his own, or with some assistance. Even if we knew the precise weather conditions to be encountered, the abilities of the pilot-to-be, the site conditions and all relevant factors we could not design a specific style of training model — life is not like that!

Paying a visit to a local model club to watch the members flying their R/C aeroplanes may give you the impression that it is easy to fly the models. Indeed, it may even appear that the faster, aerobatic types are the easiest of all to fly because they can be so precisely controlled. And scale models, too, the ultimate aim of many R/C modellers — the flyers seem to be coping with them without too

At the local flying site you will probably find a wide variety of models, modellers and flying skills. Don't be fooled into thinking that it is all too easy — or too hard!

many problems. It is, in part, an illusion and it will have taken a good deal of time to reach the standards they are demonstrating. Don't be put off by this fact − if they can do it, so can you, but don't expect to be able to conquer the skills in a week or two. Learning to fly requires a deal of devotion and patience and the rewards are the greater for it not being a 'quick fix'. One of the principal aims of this book is to take the uninitiated through the first faltering steps to, we hope, a full and active participation in the hobby.

There is also no such thing as an 'uncrashable' model. Some modellers, when they start out on the hobby, believe that by using stronger materials, more glue and a tougher structure, the model will not break so easily. In one sense this is true but, unfortunately, the reverse side is that it will have to fly much faster − if it flies at all − and this alone will make it more difficult to fly. It will also crash harder. The actual truth is the complete opposite − the lighter the model is, the better it will fly (with a few specialist exceptions).

Having rid ourselves of a few misconceptions let us now consider a few definite NO-NOs before going onto the constructive considerations. So many beginners want to start their R/C activities by building and flying a Spitfire. Why not? They may have seen them being flown at a display and they perform beautifully and look fabulous in the air. Absolutely true, but the flying skills needed for that type of model are not inconsiderable and in the hands of a beginner a flight wouldn't last a minute. After all, if you are learning to fly a full-size aeroplane you don't start with a fast aerobatic type − never mind a fighter − you begin with a more sedate and easy to fly Cessna or Piper. After logging many hundreds of hours on different types of aircraft you may move on to the more exotic aeroplanes − if you can afford the not inconsiderable cost.

Keep away from complex models; the trainer is there for one purpose only, to teach you the rudiments of flying. It should be simple to build and repair and looks are not that important either. Having said that looks of the model have no importance I now realise that many newcomers expect even the basic training model to at least resemble a full-size aeroplane to some degree. Many years ago I designed and kitted a training model called the 'Pronto', a simple slab-sided

Square and ugly, the 'Pronto' flew well but didn't look like a 'real' aeroplane and was not popular.

model with no pretence to being modelled on a full-size aircraft. It never sold in great numbers but another of my designs, the 'Tyro' (and 'Tyro Major') which was essentially similar to the 'Pronto' but had a fuselage with a rudimentary cabin (the windows being painted rather than glazed) sold by the thousands. In the end, the customer is right.

Few of us have limitless pockets and a visit to the model retailer may provide many temptations. Of course it is the job of the retailer to sell, but it is your responsibility to keep a sense of reason about the purchases. It is a hobby we are talking about and not the essentials of life and we have to put it into perspective. Make out a budget for your initial costs and how much you can afford to spend monthly on running costs and new purchases. Try to keep within the budget figures − it certainly isn't worth wrecking a marriage or ruining a good friendship through overspending on your chosen hobby. It has happened.

WHICH WAY TO GO?

My job is to advise you on the options available for training models, and also to give some preferences. What, if all other things were equal (which, of course, they never are) would be my principal recommendation for a trainer and teaching system? It would be based on the premise that the model club, of which you were a member, owned and operated the training models with qualified instructors and a properly instigated training scheme. I have to admit that such facilities are very few and far between, although they should not be as most clubs have the money and potential to organise such schemes. The models would be quite large by normal standards, at least eight feet (2.5m) wing span and powered by a spark ignition engine.

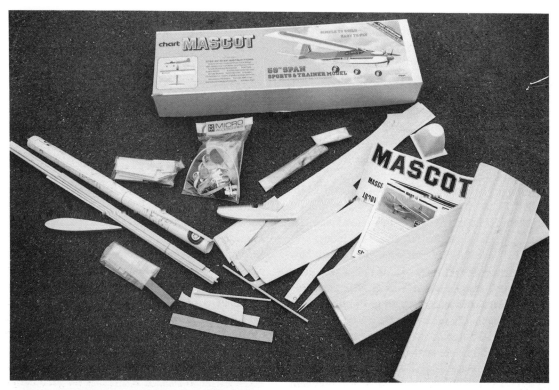

Make the trainer into a high wing design, have a painted cabin and the modeller finds it more attractive and desirable.

Larger models fly better (the aerodynamics lead to more efficiency and sensible wing loadings are possible without sacrificing strength) and they are also much easier to see. Being easier to see is a definite advantage for the older flyer, but it also allows the model to be flown at greater distances without losing the orientation. Spark ignition would be chosen because they are easy to operate and cheap to run with a petrol/oil fuel mix.

For this type of model and the training scheme envisaged it would be essential to use a buddy-box arrangement for the transmitter whereby the instructor operates the master transmitter and this is connected with a control lead to the pupil's 'slave' transmitter. Control can be passed over to the pupil, or taken back, by the flick of a switch on the instructor's transmitter. The advantages, in normal training circumstances, are considerable. With a large model it is essential but has the bonus of allowing the model to be less inherently stable and more suited to a variety of weather conditions — not just calm winds. It would be unreasonable to expect a trainee modeller to equip himself with an arrangement such as this — the cost would probably be prohibitive and transport and storage would cause difficulties. It would also be potentially dangerous for an individual to attempt to fly such a model.

So, we may not be able to have our first choice, but what of the alternatives. If cost isn't a barrier then I would recommend going to a professional training course. There aren't many of these at present, but you will see them advertised in the small ads in magazines such as *Radio Control Models and Electronics* and *Radio Modeller*. Here you will be able to have training on a one-to-one

This would be the best type of model for training at a club, with buddy-box facilities — an enlarged 'Pronto' with a spark ignition engine.

Early R/C models were little more than guided free-flight types, but they allowed the aeromodeller to achieve success with very basic equipment.

basis, either with the model provided or with your own model. Almost as good is to join the MPA (Model Pilots Association) and go along to one of their residential flying weeks at the beginning and end of the summer season. You will be able to attend building courses and have experienced aeromodellers advise you on all aspects of the hobby. There will be flying sites for powered models and gliders and instructors on hand to give you assistance.

Most clubs will be able to offer some training facilities, although the standards and availability may vary — make a point of finding out what is on offer as this may affect your selection of model. From having a reasonable amount of assistance with your flying training let us consider the other end of the scale, where you have no experienced help, only a friend who may be willing, but not very able. I am on record as stating that the chances of learning to fly an R/C model without any form of qualified help is very slim indeed. It is not impossible; I, and many of my generation taught ourselves to fly R/C but we had the very definite advantage of being experienced with free-flight models and how to trim them for flight. Our first R/C models were little more than guided free-flight designs. If you are totally committed, have good stamina, can take disappointments and make some sensible selections then, you can do it. In the chapter on first flights (p. 141), there is a section dealing with this challenge and the type of model to select.

Age and competency must also be factors in the selection of the training model. Give me a ten year old, used to operating computers and with good manual skills and I will teach him or her, weather permitting, to fly an R/C model in a matter of weeks. Give me a sixty year old and, unless he's found the 'elixir of life', it is going to take a whole lot longer. As we get older our reactions become slower, our eyesight less perfect and, mentally, it takes longer to acquire skills. It is no good denying it, we must accept the facts and select our training — and subsequent — models accordingly. Larger, brightly coloured, slower flying types will be more suited to 'senior citizens'. It doesn't mean less fun, the satisfaction will still be there — probably even more so. It may mean that we have to select our weather conditions a little more carefully, but we will probably have more free time than our younger compatriots anyway.

PLAN, KIT OR ARTF

Plan, kit or what? ARTF stands for 'Almost Ready to Fly' and while it is not a new conception it has changed considerably over the past few years. In the early days of ARTF the designs were mostly poor, the models overweight and few could be recommended as genuine trainers. Now, manufacturing techniques have improved (they are still quite labour-intensive and most are produced by Far East countries) and the designs are vastly improved. There is a tendency by the 'true' aeromodeller to be scornful of the ARTFs. It is not proper aeromodelling, they will say. Sheer nonsense, if it is a good way to get someone into the hobby and give him success both he and the hobby

Youth gives the advantages of rapid reactions and learning ability − as you get older you need a little more patience to master the R/C flying skills.

will benefit. That person will go on to build and fly many more models, a failure will fall by the wayside. Consider these facts. The ARTF model has been professionally built and it is unlikely, therefore, to have any poor construction or warps. It is almost finished, just the radio and engine to fit, so the balance point is almost sure to be right and the control surface movements correct. Within a week you should be ready to go flying − your input may not have been great, but you have still contributed to the final result. The finished model

will certainly look attractive as the manufacturers are able to incorporate colours and markings far more flamboyant and eye catching than we are likely to achieve from a kit or a plan.

Now consider the alternatives, building from a plan or a kit. Unless we are particularly competent with our hands, or have had previous experience modelling, are good at reading drawings and are more than averagely good at gluing, wire bending, wood cutting, soldering, covering etc, we are less likely to finish up with a sound, flyable model than

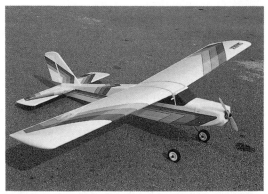

Modern ARTF trainers tend to be well designed and built, attractive and offer a quick means of getting to the flying stage − ignore traditionalists who claim that it is not 'proper aeromodelling'.

if we bought a good ARTF type. It will certainly give us more satisfaction, particularly if we like building, but the initial aim is to get flying.

POWERED MODEL, GLIDER, ELECTRIC?

Flying site conditions will obviously have a bearing on the type of models you fly and those used for training. If you are fortunate enough to live near to a good slope soaring site, then gliding is one option open for R/C flight training. It is perfectly possible to learn to fly using a simple slope soarer and then to move on to powered models if you so wish. Gliders have a number of natural advantages – they are clean, quiet and inexpensive to operate. You need only purchase a two function, rudder and elevator control, radio outfit in the first place as there is no engine control to worry about. There is a further saving by not requiring an engine – or fuel to operate the motor. On the down side are the need for good lift conditions – not all slope sites are suitable for a wide variety of wind conditions – and the top of a hill is not always the most comfortable of places except in warm summer conditions. Learning to land on a

You can learn to fly with a simple two-function glider if there is a good slope site near to you.

slope site calls for different techniques and judgements to powered flying but, with a little advice and assistance from an experienced flyer they can soon be learned – and unlearned again when the time comes.

Nearest to slope soaring with an IC (internal combustion) engine is the powered glider. Designs of gliders, or sailplanes, for operation from flat flying sites differ in that they must be able to take advantage of lighter lift conditions or be able to stay airborne for reasonable periods in no-lift situations. Models, for training and sports flying, have quite light wing loadings and wing aerofoils with high lift coefficients. They are generally slow flying, no bad thing for a trainer, but have to be towed to height on a tow line. This period of flight, when the model accelerates and climbs rapidly can be a little disconcerting for the learner. Also, in still air conditions, the flight time from the release from the tow line to landing is too short to get in sufficient useful training. If thermals (upward air currents caused by temperature rises) are present during the flight, the airborne time can be considerably extended, but you cannot rely on thermals being present at the times when you are training.

An excellent compromise is to use a powered glider for training. This uses the standard two function 'thermal' soarer, but it is fitted with an auxiliary engine, either on the nose or on a power pod on top of the wing. With this system the engine will give enough power to take the model gently to a height at which, when the fuel is used up, the model will continue as a glider. Flights of eight or ten minutes are quite common with this arrangement, more than enough for basic training. Being lightly loaded the models are more suited to calm wind conditions, but given this limitation the powered glider approach has much to offer for the initial training stages. Although IC engines are often used as the power plant (diesels often being favoured as they are more tractable and can be adjusted for power more consistently than glow engines) another alternative is to use electric motor power.

Electric powered R/C models have become highly favoured over the past decade as efficiencies of nickel cadmium rechargeable cells (and more recently, nickel hydride) have improved dramatically. With equally beneficial improvements in

The alternative to a pure glider is to have a powered glider for flat-field flying. It can be powered by an electric motor or a small diesel or glow engine and still be controlled with two-channel radio.

miniaturisation of the radio control airborne equipment, electric flight has been transformed from a specialist subject to a form of R/C flying suited to most aspects of the hobby. In particular, it has been used to great advantage by the ARTF manufacturers as efficient, low drag, mouldings can be produced and designs suited to this form of power introduced. There is still a slight price to pay for using this clean, effective and 'green' form of power. The battery complement is still relatively heavy and the models, many designed for sports flying than pure training, are a little faster than is ideal. However, there are good compromise models available, in plan, kit or ARTF form, and for those who like instant start, no fuss, no mess power flying, electric could be the answer. For those of you who like a modicum of noise, perhaps a little oil and smell, read on.

START ENGINES

The majority of all R/C modellers will cut their 'flying teeth' on a training model powered by a glow or diesel engine, more frequently the former and the pros and cons of these engines are discussed later. There has been an ongoing controversy as long as I can remember as to whether it is better to learn to fly with a three function

(rudder, elevator and engine) control model or to go for a 'full house' four function (i.e. with the addition of aileron control) right from the beginning. Much will depend on the degree of assistance the trainee can rely upon in the first instance. If he has an instructor standing by he can afford to go for the four function system, with a slightly more advanced trainer, knowing that his mentor can get him out of trouble if he makes a mess of any particular part of the flying. If, however, you are going to be left to your own devices for much of the time you would be better off with a three function stable model which will, in part at least, get itself out of trouble providing you remember to throttle back the engine and let go of the controls.

You have the choice of a stable, three-function (no ailerons) trainer with generous wing dihedral or a 'full house', four-function model with slightly less inherent stability — but still a forgiving flyer.

For the 'self-help' type of model you will be looking for good positive stability and this will be found in a model with a high or shoulder wing location, generous dihedral and a light, built-up structure. Many of the 'vintage' cabin designs from the 1950s and 1960s incorporated these features and you can do a lot worse than to select one of these plans. There are also some kits available for this gentle form of introduction to R/C flying. There are also plenty of modern designs that follow the same patterns and make for relaxing flying, but again with the limitations of fine weather performance, they do not make too much headway against the wind and it is all too easy to finish up way downwind. The next compromise is for a model, still preferably using a built-up, balsawood and plywood structure, having similar, but less pronounced, stable features. The wing dihedral will be rather less, the nose and tail moments will still be long and the tail surface proportions generous, but the inherent stability will not be there to the same degree i.e. you will have to control the model for a little more of the time. It may be that instead of incorporating a flat bottom wing aerofoil it will use a semi-symmetrical (the lower surface gently curved) which will also make it more suitable for a wider range of wind strengths, with a trade-off of lower positive pitch stability.

I refer to built-up structures, which may be incorporated in ARTF models, in preference to the moulded fuselage and veneered foam wing types simply because the latter versions can be rather on the heavy side. This is not always the case — you have to be a little careful when selecting a 'glass and foam' trainer. The last thing we want when we are at that critical stage of learning is a model which comes in to land at a high speed and drops out of the air without much warning. Remember, it may produce a stronger

Built-up airframes, as opposed to GRP mouldings and veneered foam wing types, have the advantage of lower weights, but many modellers prefer the latter for ease of construction and more rapid assembly.

airframe, but it will hit the ground harder.

The final form of trainer is the 'full-house' primary trainer, typically featuring a tricycle under-carriage, shoulder or high wing and designed to resemble a full-size aeroplane. A '40' sized engine (6.6cc capacity) and wing span of around 60in. (1.7m) is average. It is a good compromise between the too small − and fast − and the larger, more expensive and less convenient models. It probably represents the most suitable training model for Mr Average who will then go on to use the radio equipment and engine for future projects.

It is impossible to give absolute advice on whether to build from a plan or a kit, much will depend on the facilities available at home for constructing and finishing a model, and whether this part of the hobby is really enjoyable (to some enthusiasts it is as important, almost more enjoyable, than the flying). Only you can provide the answer to this question. If you have only modest facilities for building then the kit, with most of the parts pre-cut and pre-formed, may be the sensible approach. There is a marvellous variety of kits to choose from, the selection is almost overwhelming. From time to time model magazines publish lists of available kits for trainers

and sports models, which should give a lead to the availability and cost of suitable types.

For those of you deciding to build from a plan, or drawing, the selection is even wider. The Plans Services associated with magazines will have handbooks and catalogues listing the plans of the models and often grading the designs into categories of building difficulties. They will also advise on engine suitability. In this book the intention is to cover all the forms of constructional methods.

SO WHICH ONE?

As I said at the beginning of the chapter, there is no such thing as the ideal trainer candidate. You will have to make the final decision but don't rush into that selection. Visit your local model club, ask questions − of experienced flyers and yourself − and when you have sorted out the direction in which you wish to go, that is the time to make your purchases and start the hobby. You are coming up to one of the most exciting phases of any hobby or sport, you don't want to spoil it by making the wrong decisions − I envy you the experience.

CHAPTER 4

Workshop Tools

Not everyone will be fortunate enough to have their own workshop purely for the purpose of building models. It is, though, an ideal to aim for. A properly laid out and equipped workshop will not only make for more efficient building but will make it far more pleasurable too. Assuming that you are going to be able to commandeer a small area of the house for a permanent working area here are a few hints.

Try to plan the work area carefully before rushing in only to find out later that the arrangements are inconvenient. It is impossible to suggest a layout, as all workshop areas will vary in size and shape, but think logically before finally deciding on the permanent position of fixed items. Remember that if the building board is hard up against a side wall it may be impossible to build large one piece wings or join wing panels, because of the lack of overhang. A vice must be positioned so that there is a reasonably clear area all round to allow for bending long pieces of wire. Most power tools, although most useful in reducing building times, also take up quite a lot of space because of the need for free areas around pillar drills, sanders, band saws etc. Unless you have a generous workshop area power tools are best limited to the portable types that can be put away under the work bench when not in use. Good lighting is essential for a workshop area. Fluorescent lamps give an excellent even light and can be augmented by an adjustable spot lamp. Never use just a spot lamp on its own, without background lighting, as this is very tiring on the eyes.

Power socket outlets are best situated at the front of the bench, just underneath, and at the side walls. With these positions you can avoid, as far as possible, having electrical flexes trailing across the bench top.

The primary essentials of the work bench are that it shall be perfectly level, flat and rigid. Without a flat and level surface, that will stay that way, it will be impossible to build warp free structures. Flush doors make a good basis for a workbench and this should be adequately supported at all edges. Small cleats, say 1in. × 1½in. softwood, can be used where the bench abuts the wall but a larger timber member must be used to support the free edges. Position the bench at a suitable height. I prefer to do most of my building standing up, and have the bench level quite high, but also have a high stool for the easier and more repetitive work. Also of prime importance is the building surface; it must be possible to push pins into it without too much effort and it must 'retain' them sufficiently to hold down 'difficult' pieces of balsawood. The best form of board I have discovered is known as 'K' quality hardboard (used extensively for pinboards in schools). Unfortunately this is not generally available at DIY shops but should be available from larger timber merchants. The board is in ¼in. and ⅜in. thicknesses and can be pinned, screwed or glued to the bench with contact adhesive.

In addition to the workbench we need as much storage space as we can obtain, not only for tools and materials, but also for models. One of the problems of storing completed models in the workshop area is that they will get covered with balsa dust during construction. Models are generally bulky and so it is not easy to fit them into cupboards. An alternative, assuming you are not allowed to keep them in the bedroom − my wife is extremely understanding − is to put the models in plastic bags before storing them in the workshop. Large clear polythene bags are sold at most household stores and are excellent for this purpose; slip the model inside and put a rubber band around the neck of the bag.

Simple shelves, supported on pressed steel brackets, will store dopes, boxes and general paraphernalia and a pegboard, with wire clips, fixed vertically on wall framing is ideal for holding

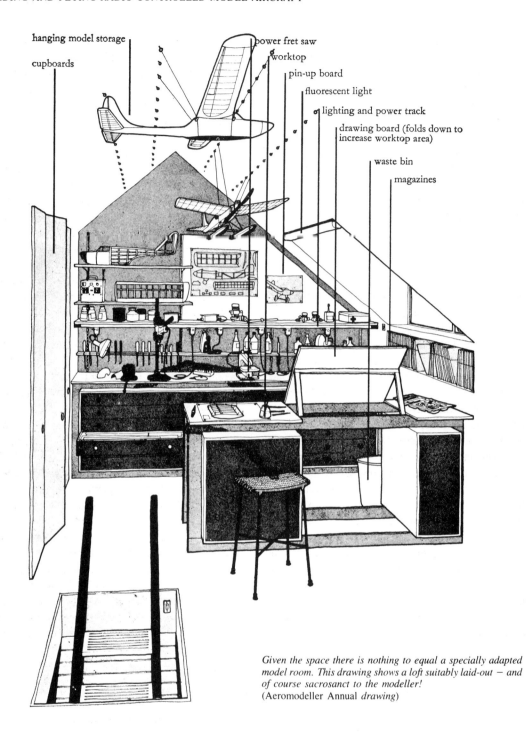

hanging model storage

cupboards

power fret saw

worktop

pin-up board

fluorescent light

lighting and power track

drawing board (folds down to increase worktop area)

waste bin

magazines

Given the space there is nothing to equal a specially adapted model room. This drawing shows a loft suitably laid-out − and of course sacrosanct to the modeller!
(Aeromodeller Annual *drawing*)

large hand tools. For smaller hand tools, screw-drivers, spanners, pliers, etc. wall racks are best, either commercial wire or plastic types or purpose-made from hardboard or plywood. A cupboard will be necessary for storing radio control equipment, engines and other items that must be kept

clear of dust. Small parts storage, nuts, bolts, washers and screws can be stored in screw-top jars, with the tops screwed to the underside of a shelf, or in the interlocking plastic storage boxes available from large stores and ironmongers. Balsawood can be stored in a vertical or horizontal rack. I prefer to store sheet flat and strip in a subdivided (egg carton type divisions) vertical storage rack. A final consideration of the workshop area should be ventilation. When doping and painting is to be carried out in the workshop you will be most unpopular if you let the fumes spread into the house or 'corpse' yourself through lack of adequate ventilation. An electric extractor fan is fine for ventilating the workshop as it gives immediate control of the atmosphere. Most of us, however, have to be satisfied with opening or closing a window to provide the degree of ventilation we need.

HAND TOOLS

Most books on modelling start in the first chapter with a statement to the effect that the only tools required for building are a razor blade, a pair of multi-purpose pliers, a packet of pins and a tube of glue. In reality this is over-simplification. Nothing is more frustrating than not having the correct tool for the job. To anyone just commencing aero-modelling I would suggest they build up, at the earliest possible opportunity, as comprehensive a stock of tools and materials as possible. Do not, however, fall into the trap of buying inferior tools. This is a false economy as top quality equipment should last a lifetime. You should not have to 'pay the earth' for these tools; some good ex-government surplus stock is obtainable or the auction sales can also provide second-hand tools at very reasonable costs. The main aim should be to acquire a wide assortment of files, screwdrivers, pliers, drills, etc.; the better equipped you are the quicker and more pleasurable becomes the building.

The one 'basic' tool required for aeromodelling construction is a very sharp cutting edge. Opinion is divided as to whether a razor blade or modelling knife is best for cutting balsa strip to length and cutting out sheet parts. The principal advantage of a razor blade is that it has a sharper edge; but it is, of course, a more hazardous tool to employ and the fact that it is flexible makes it difficult to cut thicker sheet accurately. A modelling knife has the advantage that it can take different shapes of blades for different work; or even a razor saw for cutting thicker sections of strip wood.

In fact, both tools are really essential. In the case of razor blades, some people prefer the stiffer (and safer to handle) single-edged 'backed' type; others the more flexible double-edge type either whole or broken in half to form an angled cutting point. Choice is largely a matter of individual preference, although double-edge types usually appear to stay sharper longer — but perhaps this is only because they have two usable cutting edges! In all cases, however, it pays to buy new blades and throw away blades as soon as they lose their edge. It is not worth the trouble of trying to re-sharpen razor blades as the results obtained are seldom satisfactory.

With regard to modelling knives, again choice is rather a matter of individual preference. The slim handled knife with tapered, pointed blade is best for light cutting and trimming work. A heavier handle, either plain or enlarged into a 'grip', will take a stouter and wider straight tapered blade for cutting thicker sheet, etc. or various carving blades. It should be noted that the blades for knives vary considerably in quality. Blades used in the surgical type knives (designed for surgeons rather than specifically for modellers) are of the highest quality steel and keep their edge over a long period — and re-sharpen well. Heavier duty, general purpose knives have blades of much

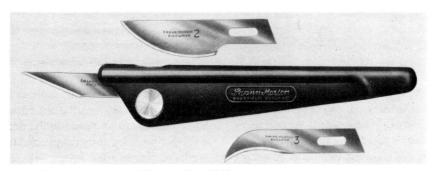

One of the many types of modeller's knife available.

lower quality and they have to be changed more frequently. When it comes to heavier carving work, however, a separate knife is usually better than a long carving knife in a modelling knife handle. This can be an inexpensive kitchen-type knife, sharpened to a really keen edge — and kept sharp. A long modelling knife blade can snap if used for 'heavy' carving and the fact that it will also tend to flex makes for less accurate carving work. Another invaluable tool for planing block balsa is the razor plane. This simple and cheap device will save many laborious hours of carving with a knife and is far more accurate a tool for shaping leading edges etc.

For other cutting jobs a variety of saws will be handy, and in some cases essential. Thus a fretsaw or coping saw is essential for cutting out parts in ply thicker than ¹⁄₁₆ in. Ply of ¹⁄₁₆ in. thickness or less can be cut more accurately with a modelling knife — but more easily with a saw. A small stiff-backed saw and a small hacksaw are also other handy tools — also a hacksaw blade fitted with a handle made from a length of dowel split in half. None of these is an expensive item to buy and all are worthwhile additions to the modeller's workshop equipment.

The razor saw, which is like a small version of the stiff-backed saw but fitting a modelling knife handle, is also well worth having. Its very fine teeth produce a clean cut across the grain when parting off thicker strip, and it can also be used on ply and hard sheet plastic. It is not so suitable for cutting materials of any appreciable thickness, however, as the blade tends to jam in the cut.

Other useful cutting tools are a set of small files, although these will have more limited application. Fine flat files are very useful for accurate slotting work — such as slotting a trailing edge to accommodate inset ribs. Choose a thickness the same as that of the rib sheet and be sure to buy files that have a cutting surface on the edge as well as on the face! A small triangular file will also be useful for cutting thicker steel wire to length — cutting pliers usually 'give up' on this sort of job on 16swg wire, or thicker.

You will also need some 'marking out' tools, such as a steel rule, small metal T-square and a 30–60 or 45 degree set square. Beside measuring, the steel rule can also be used as a guide for straight cuts with a razor blade or modelling knife.

The T-square is for marking out right angles on sheet or block (or larger strip sections). The set square is a necessary instrument for checking the squareness of the alignment of box fuselages when assembling the two side frames.

A collection of good pliers is always useful, but this can be built up as you go along. Most of the wire bending and cutting requirements can be tackled with a stout pair of general purpose pliers, since hooks and similar shapes are most accurately formed by pulling and bending wire around a suitable mandrel (e.g. a piece of metal rod held in a vice).

Cutting pliers have their uses for cutting piano wire up to 16swg, but not larger, and even then need to be of first class quality to withstand notching, or even breaking. Round-nosed and snipe-nosed pliers are very useful for manipulating bends in soft wire or piano wire up to 20swg.

A hand drill is one of those tools which is an essential part of most home workshops, together with a suitable selection of good twist drills. For working with the smaller drill sizes — ¹⁄₁₆ in. and under — a pin vice is easier to handle than a hand drill and far less likely to produce broken drills.

A medium size vice, substantial enough for bending up to 8swg piano wire, is essential. Mount it on the bench near an upright to ensure it is rigid enough. 'G' clamps are also useful for some forms of construction as are 'bulldog' clips and ordinary household plastic spring pegs. Working on your own you often feel the need for a 'third hand' and all these forms of clamps can assist you; another excellent hand tool is a mole wrench which has the facility to 'lock' on to materials.

Screwdrivers are required not only in different sizes but also for both normal single slot and Phillips head screws. Always use a screwdriver that is large enough for the task, trying to undo a 4BA screw with a small 'electrician's' screwdriver will cause frustration and damage to the screw-head and probably you as well. Special screwdrivers, with screw holding devices, can be useful for some difficult situations and another tip is to magnetise a long-shanked small screwdriver to enable it to 'hold' small screws when they are being inserted in awkward spots. Some engines, and other pieces of equipment, use Allen bolts and for these you will need a set of Allen wrenches unless a wrench is supplied with the equipment.

A purpose-made modeller's vice with alternative jaws, fully swivelling, and clamp on base.

At the time of publishing this book the most commonly used range of nuts and bolts is the metric range. It would seem very likely that, within a short time, the metric system will supersede the BA range. This means that you may have to invest in both sizes of spanners for the present. A set of open ended spanners will look after most jobs but you will find that box spanners will also be required in some situations. The 'cheap' variety of box spanner sets, with changeable socket ends and a plastic handle, will suffice for our purposes.

Although not used very often, we hope, a small hammer will be part of your equipment; a 4oz hammer should be heavy enough for all of our purposes. To go with the hammer a small centre punch will be of great assistance when you come to drill holes in metal and plastics.

Sanding blocks and sandpaper are, whether we like it or not, going to be necessary during all phases of construction. Common sandpaper is a fairly inferior product for our purposes and much more preferable is garnet paper or some of the new 'anti clogging' papers. For finishing on paintwork wet or dry paper may be used and this is obtainable in grades from about 200 to 600. Sanding blocks can easily be made from pieces of softwood. The sanding paper should preferably be glued, with a contact adhesive, to the wood to prevent the sanding paper from tearing and digging into the surface of the model. A variety of small sanding blocks should also be made from odd scraps of dowel, triangular section, square hardwood etc. for sanding those awkward corners that cannot be reached with the large sanding block.

To complete your selection of tools and accessories you will also need the following miscellaneous items.

Pins — both steel dressmaking and glass-headed

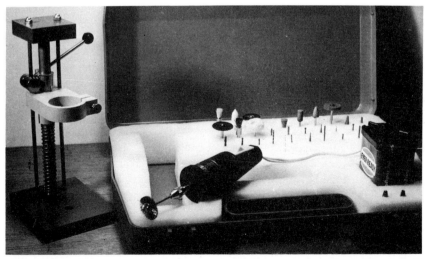

Although relatively expensive, a power jigsaw and attachments can prove a boon. That shown is fitted to a Unimat Mk. 3 miniature lathe.

Small battery driven drills and accessories such as the Precision Petite have a great appeal and can be used anywhere.

pins. Beware when pushing in glass-headed pins; the glass can shatter and the pin pierce your finger.

Masking tape, clear adhesive tape and electrical tape.

Ball point pens, soft pencils and a Chinagraph pencil.

Soldering irons − a heavy duty one for large diameters of piano wire and a small one if electrical soldering is to be undertaken.

Solder − resin core solder *only* for electrical work although acid core solder can be used for piano wire, tin plate, brass etc.

POWER TOOLS

Power tools are not strictly essential for building radio control models but do make many chores a lot more pleasant. One of the most useful, and versatile, of the power tools is the Dremel fretsaw with attachments. The attachments include a flexible shaft, which fits into a take-off point on the saw, and many accessories such as a buffing wheel, sanding disc and grinding wheel. It can also be used for drilling. Dremel also produce a Moto-Tool which is a small powerful hand electric drill, again with a number of attachments available including a drill stand and router.

DIY power drills and stands are equally useful for the modeller, the two speed variety giving more control for drilling plastics, wood and soft metals. Having one hand free to support the work, with the drill mounted in a vertical stand, increases the accuracy of the work and reduces the time taken to drill the holes. Band saws are of less general use than a fretsaw (you cannot cut internal holes with a bandsaw) but they are excellent for cutting block wood and multiple layers of sheet (wing ribs) where the extra power and throat depth is an advantage. Whether you invest in a lathe will probably depend on your aptitude as an engineer. They are undoubtedly invaluable for turning parts for special silencers and many other metal parts, but the cost of a good lathe cannot be justified purely by the amount of work done on the machine. A belt sander or vibratory sander will certainly take a lot of the 'elbow grease' out of sanding and is desirable for the modeller expecting to do a lot of building.

When you know that you enjoy the building and construction phases of the hobby you will find many tools, both hand and power variety, that will make the modelling tasks easier and more enjoyable. There are some purpose designed modelling tools that, once used, seem almost indispensable. In this category I would certainly include the Permagrit tools, which are 'sanding' implements featuring a welded-on abrasive material, in the form of bars, blocks, wheels, needle files and saw blades in a variety of grades. They are extremely long lasting, very effective and a 'must' for serious modellers.

One problem you may find when purchasing strip materials such as balsawood, spruce or obechi, is obtaining stock of similar consistency. One way of overcoming this problem is to cut your own strip material from the sheet, providing that the sheet is of consistent density and character throughout. It is, in any case, worthwhile marking, with a felt tip pen, one end of the sheet so that the strip ends can be sorted after cutting. Although balsawood strippers, with a knife blade, will cope with thinner, softer varieties of balsawood, harder woods and greater thicknesses will require a circular saw for good results. On the market there are ranges of mini-tools which include a small circular saw attachment. Beware of the smallest

– and cheapest – of these systems as they are not man enough for the job as far as our modelling is concerned. There are larger versions which will cope with materials up to ¼ in. thick and produce a clean, square cut (or angled if required) – these are ideal for our needs.

Visit the Model Engineer Exhibition held in London each year at the end of December to see the tool ranges available. You will be able to inspect a vast range of tools and materials and have the bonus of seeing some of the best made models in the world. There is a good chance that you will also be able to witness some indoor R/C flying, a truly exciting challenge.

This list of tools may sound a little formidable but the handyman will already have many of them. Also, looked after properly, most of the tools will last you a lifetime.

Few modellers will have the benefits of a separate building for modelling activities but it makes the building and storage of large models very much easier.

CHAPTER 5

Materials

WOODS

Despite the introduction of many new materials, such as glassfibre and plastics, one building material has remained 'King' over the thirty or so years that radio control models have been built. That is a material with many excellent properties. Combining strength with light weight, easily cut and sanded, available in various grades and yet a naturally produced material − it is balsawood.

Although, botanically at least, balsa is only about the fourth or fifth lightest wood in the world it is the first of all the woods which combine strength with lightness. On a strength/weight basis, in fact, balsa compares favourably with most other woods − even oak. This is one of the main reasons why it is so suitable for aeromodelling, where strength is required with minimum weight. Many other materials which are as light as, or lighter than balsa, also fall down on this question of combining strength with lightness and cannot be used in small sections − expanded polystyrene, for example. As it has a fairly open structure, glues impregnate and adhere strongly to balsa with the result that properly made glued joints are as strong as or stronger than the wood itself. With balsa readily available in a wide range of sheet, strip and block sizes, very few tools are required for working balsa, either in solid form or for the assembly of built-up frames, etc.

The actual density of balsa can vary from as little as 4lb/cu.ft. to as much as 24lb/cu.ft. (which is about the same as obechi). Practically all the commercial balsa available, however, falls within the range of 6 to 16lb/cu.ft. with the overall average tending to run about 9−10lb/cu.ft. The strength properties of balsa vary directly with density − the denser the wood the stronger it is.

Balsa is normally graded by density, although the actual descriptions are largely arbitrary and not always identical between different suppliers,

or different model designers specifying grades to be used. The most general commercial classification is 'light', 'medium' and 'hard', as follows:

Grade	Light or Soft	Medium	Hard
Density lb/cu.ft.	6−8	9−12	12−16

Logically one selects the lightest grades for the lightly stressed parts (e.g. block wing tips, sheet fill-in, etc.) and the heavier grades for spars and longerons. Even here, however, practice can differ. Some modellers prefer to use very hard balsa for longerons and spars and keep weight to a minimum by reducing the actual size of the sections used. Others prefer to use a lighter grade and compensate for strength by using a larger section.

Both systems have their advantages and disadvantages. The use of hard grades and small sections actually gives the best overall strength to weight ratio. On the other hand, the smaller size spars may be more difficult to handle for building and also lack local stiffness. Using larger sizes normally gives greater stiffness and local strength, although it is also easy to add excess weight as well unless the grade is carefully selected. Also if too light a stock is chosen in the interests of saving weight, the resulting structure may be weak. For most purposes, however, Table I can be used as a guide for balsa grade selection.

Obechi

Obechi was used as a substitute for balsawood during the war when balsawood could not be imported for modelling. Weightwise, it is equal to the heavier grades of balsawood and the strength is

Opposite: Some of the right and wrong ways of cutting balsa. Right ways, of course, are on the left.

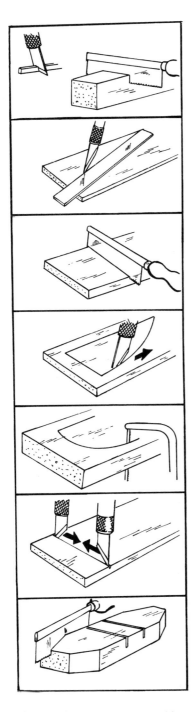

similar. Because of these similarities, and because balsawood is more easily available, obechi is now little used for general building construction. In veneer form, obechi is used as covering for expanded foam wings as it is less expensive, more convenient and more 'dent' resisting than balsa sheet.

Spruce

Spruce, or hemlock, can be purchased in sheet or strip form although it is in the latter form that it is mainly used for modelling work. Spruce strip can be used to advantage for wing spars where the wing thickness ratio (depth/chord ratio) is low, and

Table I. Recommended applications of balsa grades

Grade	Application(s)
Light	Sheet fill-in on built-up fuselages. Semi-solid or hollow log fuselages. Sheet covering (fuselages and wings) – Small models. Wing leading edge sheeting. Cowling blocks.
Light–Medium	Sheet fill-in on larger models. Large section leading and trailing edges. All-sheet tail surfaces. Solid sheet wings. Sheet-box construction (e.g. fuselages),
Medium	Spacers on box fuselages. Trailing edges. Longerons of generous section.
Medium–Hard	Wing spars of generous section. Auxiliary wing spars. Longerons. Small section trailing edges.
Hard	Main wing spars. Longerons of small section. Auxiliary spars of very small section.
Extra-hard	Inset leading edges on side sheet wings. Wing mainspars of small section.

Table II. Recommended applications of balsa 'cuts'

'Cut'	Application(s)	NOT to be used for
Quarter-grain	Ribs cut from sheet balsa (all sizes and types of models). Trailing edges (cut from sheet). Fuselage sheet covering.	Sheet, curved or curved surfaces
True tangent cut	Sheet tail surfaces. Sheet covering wing leading edges. Covering curved surfaces.	Ribs, sheet, tail surfaces.
Random	General application, but select for suitability by individual test as characteristics will vary between 'quarter-grain' and 'tangent' cut.	

as is the case with scale models of early aeroplanes. The superior strength, and consistency in small sections, makes it also superior to balsawood for

scale open frame fuselages where, for scale reasons the size of the members must be kept to a minimum. Other minor uses of spruce are for strip ailerons, on small aircraft, elevator joiners, undercarriage fairing and wing struts.

Beech

Beech is used for two primary purposes in modelling: engine bearers and dowels. For engine bearers the beech is available, from model shops, in a variety of sizes from ¼ in. × ⅜ in. up to ½ in. × ¾ in. in lengths of 12in. or 18in. Because it is a close grain, hard and tough wood it will stand the stresses and vibrations of a radio control engine bolted to a surface without showing undue wear and tear. It is also reasonably impervious to fuels, although it should always be doped and fuel proofed. The strength of beech is also the reason that it is used as dowels for retaining wings, tailplanes and undercarriages by rubber bands. Beech, though, is also relatively short grained and care should be made in selecting the dowel to avoid any crossgrain that will cause the dowel to break easily when stressed. It is for this reason that birchwood is frequently used for dowels instead of beech. Birch is not as hard but is much straighter grained than beech and is strong enough for most of our purposes. To increase the strength, and fuel resistant properties of dowels, they should be immersed, one end at a time, in clear dope for a period of twenty-four hours, removed, allowed to dry and sanded and this operation repeated two or three times.

Ramin

You will probably not be able to purchase ramin in your local model shop but it is available, in sizes from about ⅜ in. square upwards from timber merchants. Limited in its application to modelling it is nevertheless useful for engine bearers and mounting blocks for undercarriages, cabane struts etc. which are reasonably highly stressed.

Plywood

Aircraft grade plywood is the best type to use for radio control models. Unfortunately this material is not easy to come by and, when you can get it, it is very expensive as it is specially 'cleared' by government inspectors for aircraft manufacture. The best alternative is high quality resin bonded. Finnish plywood which is a very 'clean' and consistent material that cuts well. Normal thicknesses are .8 or 1mm (1/32 in.), 1.5mm (1/16 in.), 3 and 4mm (−1/8 in. and +1/8 in.), 5mm (3/16 in.) and 6mm (−1/4 in.). Plywood is used for highly stressed parts such as engine bulkheads, undercarriage plates and doublers, formers with large access cutouts, wing dihedral braces and, in the thinner sizes, full length nose doublers. Mahogany plywood may also be used but is more difficult to cut; it also tends to have a coarser texture to the surface. The direction of the outer face grain is frequently important to consider when cutting out parts. Most of the plywood we use will be 3-ply, i.e. the grain is in the same direction on the outer faces and the centre veneer has the grain running at a right angle to these. For items such as dihedral braces we need the maximum strength lengthwise and, therefore, the outer grains should be in this direction.

Veneers are mostly used for covering polystyrene foam wings and usually are of obechi or mahogany about 1/64 in. thick. Veneers can also be useful in scale models to simulate the mahogany plywood and wooden dashboards used in the full-size aircraft. Contact adhesives are commonly employed for gluing veneers to other materials and it is advisable to slightly spray dampen mahogany veneers before they are glued into position.

METAL WIRES, TUBES AND SHEET

Piano wire

Piano wire is a high tensile steel wire which, because of its strength, 'spring' and bending qualities, make it ideal for modelling purposes. Sizes are going to be a problem with the change over to metric sizes, the normal modelling range is at present from 20swg (about 1/32 in. dia.) to 8swg (5/32 in. dia.), in even gauges, and in lengths of 36in. The wire tends to vary in strength, brittleness and bending quality, not only from one manufacturer to another, but also in one particular batch. Wire should never be bent over the sharp edge of a vice jaw, or it may fracture; use soft metal facing plates to the jaws. Commercial bending tools, specifically designed for the model business, are readily available and, if you propose doing a lot of building from scratch, it would be worthwhile purchasing one. Bending jigs are essential for producing nosewheel legs incorporating a spring coil.

Thin sizes, 18 and 20swg, can be cut with heavy duty pliers and wire cutters but larger sizes must be cut with a hacksaw (high speed cutting blade) or a triangular fine cut file. Pliers, flat jaw or round nose, are also substantial enough for bending the lighter gauges but larger diameter wire should always be bent in a vice or bending jig.

Soldering piano wire is not difficult providing two considerations are borne in mind. Cleanliness

Large models, such as the 10-foot wing span twin-engine model, shown above, may feature balsawood construction or GRP and foam methods.

is essential for satisfactory soldering; the oil film must be wiped from the wire and the area to be soldered is then burnished bright with steel wool. The second consideration is a hot, and sufficiently large, iron. You will never solder the heavier gauges of wire together, and produce a strong joint, with a small electrician's soldering iron. It is advisable to 'tin' the surfaces of the piano wire to be joined before commencing the joint, i.e. a thin film of flux cored solder is flowed over the wire. For joints of undercarriage assemblies, wing cabane struts, and other areas of high stress, the joints should be bound together with copper wire, after tinning and before soldering. Ready tinned copper wire of various gauges can be obtained from electrical stores, about 24swg is correct for most of our purposes. The wire is bound round the joint and the solder flowed into the joint. Hold the iron under the joint and apply the solder to the top surface to be sure the whole of the joint area is hot. The solder fills the gaps between the piano wire and the binding wire making a 'full' joint. File down the rough 'blobs' of solder and ends of binding wire to give a smooth finish.

Dural dowel

Instead of using wood dowel, for wing and under-carriage retaining purposes, dural dowel can be used as an alternative. It is a little heavier than the wood dowels but is very much stronger and often a size smaller can be used. Epoxy glue should be used for fixing it into the fuselage and the exposed ends can either be painted or burnished.

Tubing

Brass tubing is available with internal diameters to match all of the piano wire gauges. The tubing is used as the housing for piano wire 'dowels' for detachable wing fixings. Although the internal diameters of different makes of brass tubing are constant the wall thickness may not be; choose the wall thickness required for the purpose, i.e. a large diameter tubing for a wing fixing should have a reasonably thick wall.

Most sizes of brass and aluminium tubing can be cut with a spare, straight edged knife blade. The tubing is placed on a flat surface, the knife blade positioned 90° to the tubing and the tubing rotated under the blade with a rolling action. As soon as an incision has been made the tubing can be snapped apart with a clean break. Bending thin walled brass and aluminium tube presents some difficulties but commercial benders, in the form of heavy duty springs, are available at a reasonable cost.

Copper tubing, being much softer by nature, is more suitable for fuel tank pipes in clunk tanks. It is easily bent and, unlike brass tubing, does not tend to 'collapse' at the area of the bend. The same conditions for soldering piano wire apply; the tubing must be clean and the iron hot.

Metal sheet

Aluminium, dural, brass and tinplate sheet all have their minor places to take in the construction of radio control model aircraft. Try to build up a stock of different types and thicknesses.

SYNTHETIC RESIN BONDED LAMINATES

The best known of these plastics are known under their brand names of 'Formica' and 'Warerite'. This material, about 1/16 in. thick and normally used for kitchen worktops and tables etc., is useful for cutting out special control horns and cranks. It is not strong enough, unless doubled or tripled in thickness by having different layers, for engine plates.

Paxolin sheet is more frequently used for engine plates. It is available in thicknesses, for our purposes, of 1/8 in., 3/16 in. and 1/16 in. and is a synthetic resin bonded paper. Tufnol sheet manufactured using a cloth is also available; this is much stronger than the Paxolin but is not so suitable for engine mounting plates. The name given to engine plates originally was 'break-away' plates for the obvious reason that, in a severe crash, the plate would break rather than the engine be damaged. Today this reason seems to be very much overlooked but is, I think, still very valid. It is better to go to a size thicker in Paxolin − 3/16 in. should be sufficient for larger engines − than use a thinner SRB fabric.

ADHESIVES

The problem these days is in keeping up with the

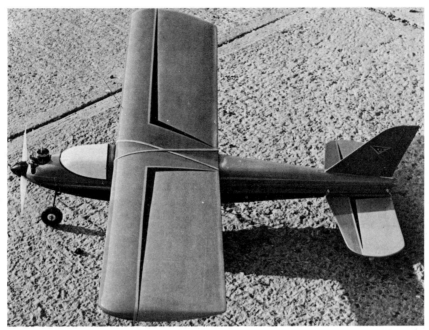

This commercial ARTF (almost ready to fly) model features moulded plastic and expanded polystyrene in its construction.

number of commercially available adhesives and knowing the qualities and limitations of each. There must be an adhesive obtainable for sticking just about any material to another but we can narrow the field down to about five types. They are:

1. Balsa cement.
2. PVA white glues.
3. Epoxy adhesives.
4. Contact adhesives (where two surfaces are coated and the adhesive allowed to dry before mating).
5. Styro foam/veneer adhesive, also contact, of the 'Styro bond' type.
6. Cyanocrylate − 'instant glue'.

Balsa cement, one of the original adhesives for balsawood, is faster drying than most other glues used in modelling. It is suitable for balsa to balsa joints and has certain gap filling qualities, i.e. if there is a slight discrepancy of the mating of the two balsa surfaces the cement will fill the gap. It is difficult to use for securing large sheeted areas as the cement dries before the sheeting can be positioned and pinned. When a particularly strong joint, using balsa cement is required, pre-cementing is recommended, i.e. coating the two surfaces with cement first and allowing it to dry before recementing for the final joint. Balsa cement sands easily but is not fuel-proof and is not recommended

for hardwood or wood to metal joints.

PVA glue has to a very great extent taken over from balsa cement as the main adhesive for balsa wood construction. Being a water soluble adhesive it should not be used for floatplanes or flying boats. For most conventional airframe construction it is ideal, providing one takes the trouble to make sure all the pieces fit together well − it will not fill gaps readily. For sheeting work such as balsa leading edge sheeting, its use is almost imperative due to its slower drying characteristics. Using PVA glue for larger sheeted 'doubler' areas, where two sheeted surfaces are to be glued together, presents certain problems. The water base to the adhesive tends to 'warp' the balsawood and the unit must be very securely clamped and pinned during the drying period − this can be very extended as little air is present at the centre of the two sheeted areas to allow the glue to dry. Some PVA glues never seem to dry completely 'brittle' hard and, although structurally this is no problem, it can make difficulties during sanding operations. Unless one is careful − and a sanding block should always be used − a ridge can be formed at a joint where the glue is resisting the sanding more than the balsa. The cost of PVA glue is very much less than other types, particularly when bought in large bottles.

Epoxy adhesives are now produced, for domestic

and modelling uses, by most major manufacturers of adhesives. These are 'two pack' adhesives with one tube containing the adhesive and the other hardener; they are mixed in equal parts. Two types are available, the standard and the quick setting − drying time about ten minutes. The quick setting variety has become very popular with the modeller because it can speed up the building operations without sacrificing any strength. In fact it is probably used in many places where, from the strength consideration, it is not really warranted. Epoxies are particularly good for gluing hardwood and metals They are fuel-proof and fairly easy to use. When squeezing out the adhesive from the tubes take care not to get any of the hardener on the end of the adhesive tube, otherwise the cap will stick in place.

Contact adhesives are not suitable for general building operations but are ideal for joining sheeted doubler areas together. The setting time is quite good, about fifteen minutes for the separate glued surface to dry, and once the surfaces are placed together a bond forms. This immediate bonding

feature can also be a disadvantage. Unless you position the sheeted surfaces accurately first time they are impossible to move again. One way to ensure that the parts to be glued are correctly lined up is to lay a piece of tracing paper, or clear plastic film between the two surfaces, when they have dried, and gradually withdraw it as the parts are lined up over each other.

Fixing the plywood template of wing section.

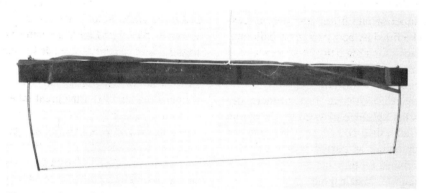

The cutting bow with heated platinum tensioned wire.

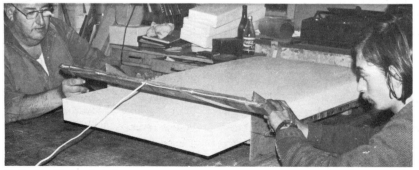

Cutting the block to basic size.

Also a contact adhesive, but with a different base and solvent, is the adhesive for adhering veneers to foam polystyrene cores. It is essential to use these special adhesives, or Copydex, when covering foam cores.

One of the growing range of 'miracle' adhesives is cyanocrylate. This is a one part adhesive which relies on the water present in the material, or air, to achieve its 'set'. Being extremely strong it gives, used correctly, a joint strength in excess of most of the materials it will glue together. The bond is made within seconds of introducing the adhesive and maximum strength is achieved quite rapidly. It is particularly useful for gluing 'difficult' materials such as nylon, rubber, silicone, PTFE, metals, etc., and it will normally join any combination of these. Cyanocrylates should be treated with respect as they are capable of gluing together skin/skin and skin to other materials. Being also an expensive adhesive it should be used only in areas where other adhesives are not suitable or for very specific purposes; i.e. rapid field repairs. Although the standard cyanocrylate adhesive has instant bonding properties there are also types available with slower setting qualities; these also tend to have superior gap filling abilities. Excessive gaps can be filled by applying glass balloons, or baking soda, to the area before the adhesive is deployed. Greasy or oily parts are notoriously difficult to join with any form of glue but one type of cyanocrylate, two part adhesive (commercially known as 'rocket' glue) will even achieve this miracle. The adhesive comes with an aerosol spray hardener and it is particularly useful for repairing models where they have been damaged around the engine or fuel bay area.

There are constant additions to the adhesives range and most of them have some application to the model hobby sphere; do not be afraid to try new ones for suitable applications. When you are unsure of the suitability of an adhesive for a particular purpose the best answer is to make a simple practical test using scrap materials.

GLASS FIBRE

Glass fibre and resins, their uses and methods, is a large enough subject for a book, indeed there are separate technical books on the subject. I will content myself here with making some general comments on this versatile material.

Glass Reinforced Plastic (GRP) consists of the resin and the reinforcement, either chopped strand mat or woven cloth. In modelling terms it can be used to reinforce local areas where hard treatment is anticipated, i.e. on the underside of the nose of a model, or for joining parts together and reinforcing the joint, i.e. jointing two foam wing halves together. The second, and main purpose, of glass fibre work is to mould it into fuselages, wheel spats, cheek cowls, nose cowls and many other model aircraft parts. Providing weight considerations are not too vital, and the material is used sensibly, glass fibre fuselages are both practical and very strong. With no limitations in complex curves, fairings and general 'lines' glass-fibre mouldings can produce fuselages that are very beautiful and would be almost impossible to produce by conventional constructional methods. Commercial fuselage mouldings are available but it is perfectly feasible for the lone modeller to produce his own master mould, female mould and finished GRP mouldings. It involves quite a lot of work for a 'one off' fuselage but makes an ideal club project where a number of modellers wish to make the same model. Resins are either of the epoxy or polyester types, the latter version being slightly easier to use as it tends to 'stay put' more readily than epoxy resin. Epoxy based GRP mouldings offer slightly increased strength, weight for weight, but the great inherent strength of these mouldings makes this advantage less important, apart from specialised purposes such as scale models and helicopter fuselages. With the reduction in building time offered by GRP products, and the consistency of the mouldings, they will undoubtedly be a popular alternative to conventional structures.

For reinforcing vulnerable areas fibreglass resin can be used on its own (it is excellent for coating the engine and fuel tank bay areas) or with the glass cloth. The resin penetrates the balsa surface and adds strength, hardness and abrasion resistance; with the cloth and further coats of resin the strength is further increased. Glassfibre is, because of its hardness, difficult to sand and, therefore, it is more simple to fill in any pores or holes with a filler, again using the resin as a base. Glassfibre fillers can be purchased from car accessory shops as it is used extensively for car body repairs.

MODERN LAMINATES

Advances in finding new materials for composite materials continues at a bewildering pace. No sooner have we got used to the idea of using materials such as carbon fibre, than along comes Kevlar and after that boron. All of these materials have their uses in R/C model aircraft building, but more so in some of the specialised fields. R/C helicopters is one of the obvious areas where these 'space age' materials can be used to great benefit. Components where high strength is required, or maximum rigidity, can gain a lot from using the new materials and moulding techniques. Competition sailplanes, pylon racers and sophisticated scale models are other types of models where good use can be put for plastic laminates.

There is no doubt that, in common with full-size aircraft where designs as diverse as airliners and VTOL fighters make considerable use of plastic composites, the use of plastics will increase in modelling where efficiency and performance is at a premium. Specialist books are available on the materials and processes and there are also frequent articles on the subject in the specialist hobby magazines.

STYROFOAM

Expanded styrofoam was originally produced for the building industry and was 'adopted' for the modelling hobby. It is mostly used as cores for veneer covered wings. Styrofoam can also be used for non stressed areas such as fuselage 'turtle' decking. Cutting and covering veneered foam wings is well within the capability of most modellers and the only specialised equipment required is a hot wire cutter. Commercial cutters are available, they consist of a bow and ni-chrome wire for cutting, or they can be made from hardwood dowel and piano wire. A variable output transformer will allow cutting speeds to be varied and different length cutting bows to be used. Wing root and tip templates are cut from plywood or sheet plastic and the edges should be sanded very smooth to prevent the wire snagging during the cutting operation. Obviously, only parallel or straight taper wing panels can be cut by this method and curved plan forms (i.e. elliptical wings) are best produced with built-up construction.

Expanded polystyrene foam can be purchased in various densities, averaging about 1lb cu.ft. In addition to the standard quality (suitable for relatively thick section wings) heavy duty and extra duty qualities may be obtained and are suitable for smaller sectioned wing panels. 'Blue' foam has a higher density and finer texture than the white materials (formed from the fusing of expanded polystyrene beads) and is sufficiently rigid to be used, in some cases, without additional veneering.

Balsawood and obechi veneers are the most common materials for covering foam cores, the former material gives a lighter finish but obechi is easier to use (it is available in widths in excess of 12 inches) and cheaper. For a very high strength wing the core can be covered with .4mm thick plywood, although there is a weight penalty in using this material. Leading edges are either balsawood or, with a reasonable leading edge radius, the veneer may be wrapped completely around the front of the wing. Great care must be taken when the covering is applied to the foam core to ensure that no twisting takes place during this operation. It is virtually impossible to remove any twists or warps from this type of construction after the veneer has been fixed in place.

In addition to foam wings made by cutting the foam from blocks it is also possible to purchase moulded foam wings. Although, being moulded in one piece, they have the advantages of being 'finished' as bought, they are only practical for models of about 44in. span. With no surface sheeting to add rigidity and strength to the wing they rely to some degree on flexibility for their strength and, with larger sizes and greater loads, would be likely to fail. Finishing techniques with moulded foam wings are rather different to conventional balsa constructed wings or veneer covered foam wings, and instructions are included when the wings are purchased.

ABS PLASTIC SHEET

ABS plastic sheet is widely used for producing vacuum formed parts for model aircraft from fuselage shells to wheel spats, wing tips, radial cowls and, in some cases, complete ARTF (almost ready to fly) models. A disadvantage with vacuum formings, compared with glass fibre, is that the

Cutting styrófoam for wing core with a heated wire.

Carefully positioning the foam core on the veneer after the adhesive is touch dry.

Trimming the lower part of the veneer.

Wrapping the foam core leading edge around the veneer.

Pressing the upper side of the core onto the veneer.

(Photographs taken at Aviette Kits, Newport Pagnell.)

moulding cannot be integrally strengthened at high stress points. To overcome this a certain amount of reinforcing is required for fuselages in the form of plywood, balsa wood or additional ABS plastic mouldings. Gluing moulded parts together can be carried out with a clear adhesive (e.g. Bostik Clear Adhesive) or with a special solvent. The solvent softens the plastic sheet to an extent that with the two surfaces welded together a 'welded' joint is formed. This gives a very strong joint but the solvent must be applied to strict limits otherwise the sheet will be over-softened causing distortion and, possibly, melting.

The author with one of his large scale models, a ¼ size 'Bleriot XI', developed from a design used in a television series.

CLEAR PLASTIC SHEET

For windscreens and cockpit covers there are a number of types of clear plastic sheet on the market. Unfortunately, with so many new plastics being invented all the time, it is difficult to tell which type of sheet one is buying. They all have slightly different properties and acceptance of types of adhesives. Acetate sheet is easily secured, and is softened by, balsa cement but it is not fuel-proof and must be hot fuel-proofed before the model is flown. Butyrate sheet is fuel-proof and

can be glued with balsa cement or epoxy adhesive. Some of the other clear plastic sheeting, especially PVC types may be difficult to glue with anything other than clear adhesives. If you are uncertain experiment with scraps of the material.

DOPES, PAINTS AND COVERING MATERIALS

All of these items too, will be covered in later chapters.

MISCELLANEOUS

You will need in your stock a selection of various sizes of nuts, bolts, screws and washers including, if you can get them, high tensile bolts for under-carriage fixings, solder tags, blind and anchor nuts and a candle — the use of the candle will be explained in Chapter 6.

To assist the modeller in having an easier, if slightly more expensive, life a wide range of accessories are available and it is worth purchasing the catalogues produced by the major manufacturers to see the items from which you are going to benefit.

Construction

How much you like, or dislike, actually building the model will probably determine whether you build from a plan or from a kit, or, for that matter, purchase a completely ready-to-fly model. Building from 'scratch' has the advantage of allowing you to select your own materials, the grade and quality of balsawood, assuming your model shop has a good stock, of course. It is more time consuming — most kits contain a lot of pre-cut parts — but gives a much wider choice of model subjects.

Kit manufacturers try hard to select balsawood of suitable quality for the different parts. In some respects they can carry out a better selection than the individual purchasing balsa from his model shop. It is sometimes possible for them to put 'matched' pairs of fuselage sides into a kit because the sheets of wood are cut adjacent to one another from the log. Leading edges, cut from thick sheet can be 'paired' to ensure equal density and strength for both wing panels. Inevitably, however, a piece of wood that is the wrong grade, or slightly sub-standard, may get into the kit. Do not go ahead and use this wood but replace it, you will probably save yourself a lot of time and trouble later on. Examine a kit carefully before you start building it. This inspection is not only to sort out the right grades of strip and sheet wood for the various uses but to identify all parts and to check that there is nothing missing. You should not run out of strip-wood before you complete the model, although this can happen when fuselage uprights and cross pieces are cut from the wrong lengths of strip. If you are not satisfied with the kit or have some constructive criticism to make do write to the manufacturer and tell him, it may help him to improve the kit and make life easier for future builders.

For the modeller with limited building facilities and tools (the kitchen table-top builder) I would certainly recommend building from kits rather than plans. He has less work to do, less mess to clear up, will need fewer tools and at least has the kit box and lid to put the pieces in when it comes time to move for the supper to be prepared. The cost of building from scratch should, in theory, be less than from a kit. It does not always work out this way as there is always a lot of waste when purchasing materials by the sheet or by the yard. A model with a wing span of 40in. may use wing spars of 20in. length and, as the strip is only obtainable in 36in. lengths, there could be a wastage of nearly half the material if it is not utilised elsewhere. On the other hand bear in mind that the manufacturer has not only to charge for the materials and plan he supplies but for the printing and advertising costs, wholesalers and retailers profits, as well as a cut to the tax man.

AIRFRAMES

To build a successful airframe, one that will allow the radio control equipment to operate the model accurately, it is important to pay attention to what I call the three As.

Accuracy — Cut all parts as accurately as possible so that they fit without gaps or having to force fit the joints.

Alignment — Square and true construction at all times and correct alignment of wings and tail surfaces on the completed model.

Avoirdupois — Weight! Keep it as light, consistent with strength, as possible.

I am a believer in the old aeronautical saying 'simplicate and add lightness'.

Designers all have their own 'pet' ideas on construction and it is not possible, in this book, to cover every conceivable form of construction. In this chapter I shall try to give some general hints and suggestions on methods of building the various components of a radio control model airframe.

There are so many different forms and types of construction that it is impossible to include detailed explanations of all of them. Part of the fun in building models is learning, or inventing, new techniques and experimenting with new materials. Never be afraid of having-a-go with a new idea — it may not work out, but it might prove to be a valuable idea which will be incorporated in many models in the future. Although I have designed models by the hundred I cannot claim to have contributed many unique methods and systems, but a few small ideas and adaptions of existing products have proved to be worthwhile.

Perhaps the most destructive factor to come into the building of the airframe was the result of the development of more powerful engines and more effective and lighter radio control equipment. In the early days of radio control the primitive radio control equipment was so heavy and the power outputs from the engines so limited that it was essential to design and build efficient airframes. No excess materials and unnecessary weight could be accepted, otherwise the model would not perform and it was essential to design the structure with due consideration to catering for flying loads, absorbing landing stresses and eliminating any wasted material. As a result of the engine's increased power output and the smaller payload of radio equipment, saving weight in the airframe became less important. This is unfortunate as there is no point in carrying around unnecessary ballast in the form of materials which are not structurally required. Good design remains good design and lighter aeroplanes, as I will remind you time and again, really do fly better.

PLAN

Usually the plan when you receive it is folded and creased, for ease of packing or posting, and the creases should be removed as far as possible before it is pinned on to the building board. Ironing, with a domestic iron, will usually assist here and make the plan much easier to stretch tight onto the board. Masking tape is better than drawing pins for securing the plan to the building board as the plan tends to tear through the pins when it is pulled. As many of the components are built directly on top of the plan we must prevent the glue from sticking to the plan during building. Going over the plan, where joints are to be made, with a candle, or piece of hard soap, is one way

of achieving this; another is to cover the whole plan with a transparent material such as tracing paper or a thin clear plastic that model glues will not adhere to.

When building from a plan it is necessary to transfer the outline of ribs, formers, doublers etc. on to the material to be used. Carbon paper is one method we can use (it should be the pencil grade and not the sort used in typewriters); an alternative is to 'pin' through the plan at regular intervals using the pin holes in the material as a guide to cutting or for remarking with a ball point pen. If you have access to a photocopying machine the operation of transferring the shape of a component, from the plan to the balsawood or plywood to be cut, can be more easily and accurately carried out. Take a print of the parts to be cut out and place the print, face down, on the wood. With a hot iron, press down on the photocopy and the printing will be transferred onto the wood. Although the markings will be a mirror image of the original this is no disadvantage, the part is placed in the construction accordingly. A very slight increase in size may result from the photocopying process but this is of little consequence unless large components are being reproduced. Where templates are to be used, i.e. for multiple wing ribs, the pattern can be cut from the plan and glued direct to the template. Contact adhesives are good for this purpose, particularly Cow Gum — available from stationers.

An unfortunate habit of some modellers is to modify the construction, usually by 'beefing up' in an attempt to improve the strength of the completed model. Unless you have a specific or valid reason for changing the construction I would respectfully suggest that you build it in accordance with the designer's plan and instructions. It is *not* possible to build a model that is *impossible* to break in a crash any more than it is to design a model that is *certain* to fly, regardless of how it is built. Far more important is to build the model correctly and with care, install the radio equipment as well as you can and give yourself every chance of flying successfully. In other words take the positive attitude that you are going to *fly* the model, not the negative one that the model is going to crash. 'Strengthening' the airframe will more likely add unnecessary weight that, in turn, will ruin the flying characteristics of the finished model.

Using tools correctly is largely a matter of experience but it is also important to know the correct way to use them. I have already commented on the need to use sandpaper blocks for sanding but these must be used judiciously when sanding edges of balsa that have to be joined. There is always a tendency to let the sanding block 'rock', as it moves forwards and backwards, leaving a surface with rounded edges. It needs a conscious mental effort to avoid this. Another failing with builders is using the wrong method of cutting with a fretsaw causing problems with accuracy. The humble hand fretsaw, properly handled can give a very accurate cut with a variety of materials. Yet I have watched modellers struggling over a fretsaw, only too thankful to finish up with a shape vaguely representing the required part. Most frequent of the mistakes in fretsawing appears to be in trying to turn the saw around the corners instead of turning the material being cut. The saw blade should be moved up and down at a steady rate, although the cutting action is always on the down stroke, and the material moved into it without too much pressure being applied. To keep accurately on the line to be cut look slightly ahead of the saw blade and not directly at it. (This applies to all methods of cutting incidentally, and drawing freehand lines.) Finally, use a substantial saw table well fixed to the table or bench and allow yourself plenty of elbow room.

Sanding, to me, is one of those necessary evils; it can be likened to having your hair cut, you have to pay to lose something. To keep sanding to a minimum try to cut all parts as accurately as possible including spars, longerons, wing leading edge sheeting etc. It is amazing how much time can be saved in this way particularly if *all* the parts are cut out before construction is commenced. Never cut parts over the plan, you will cut it to ribbons and you never know, you may wish to build a second model from the plan or use it for reference for repairs to the model.

There are a number of time-saving 'tricks' to be learnt in building models. Many of these will become apparent as you get more experienced at building, and you will no doubt find some of your own methods, but here are one or two tips.

'BLOCKING' WING RIBS

Cutting out identical wing ribs can be something of a chore even when a metal template is used for

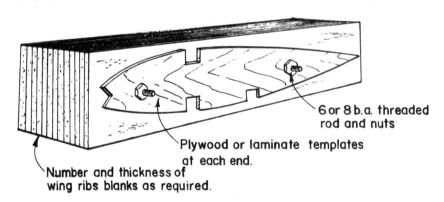

6 or 8 b.a. threaded rod and nuts

Plywood or laminate templates at each end.

Number and thickness of wing ribs blanks as required.

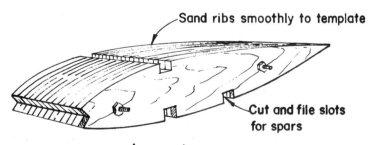

Sand ribs smoothly to template

Cut and file slots for spars

Method of 'Blocking' Wing Ribs.

cutting around. An easy, and accurate, method of producing large numbers of wing ribs is by using two templates, plywood, metal or plastic laminate and sandwiching between them the required number and thickness of balsa sheet for the ribs. The balsa sheet rib blanks need only be roughly cut to the dimensions of the rib as the full circumference of the rib is cut and sanded. Although the templates may be pinned in position to the ribs a better way is to drill through the templates and blanks and secure the whole 'block' with studding and nuts. With the 'block' firmly secured the balsa is trimmed, to within $\frac{1}{32}$ in. or so, with a razor plane and finished off with coarse and fine sandpaper to the outline of the templates. Slots for spars can be cut with a small hacksaw and finished with a square-edged fine file.

Wings with a tapered profile can also have ribs cut by the 'blocking' method providing that the rib spacings are all equal and that the taper is not too pronounced. Remember to include rib blanks for both the port and starboard wings and that the templates should be for the root and tip ribs.

WINGS

Building wings without warps is simple enough with flat bottom wings provided the balsawood is reasonably evenly graded. With symmetrical wing sections it is often necessary to block up the leading and trailing edges and this must be done accurately and at close enough intervals to prevent any bowing between supports. Wing designs using large balsa leading edges (say $\frac{1}{2}$in. × 1in.) rely on a constant leading edge section throughout the wing for good flight characteristics and it is worth making a leading edge template to give a check on the profile. The correct balance of the wings is also important; both panels should be of identical weight so that the wing balances around the centre line. Try sanding down the heavier wing, particularly around the tip area where the reduction in weight will have most effect, but, if needs be, add some ballast to the tip of the light wing. Many modellers seem to think that foam wings are the answer to all warp problems but this is not quite true. I have seen veneer covered wing panels with quite severe warps — and with no remedial action possible — but the biggest danger is in the joining of the two panels. A fraction of

an inch out at the leading or trailing edges of the two panels and you have a permanently twisted wing. Care and caution will prevent this.

For the bi-convex section wing (semi-symmetrical or symmetrical) we can make a simple jig using two jig blocks. These blocks are carved from balsa to the shape required to position the leading and trailing edges at an equal height above the plan and simply pinned down over the plan on the baseboard or building board. It is then a case of normal pin-in-place and cement working for assembling the wing, sighting or marking the rib positions, as preferred. Rib slots provide alignment for the spars, and top leading edge sheeting and cap strips, if called for, can be added whilst the wing is still pinned down. By that time the assembly will be quite rigid, so it will not be pushed out of true by adding bottom sheeting when removed from the jig — this part of the job being done 'freehand'.

An even better jig for a wing is made from two boards, one for each wing panel, accurately hinged at the centre. The complete wing plan is then pinned down in place (or drawn on, if only one wing panel is given on the plan) with the jig boards blocked up to correct dihedral angle. Wings built in two halves and then joined for dihedral are often twisted out of true at the centre joint.

With a dihedralled jig where the two panels are set up together perfectly accurately this cannot happen, provided the wing has a simple dihedral joint at the centre.

Constructional techniques vary a lot depending on the size and type of the model. The wings for the smallest models may feature only one spar and no trailing or leading edge sheeting. Medium size sports models — around 50in. wing span — probably have one or two pairs of spars and top and bottom, or top only, leading edge sheeting. Large sports models and multi-aerobatic models feature 1½ or 2 pairs of spars and usually top and bottom leading edge and trailing edge sheeting. Between the top and bottom main spars $\frac{1}{16}$ in. sheet vertical webbing, with the grain vertical, is glued to form a complete 'D' box leading edge. On large models the sheet 'V' trailing edge is frequently treated the same way. This form of construction is fast, light and simple; the sheeted leading edge preserves a uniform aerofoil shape along the wing without

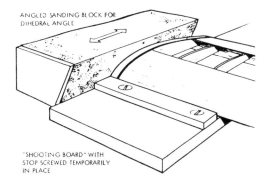

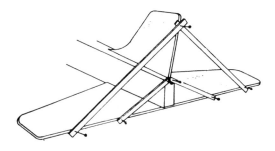

Typical tailplane and fin assembly jig.

covering sag between ribs,

In many medium sized and large models (that are not completely sheet covered) capping strips are used to minimise the rib material thickness, without reducing the strength. The rib, in cross section is in effect an 'I' beam and much of the strength is in the capping strips. The capping strips extend from the back of the leading edge sheet to the front of the trailing edge sheeting. One extremely strong method of construction employs spars which are as deep as the wing thickness. The ribs then are slotted to about two-thirds depth and a corresponding slot one-third in depth cut into the spar. This 'egg carton' form of construction is extremely strong and eliminates the need for vertical webbing between the main spars.

With the large partially or fully sheeted wings there is little risk of them warping during or after covering but this is not the case with lighter structures for small aircraft. Fortunately corrective measures are not difficult. The finished wing (unless it is covered with one of the plastic heat sensitive covering materials) can be held over a jet of steam from the kettle until the warped area is warm. It is then removed from the steam and twisted in the opposite direction to the warp and held in this position for a minute or two until cool. Warped large wings are much more difficult to deal with, and are more likely to be the result of faulty building. To successfully remove a warp in a large wing it will probably be necessary to build a jig with clamps. The wing is steamed in the same manner and then inserted quickly into the jig and clamped into the true position. A further steaming, with the wing in the jig may be called for.

If a jointed and dihedralled building board is not used one of the most difficult building

operations is the sanding true of the wing panel root ribs. This can be achieved, with a little effort by using what is known in the joinery trade as a 'shooting board'. The illustration should be self-explanatory but remember not to take the sandpaper on the underside of the block.

Before commencing the sanding of any of the components it is wise to make a final check to ensure that all joints are securely glued. Ribs, when being pushed on to the spars – and as a result of forcing the fit – may have all the glue squeezed from the joint. When the framework is finished, and the glue joints dry give it a slight twist; dry joints can be heard to part.

TAILSURFACES

Tailsurfaces are at a long moment arm from the balance point of the model and unless the design features an extra long nose, we must keep the weight of the tailsurfaces to a reasonable minimum to avoid having to ballast the nose for the correct balance point. Rigidity and security are of importance with the fin and tailplane – they must not be able to twist or, in a violent manoeuvre, become detached from the fuselage. This should not present any difficulties with smaller models, but will need watching with large aerobatic designs where aerodynamic forces are high and there is the risk of 'flutter' if flexing of the surfaces is allowed to happen. It may be advisable to fit struts or bracing construction of the tail surfaces to be employed. Equally important is the sound and secure hinging of the elevators and rudder. Any unwanted movement, excessive hinge gap or poor linkages can easily lead to 'flutter' of the control surfaces and consequent failure. Full-size aeroplanes will have static and aerodynamically balanced control surfaces by using aerodynamic horns at the tips of the elevators and rudder and these will be ballasted forward of the hinge line so that the weight balances out the mass of the control surface. To reduce the servo load, allowing the use of a less powerful servo, with less battery drain, the control surfaces on large models should receive this balancing treatment. Ailerons, too, will benefit from introducing Frise ailerons, for aerodynamic balancing and weights at the wing tip, or on a 'stalk' to bring the weight forward of the hinge line.

Solid sheet tailsurfaces are quite acceptable on smaller designs. The balsawood should be carefully selected (light but not 'pithy' or 'carroty') and use made of tips and inserts with the grain chordwise, to prevent warping and twisting. Open structures will give the same effect with less weight, but more effort and can either have a flat section or be built-up to provide a symmetrical aerofoil section. One thing often overlooked with a built-up structure is that open areas between the structural components may not follow the aerofoil of the wing, or tailsurface. On a wing, for instance, the leading edge may be sheeted to form a strong box structure at the front. On the top rear of the wing, though, the covering will sag between the ribs and may, at the halfway point, be virtually a straight line between the top and trailing edge. The 'plane' will still fly but it does show that we sometimes talk a lot of nonsense about the importance of aerofoils — they only become truly critical on high performance models with high standards of finish.

A symmetrical aerofoil to the tailsurfaces, typically a NACA 0012 or 15 section, is worthwhile with larger models and this should be carefully sheeted, or veneered polystyrene foam,

construction. For a built-up structure use the same techniques as for symmetrical sectioned wings, only using materials of smaller dimensions. Don't forget to include reinforcement blocks for the location of the hinges.

FUSELAGES

Most fuselages; whether built up from longerons, uprights etc. or sheeted, are box-like in structure, although they may have blocks and stringers added to 'round off' the appearance. Usually the main length of the top or bottom of the fuselage, or at least the wing seating area, is flat and these areas can be laid flat on the building board to check that the fuselage formers and sides are square. The most common faults in building fuselages are to get an unequal taper on the fuselage sides and to build the fuselage out of the vertical true, i.e. with a twist in it. Avoid these faults by marking a vertical centre line on all formers and lining them up on the longitudinal centre line during construction.

When cutting uprights and cross pieces for built-up fuselages cut them together in pairs; this reduces the time taken and also ensures consistency.

Of course, the ideal way to build any model is to use a construction jig but many modellers do not consider the extra cost and time worthwhile for 'one off' models. Certainly some of the commercial jigs take such a lot of setting up (and you still need care to avoid a warped wing) that the effort barely seems to be justified. There are more simple forms of jigs that do not take long to prepare, are not expensive and, for the serious modeller, are worthy of consideration. For the aerobatic competition modeller needing to build

A purpose made jig for 'Pronto' sports model; this ensures accuracy and exact duplication of models.

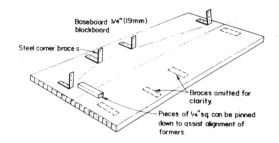

Baseboard 3/4" (19mm) blockboard.

Steel corner braces

Braces omitted for clarity.

Pieces of 1/4" sq. can be pinned down to assist alignment of formers.

three or four models, that will fly in as near identical manner as possible, a permanent jig is virtually a must. It enables a particular component or assembly to be built over and over again in it, and each construction is nearly identical with the others.

Here is a simple fuselage jig for a 'one off' design that does not entail too much work to modify it for other models.

A piece of straight, true and fairly stout timber is chosen for the base, such as a piece of 19mm blockboard about 1m × 0.3m. Mark a datum line along the centre of the face and square off lines at former positions. If these lines correspond to a face rather than the centre of the formers it helps in lining up. Now mark off the fuselage width at former positions and screw down 4in. steel corner braces; make sure these are really square. Place the fuselage sides in the jig and fit formers. The tail is pulled together over the datum and clamped; a couple more braces can be used if there is a tendency to twist. Now you should have a nice true fuselage.

This form of jig would be particularly useful for club projects where a number of models of the same design are being built.

Assuming we have the component parts of the model finished, except for covering, we must now check that everything fits together accurately. The plan will indicate the wing and tailplane incidences, even if it does not quote them in degrees or fractions of inches, and these should be checked on the assembled model. To do this it will be necessary to use a reference or datum line along the side of the fuselage. If there is no obvious datum line shown on the side view of the fuselage, on the plan, I would suggest using the centre line of the tailplane as the basis for the datum as this is normally set at 0° incidence. Incidentally, if you are using incidence measurements in terms of degrees remember that the incidence angle of a

flat bottom wing is measured from the centre of the leading edge to the centre of the trailing edge and not the bottom of the wing. With the datum line marked on the plan it is possible to measure off the distances to the wing leading and trailing edges, and by marking the fuselage in a similar way (using masking tape to avoid spoiling the surface) the incidences can be checked.

Commercially available incidence meters can be used to check the incidences of wings, tailplanes and engine thrust lines. These give very accurate references and are especially useful for checking scale and aerobatic models where precise incidence settings may be vitally important.

At this stage of the rigging procedure it will be helpful to prop the model up, with blocks of wood or books, so that the datum line is parallel to building board, or other true surface you are using. Incorrect wing incidences or wing seatings that are untrue, can be corrected by attaching a piece of sandpaper to the sheeting wing centre section and using this as a contoured sanding block. It is now a matter of measuring the extremities of the models from a fixed point to make sure that all pairs of measurements (i.e. wing tips to fin tip, tailplane tips to centre line of fuselage at nose − not the engine if side thrust is used − heights of tailplane tips etc.) are all equal. It is helpful if a centre line with lines at 90° at the positions of the wing and tailplane can be marked on the surface used for rigging purposes. This is not essential, and may not be popular if the dining table is used, but will be a very useful guide when used in conjunction with a large set square.

Is all this rigmarole worthwhile? I certainly think it is worthwhile for any model. It becomes increasingly important with fast flying models. With slow flying types you can get away with the odd twist or warp but not with a model that will be flying at 60 mph plus. It will certainly make your life easier when it comes to test flying if you are confident the model is exactly as it should be, including, of course, the correct C of G position.

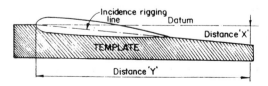

Incidence rigging line · Datum · Distance 'X' · TEMPLATE · Distance 'Y'

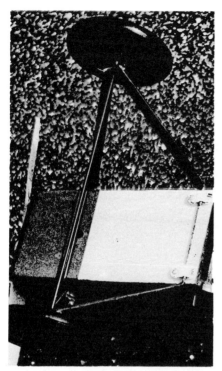

The author's 'Mannock' biplane uses 'bungee' springing on the axle. Note the relative forward position of the wheels.

UNDERCARRIAGES

The prime purpose of the undercarriage is to allow the aircraft to take-off and land with only radio control assistance from the pilot. This may seem to be a very obvious statement, but I make it so that you can more logically consider the next point. Does the field that you will be flying from have a sufficiently good surface to allow the model to perform these actions? Many of us have to fly from rough pasture land where there is little or no hope of taking a model off and the landings invariably finish up with the model being tripped up by its undercarriage. Is an undercarriage really necessary — after all gliders do not have them? Some models of the semiscale variety look so ridiculous without them that, even if they are performing no real function, they are retained for the purpose of appearances. Other models look perfectly right without undercarriages, in fact some are definitely improved — witness many multi-aerobatic models now fitted with retract gear, a vast improvement on the 'stalky, dangley' undercarriage legs. Generally speaking mid-shoulder and high wing models, preferably with

high mounted tails too, can be landed quite safely on grass areas without an undercarriage. To add puncture resistance the saving in weight of removing the undercarriage can be used by adding 1mm ply to the underside of the fuselage from the nose back to the rear of the wing position. Glass fibre resin and mat added to the nose cowls and underside block will also help to reduce damage in this area.

The configuration of landing gear can be the conventional two wheel arrangement, with a skid or trailwheel at the rear, or it can be a tricycle undercarriage with a nosewheel at the front. Tricycle undercarriages are the easiest to use for take-offs as they tend to 'track' very much straighter; and there is no gyroscopic effect of the model trying to turn that you get with a two-wheel undercarriage as the tail comes up. It is also probably easier to land a model successfully with a tricycle undercarriage. So why do we not have tricycle undercarriages on all models? Can you imagine what a semiscale 'oldie' biplane would look like with a trike undercarriage! Some models look right with two-wheel undercarriages, there is also a great sense of satisfaction in doing a true three-pointer, with this form of undercarriage, where the model stalls the last few inches on to the ground.

The undercarriage will undoubtedly get punishment, from time to time, and so it must be rugged; it must also be forgiving and not pass on all of the rough treatment to the airframe. Air, and airtrap, wheels offer a certain shock resistance but the undercarriage legs must also take their share. This is done by relying on the natural resilience of the material — piano wire and dural — and/or of mounting the undercarriage with rubber bands. I have had criticisms that the dural undercarriages sometimes supplied in kits are too soft. My answer to that is — it is easier to straighten out a bent dural undercarriage than it is to repair a broken fuselage.

Positioning of the wheels in relation to the balance point of the model is important in relation to take-offs and landings. With a tricycle undercarriage the nosewheel is normally fixed to the front plywood former as this is a convenient position structurally and is satisfactory in flying respects. The main wheels should be positioned an inch or so behind the balance point. Any

Top: *A scale triplane and* below: *a flying boat; both built by the author using traditional balsawood and plywood 'open' construction.*

further forward and the model may remain tail down when put in that position, any further back and the model will not be able to 'rotate' around the main wheels immediately prior to take-off. As we also tend to position the nose wheel so that the model has a slight negative incidence to the ground (to prevent premature take-off) this lack of rotating ability could prevent take-off completely. With two-wheel undercarriages the main wheels are normally positioned somewhere nearly in line with the front of the wing. Positioning further forward than this gives us better landings − less likelihood of nosing over − but makes taking-off

a tricky business. With wheels a long way forward there is a large moment arm (from the balance point to the centre line of the wheel) to turn against. This means that we have to put on a lot of rudder to initiate the turn but, once the turn has commenced, it also takes a lot of opposite rudder to correct it.

You can see models with this undercarriage arrangement swinging from one side of the take-off strip to the other, usually finishing up by eventually catching one wing tip and cartwheeling. For those of you that will not be able, because of ground conditions, to take-off but wish to retain a

Another of the author's models following this type of construction in the finished state.

two-wheel undercarriage the forward position is recommended. All wheels must be aligned with longitudinal centre line of the fuselage otherwise tracking will not be straight. A small amount of 'toe in', on two-wheel undercarriages, will sometimes improve the model's ability to keep straight on take-off.

Piano wire and dural are the two primary materials used for constructing undercarriages and both of these materials are suitable for the full range of model sizes. Dural undercarriage blanks are available in a variety of sizes or you can cut them from sheet or strip dural of suitable quality. Some dural may be cold bent but other, higher tensile, dural must be heated, bent and retempered. Check with the supplier of the dural on the method needed for bending and retempering as the correct methods vary considerably. The axle bolts for the wheels should be high tensile (marked with a ring on the bolt head) − mild steel will bend too easily. Because of the degree of rigidity of a single leaf dural undercarriage, particularly in the fore and aft direction, rubber bands are normally used to retain the undercarriage to the fuselage. These bands should be fixed longitudinally from dowel to dowel and not diagonally across the fuselage − this allows the undercarriage to twist. Round off the edges of the dural near the rubber band position to prevent cutting through them when the shock load is taken on landing. On small models screwing the dural leaf, via grommets, to a re-inforced plywood plate on the fuselage, is permis-

sible providing that the screw heads will 'tear' through the grommets on a heavy landing.

Piano wire is used extensively for nose, main and tail wheel undercarriage assemblies; its natural 'springiness' makes it ideal for these purposes. During bending the piano wire should be protected; a simple way is to mark off the bend positions with a pencil and wrap them in Sellotape before inserting the wire in the vice to bend. Use jaw inserts, in the vice, with a rounded edge and bend the wire, pushing on it with a hard wood block. Trying to pull, or push, the wire with your hand will result in the wire curving. For complex bending of a piano wire undercarriage component start the sequence of bends from the centre of the wing working out to the ends from each side in turn.

A combination of dural and piano wire may be used for the main undercarriage of large models, using the piano wire for the axles and to provide additional tensioning. Many wheels these days use nylon or plastic hubs. Whilst this helps as far as radio 'noise' rejection is concerned it does mean taking care not to overheat the piano wire when a washer is being soldered to the axle to retain the wheel. A tip here is to slip some aluminium foil − as used in cigarette packets − between the wheel and the washer. This will help to reflect and dissipate the heat and also prevent solder flux from being drawn between the wheel hubs and axle by capillary attraction.

Nose wheel legs are available in both the fixed and steerable version in sizes and strengths to suit all models. Unless you have the correct bending jig it is not worthwhile trying to construct these yourself. Note that the springing coil should be positioned to the rear of the leg and that the coil should be as close to the underside of the fuselage as possible.

For scale and aerobatic models retracting undercarriages are very popular. The methods of construction, fitting and actuation vary such a lot from manufacturer to manufacturer that it is impossible to cover the details here. Actuation of retract systems may be from a high power servo (with spring counter balancing), electric motor powered or pneumatically operated. Outfits are produced for the smallest (.049 cu.in. engines) models to the largest scale designs and it is imperative to choose a system that is applicable to the weight of the model and the flying surface from which it will be operated. All retracting outfits, two and three-wheel, have full instructions with them so, if you decide to fit retracts, buy them early and plan the installation before commencing construction. By nature of their complexity the retracting undercarriages are not as robust as their fixed wheel counterparts. Your flying ability and landing surface must be above average to prevent damage to the retract mechanism.

ADDITIONAL STRUCTURES

Depending on the type of model you will, of course, come across many other structural systems and structural problems. There will be struts to make, probably from piano wire with wood fair-

ings, as with the undercarriage, and this will also involve extra fittings to the wings and/or fuselage. Structural requirements for special aircraft e.g. flying boats, will require some different constructional methods and helicopters is a totally different constructional scene. Plans and kit instructions will tell you how to deal with these specialist areas, which brings me on to a plea.

Where instructions for the building of the model are included please do take the trouble to read *and* follow them. They have been written for your benefit, by persons with experience of building the model. It seems to me (having written many sets of instructions myself) counter-productive to ignore them. This is equally true of the ARTF models. It may seem quite obvious where everything fits but, get them fitted in the wrong order and you may have a nasty shock, you may have built something *out*!

HATCHES

Hatches are frequently required in models to give access to the engine, fuel tank or some radio equipment. The hatch should be securely fixed and incapable of coming loose in flight. A number of hatch fixings are illustrated here.

MOULDINGS

Having mentioned materials such as GRP in the chapter on materials it is only reasonable to mention the construction methods involved in their production. Moulded components, engine

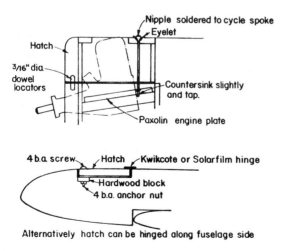

Alternatively hatch can be hinged along fuselage side

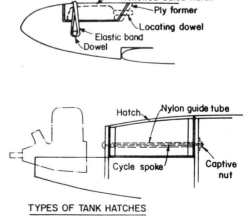

TYPES OF TANK HATCHES

cowlings, wheel spats, cockpits etc, are more suited to multi-model use. We are not talking about multi in the sense of more than one engine, or multi-control systems, but for more than one model. The reason for this is that to achieve a first rate moulding, well finished but not overweight, it is necessary to first make a mould plug.

Taking a cockpit as a simple example, we select a suitable sized piece of hard wood, mark out the plan form and side view of the cockpit on the wood and start to carve and cut it to shape. When cut to shape the surface must be sanded to a fine finish and treated (sanding resin or two-part polyurethane, for instance) to reach a polished smooth, blemish-free, finish. From this finished plug can be obtained not one, but many mouldings. Vacuum forming, with clear acetate or PVC sheeting is used, it is heated and sucked down onto the clear sheeting.

Moulding in GRP is rather different. Here we are building up a layer of resin and glass cloth or mat on the *inside* of a mould and the moulding will only be as good as the finish of the mould. The general principles involved are to produce a wood plug to the exact size and sections of the item to be moulded, say an engine cowl (the plug for a vac-formed moulding should, theoretically, be the thickness of the moulding material less than the contours of the original item − but the difference is normally too small to worry about). With the plug carved and meticulously finished a further, female, mould is made from the plug using glass fibre materials. It may be necessary to make the mould in sections (with flanges) to allow the mould plug and consequent mouldings, to be released. All this represents quite a lot of time and work, certainly for a one-off model, but becomes a sensible proposition if a number of the same model are to be produced. It also has obvious uses for scale models where it is vital to replicate cowlings and other features where conventional wood materials would not be suitable.

There is an alternative to the female mould process and that is to lay-up the glass cloth or mat directly onto the original, male plug. Again, the plug then needs to be the thickness of the material less than the original size. The layers of glass and resin are built up in the usual way, until a sufficient thickness and strength is achieved. If heavy duty polyurethane foam is used for the plug − and quite a good finish can be obtained on 'blue' foam materials − it can be melted away from the inside of the moulding with petrol or dope thinners. Unfortunately, the external finish of the moulding will leave something to be desired and it will take quite a lot of filler (lightweight variety) to build up for a smooth finish. This process can be likened to repairing car damage with glass fibre.

GIANTS NEED SPECIAL PROTECTION

As our models get larger, and more highly stressed, we have to design with the full-size aeroplane more in mind. Materials, fittings, structures become closer to prototypes the bigger we get and as most of 'giant' models are scale types we can learn a lot from the original designers. This is particularly true of the earlier prototypes featuring similar built-up structures to our own, our R/C models become miniature replicas of the originals. For modern metal prototypes we copy the full-size structures less − we tend to use different materials in reproducing these aeroplanes. But now that many light aircraft are using composite materials, it becomes a question of whether we are copying them, or they are copying us. Modellers probably made use of GRP laminates before full-size aircraft designers included the technology. However, it is no part of this book to deal in detail with specialised structural methods, there are books available on these subjects, but simply to make you aware of them.

Reduced to absolute basics, the wings provide the lift for the aeroplane, the tailsurfaces the directional control and the fuselage simply holds these components apart, plus housing the radio equipment and − mostly − supporting an engine. Our structures and construction should reflect this, the birds do it remarkably well and even include a retracting undercarriage!

CHAPTER 7

Basic Aerodynamics

The understanding of the principles of flight are important in understanding also what happens to a model during the various stages of its flight. When we are unfortunate enough to crash a model through a flying error it is important to know why it crashed, so that we can avoid making the same error again. It is not intended to pursue detailed aerodynamics for designing models, etc., but sufficient to understand why an aeroplane flies and what effect control surfaces have.

Let us first consider how an aeroplane stays up in the air. Although it seems to be the general view of laymen that an aeroplane is kept in the air by the action of the propeller or, in the case of a jet, by being pushed upwards and forwards by the thrust of the jet engine, it is, of course, the wings that create the lift to suspend the aircraft. Now, if we look at the side elevation of the model in *Fig. 1* we can see that the wing is set at a slight angle, with the leading edge slightly higher than the trailing. When the model is being propelled forward in straight and level flight the air, when it reaches the leading edge of the wing, has to divide, some passing over the top of the wing and some underneath.

At this point even the aerodynamicists disagree over the exact cause of lift production, although it is accepted that the lift created is a result of pressure differences on the upper and lower surfaces. Without wishing to become embroiled in technical and scientific arguments, that have already taken up many pages of learned discussion, it is sufficient to state here that the pressure variation is related to the difference in relative air speeds on the two surfaces i.e. the top surface will be (as Bernoulli's theory explains) creating low pressure from high air speed and conversely, the bottom surface high pressure.

The difference in the upper and lower air speeds is also equivalent to adding a rotational movement and it is this 'Circulation Theory' that has been ignored, or disbelieved, by many aviation enthusiasts. For modellers wishing to learn more about the subject, there are a number of books available on the subject, none better than *Aircraft Flight* published by Longman Scientific and Technical.

The lift created on the top surface can easily be demonstrated by holding a piece of note paper by one edge and blowing along the surface. Notice how the paper rises.

Lift is directly related to the speed of the model, and it therefore follows that if a model slows down too much there will be insufficient lift created to allow a model to fly − a most important point to

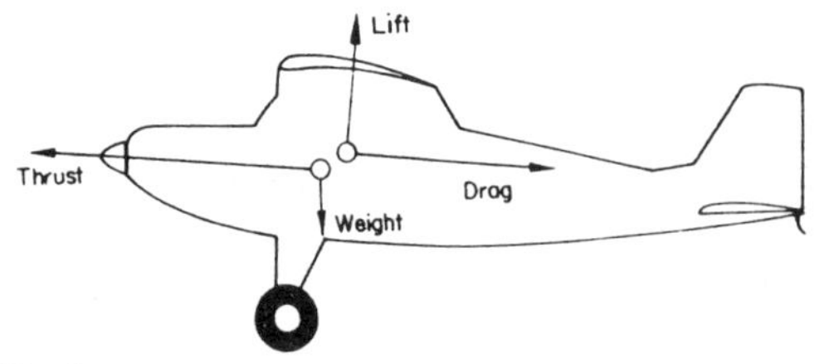

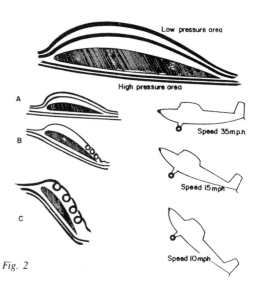

Fig. 1

Fig. 2

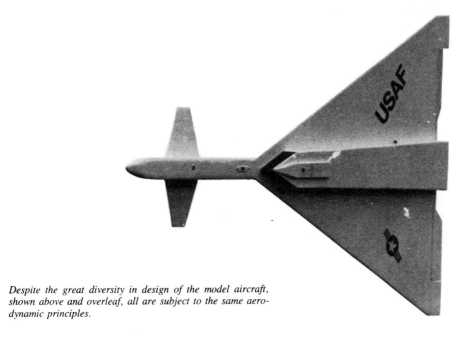

Despite the great diversity in design of the model aircraft, shown above and overleaf, all are subject to the same aerodynamic principles.

remember during the launching or take-off and landing. *Fig. 2* shows the airflow over the aerofoil (wing) section in normal conditions and in A, B and C the airflow through straight and level flight, through a climbing angle and reduction in speed, until there is a break-up of the airflow over the wing. When the break-up of the airflow is reached, the model is said to be stalled, and control cannot be attained until the model is dived and flying speed built up.

Having seen how the model stays up, we can now consider the disposition of other forces acting in flight, as shown in *Fig. 1*. Thrust is provided by the engine 'pulling' the model forwards. The speed of the model is governed by the power of the engine, the attitude to the ground, i.e. climbing

or diving, and the drag from the model; when the thrust of the engine is exactly balanced by the drag of the model, the model will cease to accelerate. Various types of drag are involved when the model is flying but, at this time, we will just consider it as resistance to air. The lift must, as stated before, counteract the weight of the model and because lift has to be increased by an increase of speed, it is important to keep our model as light as possible. A heavy model has to fly faster to stay in the air, and therefore landing and launch speeds are higher — even the slow landing speeds can seem too fast for a beginner! Notice that the thrust line and line of drag are not in line with one another, thus causing a climbing effect unless counteracted. Although the line of weight (acting through the

centre of gravity) is offset compared to the Line of Lift, to counteract this climbing effect it is often also necessary to change the line by introducing engine down thrust.

Having considered the forces acting upon our model, we will now take a look at the axes through which a model can turn. (*Fig. 3*.)

The diagrams are reasonably self-explanatory and it is sufficient to say that the control surfaces move the aircraft by creating more lift, as shown in *Fig. 4*. For the purpose of our training model we shall be considering the rudder as a method of turning. This does not mean, however, that all our turns, using rudder, will be flat yawing turns; as the yaw occurs the wing on the outside of the turn increases its speed and creates more lift (and vice-versa for the inboard wing), thus causing the outside wing to rise, and the model banks in the direction of the turn. Note that when the model is

in a steeply banked turn, the elevator in effect becomes the rudder, or turning action and, to a lesser degree, the rudder becomes the elevator. (See *Fig. 5*.) This knowledge is important when we are trying to recover from a spiral dive. In these circumstances, the application of up elevator will aggravate the condition and not improve it.

Ailerons give, when combined with elevator, smoother turns than those achieved with rudder; less tendency for the nose to drop during the turn, and better axial rolls.

Ailerons may not be so effective when the model is at lower speeds, such as on the landing approach, when rudder may be used for correction of the direction of the model. For correction in direction during the take-off run of a model, the ailerons are of no value as we need to yaw the model (the model still being ground based) and not bank the model as required in flight. All

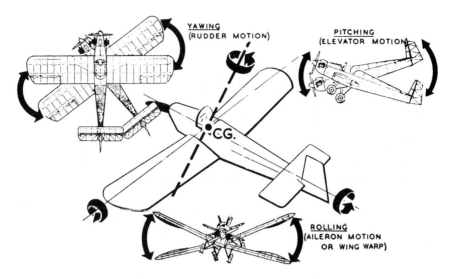

YAWING
(RUDDER MOTION)

PITCHING
(ELEVATOR MOTION)

C.G.

ROLLING
(AILERON MOTION
OR WING WARP)

Fig. 3

The three axes: yawing; pitching and rolling.

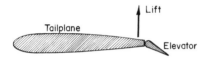

Lift

Tailplane

Elevator

Deflection of elevator downwards creates
lift causing the tail to rise and nose of
model to dive.
Other control surfaces i.e. rudder and ailerons
work in similar manner.

Fig. 4

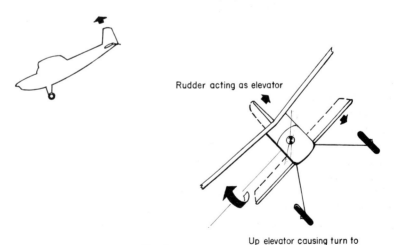

Rudder acting as elevator

Fig. 5

Up elevator causing turn to
be tightened.

competition aerobatics, and most scale and pylon racing, models feature ailerons in addition to rudder control and the only disadvantage to the beginner is the relative complexity of fitting the ailerons and linkages. I would always recommend incorporating ailerons to a second R/C model (in place of rudder if only two or three function radio is being used) as it increases the scope of flying considerably.

There we have a very potted version of basic aerodynamic principles. I have missed quite a lot of important information and oversimplified the

A typical training/sports model, for four function radio control − rudder, elevator, ailerons and engine throttle.

science of aerodynamics but I consider it is more important to supply a few basic facts, relevant to initial flights, and which can be properly learnt rather than to overwhelm the reader with a whole lot of information that cannot be digested.

Aerodynamics is very much a subject on its own and should you find it of interest by all means carry out some research at your local library.

A very useful book *Model Aircraft Aerodynamics* is published by Nexus Special Interests and written by Martin Simons. This puts the subject in perspective and is angled entirely to *model* aerodynamics.

CHAPTER 8

Installation of Hinges, Linkages & R/C Equipment

Making and flying a radio control model aircraft is like fighting — and winning — a series of battles. Each has to be won before you can commence the next battle. Installation of radio equipment, linkages and control surfaces can be considered at the last major fight before learning to fly — unfortunately it is a campaign that is often lost. It is most important to approach the installation stage with both a neat and tidy mind *and* neat and tidy workmanship. A positive and logical approach, working out positions of equipment and linkages beforehand, will always pay dividends and it is at the early stages that this should be planned. Too often the desire to 'get flying' is all too strong and the installation side is rushed, usually with dire results. Your common sense will tell you — if you take the trouble to listen to it — whether the installation is sound and if you know that, truthfully, it isn't quite good enough do something about it before it is too late. It could save you not only money but a lot of frustration as well.

This chapter on installations will be divided into four parts:

1. Hinges.
2. Linkages.
3. Special linkages.
4. Radio equipment.

HINGES

Regardless of how good and accurate your radio equipment is — and manufacturers are constantly aiming to improve the resolution of their equipment — the results can be nullified by the modeller making a poor job of the hinging of the control surfaces and installation of the pushrods and control horns. The aims to achieve a good control surface hinge are:

1. Freedom of movement.

2. Close coupling of the control surface to the wing, fin or tailplane.
3. Strength of the hinge.

Freedom of movement of the hinge action is one of the most important considerations and described in practical terms, means that without the pushrods being connected, the control surface could 'flop' from side to side under its own weight. Although modern proportional servos may have an output of $2\frac{1}{2}-3\frac{1}{2}$lb thrust this is no excuse whatsoever for taking the attitude that it does not matter if the control surface hinges are stiff because the servo power will overcome the stiffness. Certainly, the controls will still probably operate but this added load, together with the air loads on the control surfaces during flying, will be at the expense of greater battery drain and generally of accuracy too.

Misalignment of hinges adds not only to drag but also increases the possibility of failure. A warped tailplane, with an upwards or downwards or concave or convex curvature is an impossibility with regard to alignment of hinges and a cure must be found before the hinges can be fitted. See sketches. Alignment of hinge lines must be 'true' in all axes to operate correctly and the hinge must be free in itself i.e. free of glue and paint.

Close coupling of the control and primary surfaces is important for two reasons. It will allow passage of air between the surfaces, reducing the efficiency and creating turbulence. Many of the older, full-size, light aircraft had strips of linen doped loosely between the surfaces to prevent this spillage of air. The other reason for close coupling is that, with strip and thread hinges, the surface itself will have freedom of movement beyond that designed.

Most hinges, properly installed, are strong enough for all forms of model aircraft but I would not recommend thread or tape hinges for large or fast models.

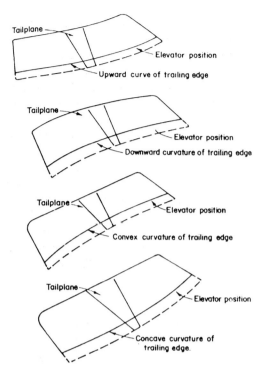

Wraps and curvatures to be avoided.

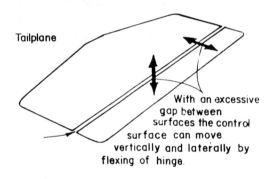

there is a length of piano wire along part of the hinge line i.e. a piano wire joiner for the elevators. With this condition it is impossible to insert a leaf or barbed type hinge but the thread can be sewn through holes behind the wire. Many modellers will decry the sewn hinge as old fashioned. It may be, but it is also efficient on small and medium sized models. We will consider hinging the elevator, although the rudder hinging will be similar.

Using masking tape, join the elevator to the tailplane at the centre and the tips. Mark off, with ballpoint pen, positions of holes at ¼in. out from the hinge lines as shown on the sketch. Note that the hole positions on the tailplane and elevator are staggered by ⅛in.

Remove the masking tape and drill the holes with a fine drill, just large enough to take the needle to be used for sewing. When using a pillar drill for this operation put a piece of rubber carpet underlay under the tailplane and elevator during drilling to prevent damage to them. On no account omit the drilling of these holes; it may be possible to push the needle through the balsa without pre-drilling but it will almost certainly result in the balsawood splitting along the grain between the holes. Fix the elevator back in position, this time using masking tape at the centre and one tip only. The most suitable forms of thread for hinging are terylene. The terylene is easy to use and can be used double so, when threading the needle, loop it right through and tie the two ends together. Start

THREAD HINGES

One of the original forms of hinging control surfaces, and in many ways still one of the best, is the thread hinge. It gives a very free hinge, is simple to install and is certainly cheap. The disadvantages are that it looks rather more unsightly than some other methods, can be excessively sloppy unless correctly carried out and, if the wrong thread is used, insufficiently strong for prolonged periods of flying. Carried out with care and thoroughness however, it will give a very serviceable hinge. It is particularly useful where

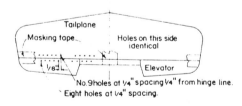

Drilling the tailplane and elevator for a sewing hinge.

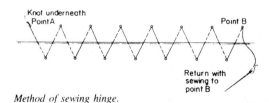

Method of sewing hinge.

sewing at the inboard hinge on the side without the masking tape. From the underside of the tailplane, push the needle through the first hole, Point A, and pull the thread through the hinge line — this can be done by 'sliding' it down the gap from the tip — and push the needle up through the first hole in the elevator. Continue in this method until you reach the last hole, Point B, in the tailplane and then back to the starting point, thus completing the cross pattern of hinging.

Construct the other hinges in a similar manner, removing the masking tape at the tip when commencing the hinges on the opposite side. Leave the masking tape at the centre in position as this will be useful when installing the pushrods at the later stage. Put a dab of glue or fuel proofer over the holes to prevent ingress of fuel.

MOULDED HINGES

Commercial hinges of various types are specially produced for model work and can provide a very neat installation and smooth operation. They do, however, require accurate positioning and alignment. Because the material used for these hinges is not readily gluable with conventional adhesive, holes are often left in the 'leaf' of the hinge for the glue to penetrate and 'lock' the hinge in position. The two main types of moulded hinges are (1) the leaf and pin hinge and (2) Mylar hinge with 'thinned' hinge line.

The Mylar type hinge will never be as free in operation as the pinned or thread hinges but the resistance is not sufficient to be detrimental to the radio equipment, providing that all other linkages are free in operation.

As stated previously, correct alignment of moulded hinges is absolutely vital and, therefore, marking and the cutting of the slots for the hinges are required for the elevator (two each side of the centre line) plus one pair for the rudder. Again we will consider installation of the hinge for the elevator. Mark the positions of the hinges on the elevator and tailplane making sure you mark a centre line along the edge of the elevator and tailplane. Cutting slots for the hinge halves must be carefully done to prevent cutting at an angle and slicing through the surface. The use of a guide (⅛in. × ½in.) will assist here to make a slot parallel to the surface. It may be difficult to cut a

slot of sufficient width with a knife and the slot must then be 'opened up' by using a jeweller's flat file or manicure sander (the sort ladies use for filing down their nails). One common mistake modellers make is that, with pinned hinges, they tend to leave the circular part of the hinge projecting beyond the control surface. The result of this, with the hinge fixed, is a gap of about 1/16 in. between the elevator and tailplane. This is not only bad from the point of aerodynamic efficiency but may also cause the elevator to flutter during flight, putting unnecessary strain on the hinges and servo. With hinges that require 'pegging' (the Micro Mold hinge N15 has a 'wedge' built in to prevent easy withdrawal) the hinges must be fitted before covering otherwise 'pegs' will show through the finished surface.

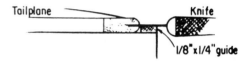

When hinges are fitted after the model has been covered, ensure that no epoxy glue gets onto the pivot part of the hinge. Either protect this part with masking tape or smear the critical parts with petroleum jelly.

MYLAR STRIP HINGES

Although generally referred to as Mylar strip hinges the actual material may be Mylar or nylon or some other suitable material. Before trying to economise too much by using some 'free' plastic sheet that you happen to have do check very thoroughly that it is tough enough and thin enough. This method of hinging relies on the inherent tensile strength and flexibility of the hinge material and a hinge that is going to fail after a few flights is worthless. Compared with the moulded hinge the Mylar strip is of constant thickness requiring a thinner slot to be cut in the surfaces making it more difficult to glue the material in position.

Mylar is, in any case, a difficult material to glue but there are two possibilities with modern adhesives. Always 'roughen' the surfaces of the hinge with sandpaper before gluing, this will give a better key.

Method number one involves the use of epoxy

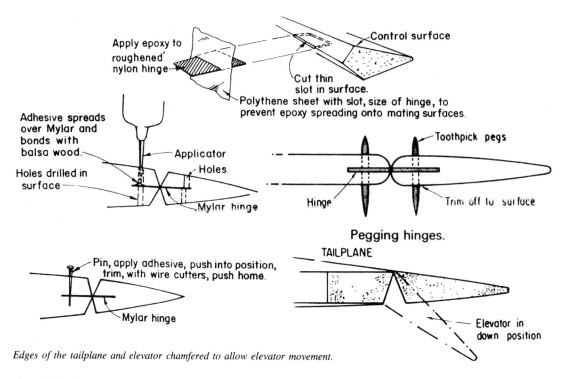

Apply epoxy to roughened nylon hinge

Control surface

Cut thin slot in surface.

Polythene sheet with slot, size of hinge, to prevent epoxy spreading onto mating surfaces.

Adhesive spreads over Mylar and bonds with balsa wood.

Applicator

Holes

Holes drilled in surface

Mylar hinge

Toothpick pegs

Hinge

Trim off to surface

Pegging hinges.

TAILPLANE

Pin, apply adhesive, push into position, trim, with wire cutters, push home.

Mylar hinge

Elevator in down position

Edges of the tailplane and elevator chamfered to allow elevator movement.

glue. This is spread onto the leaf to be inserted; I do one surface at a time and use 24-hour epoxy to give time for the glue to penetrate well. For large and fast models it is advisable to peg this hinge installation also. The introduction of cyanocrylate adhesives has improved the chances of gluing many 'difficult' and dissimilar materials together and it can be used to advantage when installing Mylar hinges. The hinge leaf is inserted in the normal way with just *one* spot of adhesive to tack it into position. Holes are then drilled from either side of the surface and a spot of cyanocrylate positioned, down the hole, onto the Mylar. This will spread sufficiently to give a strong bond.

Alternatively, or in addition, to gluing Mylar hinges, use wooden pegs (toothpicks or cocktail sticks are often used) for holding the hinges in position. The holes should be drilled slightly smaller than the diameter of the wooden peg to ensure a tight fit. Small household steel pins may be used in place of wooden pegs but a 'touch' of cyanocrylate adhesive should be applied to the pin before inserting it into the surface. The pins should not be pushed full home but left extending on one side before clipping with wire cutters and pressing home. By using pins in small models the hinges can be added after covering without

spoiling the appearance. The operation must be completed rapidly before the adhesive sets.

There are new types of adhesives coming onto the general and modelling market, almost weekly. Some of these claim to be suitable for sticking plastics that have that slightly 'greasy' feel i.e. polyethylene and polythene. By all means use them for strip and moulded hinges, but to test them first for compatibility with the different plastics and, for any sizable model, do also pin the hinges to prevent them coming adrift. You can always check on the security of your hinges on the model – just take the control surface and give it a good pull.

MOULDED POLYPROPYLENE HINGES

Thicker than Mylar hinges, the hinge line is reduced in thickness for greater flexibility. Being thicker, the slot in the surfaces must also be wider and a knife blade alone is not sufficient for these hinges – do not try to force them in as they will only split the wood. There are special tools that can be obtained from the model shop for making these wider slots, they are also used for the pin hinges. If you don't have one of these implements you must try to make two slot cuts, using a piece of

Moulded polypropylene hinges are thin but tough and inexpensive.

wood as a guide, and then pick out the wood. A small Swiss file, or lady's nail file (the type with abrasive paper) will help to finish off the slot. From this point onwards the hinge is roughened and glued in position in the same way as the Mylar hinge, although you can punch holes in the surface if none are included.

LEAF AND PIN HINGE

One of the first of the specialist moulded hinges, the hinges may be supplied already joined or as separate halves (usually identical) and the pins which must be inserted and the free end bent over to retain the pin. Gluing and dowelling is certainly recommended for the larger hinges, the smaller ones may have wedge shapes moulded on the surface which allows the leaf to be inserted, but difficult to extract.

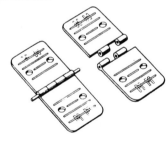

Leaf and pin hinges come in separated or assembled form.

BARB HINGES

These are probably the easiest of the moulded hinges to install as they only require a hole to be drilled, a little smaller than the maximum diameter of the barb so that it is a real push fit, and the hinge inserted. Well, not quite all because the centre portions of the hinge are square in section and the hole must be opened up to receive the square section. Failure to do so will leave you with the hinge partially inserted, but it will go no

further, and you will be unable to pull it out, because of the barbs, without ripping away the wood. To ensure that the hinge pins are aligned the free half should be dropped vertically during the installation of the first half of the hinge. If all the hinges are vertically down it will mean that the pins are all horizontal and not being strained. Barbed hinges are available with moulded, snap together, pivots for small to medium models, a very small one moulded in one piece with a thinned hinge (not the easiest to align) and nylon moulded types with a metal hinge. The latter types, in their largest format, can be used as offset hinges, for such controls as Frise ailerons, but the free projection should not be excessive.

You only need to drill a hole for the insertion of a barb hinge.

HEAT-SHRINK FILM AND FABRIC

The popular forms of plastic, self-adhesive, heat-shrinking covering materials can be adopted to form functional and free hinges. As these are also produced at the same time as the covering operation there is also a saving in time and money. Using film means that the hinge line, for ease of applications, must be on the top or lower surface; for appearance reasons it is normally the top surface of the ailerons or tailplane. To obtain a sufficient degree of down elevator travel, the edges of the tailplane and elevator must be bevelled and for strength a double thickness of covering material is required at the hinge point, the sequence of covering is shown on page 80.

To prevent the film, on shrinking, from tightening the hinge line too much a piece of scrap wood packing (.8mm. plywood or 'squashed' $\frac{1}{16}$ in. balsawood) should be inserted at the hinge line.

The underside of the tailplane and elevator are then covered as normal. For the ailerons and rudder the same principle applies i.e. using bevelled edges, but it does mean that a 'vee' joint will show on one side.

Heat-shrink fabric is even more suited for forming hinges, the material is stronger and

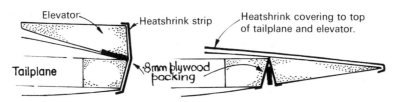

Method of forming a hinge.

shrinks less. You will probably not need to use the packing strips between the surfaces as the shrinkage is not likely to be excessive — experiment first.

Available commercially are self-adhesive fabric hinges which are pre-sewn to form the hinge line. These are suitable if the model is to be painted or if the colour of the hinge matches the covering material you are using.

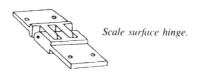

Hidden hinge.

Scale surface hinge.

SPECIALIST HINGES

Although the foregoing represent the most popular types of hinges there is a great variety of hinges, large and small, that can be used as alternatives, or are designed for specialist purposes. It would take up too much space to describe them all in detail, but a selection of them is illustrated here.

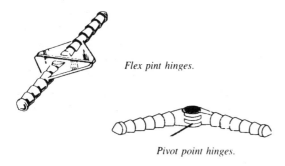

Pinless barb hinge.

Flat hinge.

Flex pint hinges.

Pivot point hinges.

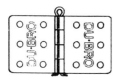

Heavy duty nylon hinge.

LINKAGES

At this stage we have to consider not just the linkages but the planning of the whole installation of radio equipment, engine, fuel tank etc. With a kit or a plan you may be lucky and have the positions of the equipment all planned for you, but in many cases it will be for you to determine where the equipment is to be located. As we will see later, one of the worst sins is to try to fly a model with a rearward balance point and it is not always that the balance works out perfectly the first time around. We can, of course, add ballast, in the form of lead weight, to the model. This, though, is 'dead' weight and can only result in a deterioration in flying performance. It is highly preferable if the equipment can be moved around to achieve the correct balance point without resorting to the addition of ballast. One of the heaviest components of the radio equipment is the battery pack and if this can be located in a number of alternative positions it gives us a reasonable flexibility. It has to be said that, due to the general layout of fixed-wing model aircraft, perhaps as many as 90% of the models finish up tail-heavy rather than nose-heavy. Although the engine is heavy in comparison with the tail surfaces the moment arm to the tail is much longer and this more than makes up for the weight difference. Therefore, there should be allowance for the battery pack to be positioned far forward to the engine bulkhead but, if the model has a long nose, to have an alternative position further back. We will look at the means of protecting the equipment later in the chapter. Servos should also be mounted fairly well forward in the fuselage, a normal position being in the wing housing area and leaving space in front of the servo mounting rails to fit the receiver. Obviously, the servos are mounted to make the most convenient linkage connections from them to the control surfaces.

The linkage between the servo and the control surface, or control function i.e. engine throttle or flaps, is the potential area for the greatest loss of efficiency and accuracy. It will be necessary, for some controls, to have a number of changes of direction and this is the most likely position for a loss of accuracy. The devices for changing direction, whether they are in the form of bellcranks or more flexible control linkages will introduce a degree of 'slop', or wasted movement. If we can avoid these changes of direction, in the main linkage or at the linkage ends, we should do so. Pushrods are another potential area for 'lost' movement. If these flex they have the effect of reducing the length of the pushrod and therefore affecting the control of the surface.

In our linkage from the servo to the control surface or function, we are looking for as little 'wasted' movement as possible, as little friction as possible and as light weight as possible. The latter requirement is a two-fold desirability. Weight, in itself, is an undesirable element in a model, but in terms of the linkage it also represents an inertia factor. If a model crashes, or makes a heavy landing, the inertia of the linkage (say a heavy pushrod) can well damage the output gears of the servo so, the lighter the better.

There are many possible combinations of linkages to achieve our eventual aim, the coupling from the servo to the control surface, which may involve pushrods, horns, bellcranks etc. It is im-possible to show them all but, by illustrating the different types, you should be able to plan your own combinations.

One word about R/C helicopters. These have very specialised installations and control linkages and they are invariably pre-planned for you. The instructions in the helicopter kit will tell you precisely where to install the receiver, servos and linkages − the mounts and linkage controls will be supplied.

CLOSED-LOOP CONTROL

I start with a description of closed-loop control linkage because, not only is it one of the oldest forms used in R/C model aeroplanes (and full-size) but also because it is one of the best systems. Ironically, although it was one of the first systems to be employed, it became 'forgotten' for many years and has only recently made a comeback. So what are the advantages? To start with, it is a positive pull-pull control and when the linkage is in tension it cannot vary − unless the control cable stretches. In other words, there is nothing to flex or distort. Secondly it is a very light system, the cables have very little weight and therefore the inertia created by the control system is exceedingly low. There we have the two principal advantages, no 'slop' and minimum mass, but what of the disadvantages? There has to be a direct line between the servo output and the control surface horns for the simplest of closed-loop control systems. However, there are alternatives in which we can still incorporate the main advantages of the cable linkage without having direct servo/horn linkages. One method is by routing the closed-loop cables through narrow diameter nylon, PTFE, or similar material, tubes. A slight loss of efficiency and increase of friction will occur, but this will still be well within acceptable limits. The second method involves using a standard closed-

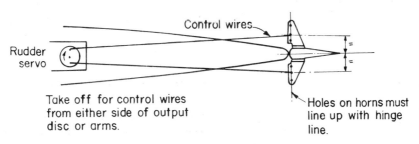

Take off for control wires from either side of output disc or arms.

Control wires

Holes on horns must line up with hinge line.

loop arrangement from the output arm to a bell-crank and then using a pushrod for the final, short, connection to the control surface.

For small to medium models the cables can be taken direct from the servo output to the control horns. Theoretically the spacing of the take-off from the servo and the control horn should be the same. In practice, I have not found having the control horn spacing larger than the servo output spacing to give any trouble (the reverse also seems to work well on the full-size 'Tiger Moth') and, for instance, will reduce the total rudder movement to an acceptable 20 to 30 degrees. What is more critical is the potential strain on the servo output bearings for closed-loop installations in large models. The air pressure created on, say, elevators or the rudder can be substantial with a large model and to transfer that load directly to the output arm may not be acceptable. To make this load an indirect one, with the possibility of also gearing down the load, an intermediate crank can be incorporated so that the initial connection to the crank is via a short pushrod from the servo. This crank can also incorporate an adjustment of moment arm and the pushrod for length.

Adjustments to the degree of movement with a direct linkage closed-loop is possible − by connecting the cables at differing spacings on the servo output arms (or at the control surface horns). However, the dual rates available in many of the R/C outfits and the infinitely variable movements available on the programmable transmitters, make the physical control adjustments less vital − but don't let that act as an excuse for not trimming out the model correctly, as opposed to the transmitter.

You will find that scale models of early, wood and canvas, aeroplanes lend themselves well to closed-loop systems, simply because these were the methods employed in the prototypes. Follow the routes of the original, which may take directional changes with the use of fair leads etc. and you won't go far wrong.

Materials for the control cables can be nylon covered fishing trace line (available from fishing and angling shops) or multi-strand steel cable. The size of the line will depend on the model but moderate size models will be OK on 10−15kg trace line, large models on 20kg − multi-core steel cable and the mega large you would have to calculate. Just for interest's sake, when going along in a car at about 60mph (88kph) open the window and put your hand out in the flat position. Then, rotate the hand and note the wind pressure − considerable! This will give you an idea of the pressures exerted on control surfaces during flight.

Joining the cables to the two ends can be done in a variety of ways − it is unlikely that we will require adjustment capability at both ends. For the nylon covered steel cable we can use the same system as the fishermen, a short length of aluminium or brass tubing, with the cable doubled back into the tubing and crimped in two places. This works well for the nylon covered steel as it grips well, but a spot of cyanocrylate adhesive onto the crimp will add security. The tubing should not have too large a diameter − ideally the tube should be slightly flattened into an oval shape and the cables a snug fit into the tube. If there is excessive room, bring the end of the cable back for a third time and fit it into the tubing before crimping.

Scale models may incorporate turnbuckles, for appearance and adjustment. These are excellent but do not omit the locking wire otherwise the turnbuckle will rotate and come adrift. For other forms of adjustment it is possible to use a clevis and adaptor for the cable fitted through and secured and the clevis adjusted in the normal way. For the connection of multi-core steel cable it can be secured by crimps, heavier wall copper tubing being more suitable, or brass tubing with the wires soldered in place. Before making the final connections in the model give the cables a good pull test to ensure that the joints are secure.

PUSHRODS

It is interesting to see how many of the terms used for our control accessories come from old engineering practices. Pushrod is just such a term and perfectly describes the method of transferring the action from, in this case, the servo, to the control horn or arm at the other end. It is a rigid rod with connectors, fixed or adjustable, at either end.

Remembering our basic requirements of lightweight and rigidity, the early pushrods were from balsawood, with a reasonable cross section, and piano wire ends. Beech dowel became popular later for medium-sized R/C models and to the ends of these were wound and glued the threaded portion of cycle spokes, or the plain end if no adjustment was to be included at that end. To the threaded end a clevis was wound on to provide length adjustment. This form of pushrod is still in general use, but is apt to flex excessively if the pushrod is long or the model fast. It is best restricted to general sports models up to 60in span.

Two materials are particularly useful for pushrods and they are thin-walled aluminium alloy tubing and arrow shaft, or fishing rod sections, or purpose-made tube from GRP (glass reinforced plastic). Carbon-fibre tubing is extremely effective as it is light in weight and mightily rigid. We have to make our adaptors for these tube pushrods and the simplest way is to fit hardwood plugs into the ends, grooved to accept the wire adaptors. These are epoxied in position inside the tubing.

The throttle linkage can be one of the most frustrating to route — it usually starts near to the fuselage, has to circumvent the fuel tank and dog leg to the throttle arm on the engine.

The linkage between the servo and the control surface, or control function i.e. throttle, is the area where there is the greatest loss of control efficiency. This is because, with the mechanical devices required to connect to the servos and control arms, plus methods of changing direction where necessary, it is possible for a degree of 'slop' to occur.

Wasted movement may happen due to flexing control rods, over-large holes in horns and servo output arms and discs and a number of other reasons. To avoid it, and obtain a greater accuracy of control, we take care to keep each connection and connecting rod as precise as possible.

There are so many possible combinations of linkages, horns, cranks, etc. that it is impossible to discuss and illustrate all of them. You will find that once you have the basic principles, and have built a number of models, it will be possible to 'permutate' the alternative to obtain the result required.

THROTTLE LINKAGES

The linkage between the throttle servo and the carburettor throttle arm is dealt with in a different way to the rudder and elevator, as there is normally insufficient space in the nose area of the model to fit in a conventional pushrod. We must also take

care to eliminate, as far as possible, the ingress of oil and fuel residues from the engine.

The nose area around the fuel tank and engine is often congested and needs careful planning of the route of the throttle linkages; this is made considerably more difficult when a steerable nosewheel is also fitted. As a general rule metal-to-metal linkages should be avoided on all control linkages. The reason for this is that, with the engine running, vibration can be set up causing the metal linkage to be constantly 'making and breaking' thus possibly producing spurious 'noise' signals that could interfere with the receiver. Some receivers are more sensitive to this type of interference than others but, for the sake of safety, it is better to avoid entirely a linkage involving metal-to-metal contact. I mention this here because on certain engines it is sometimes difficult to fit a nylon clevis into the carburettor throttle arm and still obtain clearances for the throttle to operate. If you have to resort to using 16 swg or 18 swg wire, bent at right angles to go through the holes in the carburettor throttle arm, either the wire should first be sleeved with some thin plastic tubing (from a piece of electrical wiring) or a 'no-noise' bush must be used.

To obtain accurate operation of the engine throttle we must arrange the total movement of the carburettor throttle barrel, to move through its full arc, and for this to coincide with the full movement of the servo, including transmitter trim movements. With the throttle lever on the transmitter fully up and with the trim lever also fully up the engine throttle barrel should be fully open i.e. looking down the throttle barrel should exactly coincide with the internal diameter of the intake. With the throttle lever on the transmitter fully back, but the trim lever still up, the throttle should be in a position to give the minimum safe idling revs from the engine. The movement of the

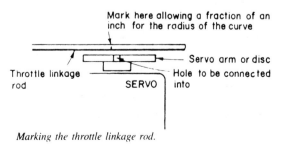

Marking the throttle linkage rod.

trim lever to the down position should then be sufficient to cut the engine completely, giving us this safety facility should it be needed during idling. All of the foregoing may sound difficult to arrange but with the different hole positions on the carburettor throttle arm it is not too difficult to find the correct combination. We must be careful not to have the servo/linkage movement too great for the engine throttle otherwise there will be a strain on the servo at the extremes causing over-loading of the servos. The opposite may be the case with linear output servos where there may be insufficient movement to operate the throttle fully. For this condition we must resort to incorporating a single arm crank in the linkage to increase the movement.

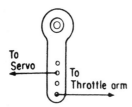

Simple crank to increase movement.

Wherever possible I would always recommend the use of a rotary servo for the throttle operation as it does give a much greater degree of flexibility.

The simplest form of throttle linkage is to use a rigid wire in a nylon tube assuming, of course, that the nylon tube will be following a straight line through the bulkheads between the radio compartment in the fuselage and the engine bay. If there are any curves and bends in this area, then a nylon tube and flexibly braided cable must be used, but avoid any bends if at all possible. It is obviously better to plan the route of the nylon tube before commencing construction of the fuselage as the holes can then be drilled in the formers at this stage. To make the holes in the formers after the

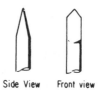

Forming drill from piano wire.

fuselage is complete will necessitate using a drill longer than is normally available so we must make our own. Cut a length of 10swg piano wire for ⅛in. dia. nylon tube, and simply file the end to a point. This makeshift drill will be quite efficient for drilling through balsa and plywood formers. The nylon tube should project about ⅛in. in front of the engine bulkhead, to avoid induced ingress of oil, and also project well into the radio compartment so that it passes the receiver position and does not allow the wire linkage to foul on the receiver packing. Nylon is not easily glued with epoxy resin adhesives and, unfortunately, some adhesives that will hold nylon are not fuel-proof. A way of ensuring that the nylon is securely held at the former positions, and still remains fuel-proof, is to first wrap the area of tube to be glued with a scrap of masking tape. The tape will adhere well to the nylon tube and the epoxy adhesive will bond the tape to the formers. Should you be unable to purchase suitable nylon tube there are some alternatives that can be used such as the internal ink tube from an old ballpoint pen. Do not however, use brass tube because of the metal-to-metal 'noise' problem.

For the connection to the servo arm one of the collet type fittings, that are fixed to the servo arm, are as good as any type. These will allow the wire to be slipped through the hole in the collet and tightened to the required length. This, together with the throttle arm and servo arm adjustments will give you all the variations you could need.

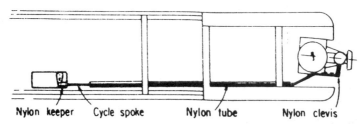

Nylon keeper   Cycle spoke   Nylon tube   Nylon clevis

Installing the throttle linkage.

AILERON LINKAGES

There are two main types of ailerons: (1) strip ailerons and (2) inset ailerons.

Strip ailerons are the simplest form of aileron to build, and attach to the wing, and have proved, in competition aerobatics, to be equally efficient as the inset variety. When used with a torque rod connection to the aileron servo, the wing can be completed before the ailerons are attached, there being no internal linkages in the wing. For small models very hard balsa, plywood, or spruce strip may be used, rounded off on the leading and trailing edges but for larger models thicker sheet balsa or trailing edge stock must be used. One disadvantage with a torque rod connection to a strip aileron is the difficulty of using a top hinge, as frequently used when heat-shrink film is employed. The reason for the problem is that the torque rod must always be in line with the hinge and this makes it difficult to obtain satisfactory fixing of the torque rod arm in the root of the strip aileron.

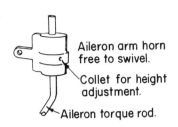

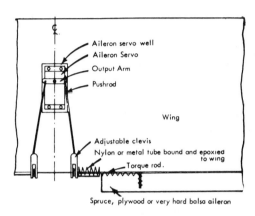

Spruce, plywood or very hard balsa aileron

Strip aileron for small model.

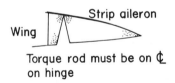

Torque rod must be on ₵ on hinge

Difficult to achieve good fixing of torque rod to aileron.

There are many commercially made strip aileron linkages available and, ideally, the aileron arm horns should be adjustable for height and free to swivel. The nylon or metal torque rod tube must be securely fixed to the wing trailing edge either by sewing and epoxying or by wrapping with glass fibre bandage and applying fibreglass resin. Clean and roughen the tube before fixing the tube to the trailing edge. Naturally, for this type of strip aileron connection to operate correctly the servo must rotate in the required direction i.e. clockwise rotation when 'left' is applied for a low or high wing model. Should all of the servos in your equipment operate in the same direction – and incorrectly for strip ailerons – the direction of rotation of one servo will have to be changed, or an intermediate bellcrank used to reverse the movement.

With large models using strip ailerons it is preferable to use commercial strip aileron linkages with wire and tube gauges of suitable strengths. For smaller models it is possible to make your own aileron linkage using standard threaded rods (cycle spokes) brass tube and clevises. Adjusting ailerons to ensure they are true with the wing is difficult and it is advisable to make a simple plywood template to check on both wing panels.

Aileron servo installations and their pushrod connections are probably among the most difficult of all installations and anything that simplifies it or makes it easier is to be welcomed. Manufacturers

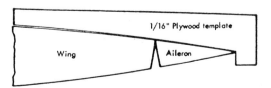

are always dreaming up new accessories to ease the modeller's burden and they know full well that we are likely to purchase them sometimes to ease frustration. Typical examples of 'useful' accessories are the aileron connectors to the rotary servo outputs.

INSET AILERONS

Inset ailerons, as the name suggests, are 'cut' into the wing in outboard section of the wings, in a similar manner to that employed by full-size aircraft. Metal pushrods (16swg piano wire) together with nylon aileron cranks, are normally used in built-up balsawood wings. This type of linkage is reasonably free from 'slop' and, properly installed, is smooth in operation without undue friction.

With the mini and micro servos now widely available many modellers prefer to fit a servo to operate each aileron. This minimises the linkages required and because the pushrod from the servo to the aileron horn is both direct and short, reduces any free play in the system. The importance of minimising unwanted free movement on aileron connections cannot be over emphasised. It is the ailerons which, if free movement is present, will start to oscillate and this can increase to cause 'flutter' which, unless the model is slowed and landed promptly, will probably cause wing failure.

On very large wings the 16swg piano wire pushrods may flex unduly and reduce control at the aileron unless they are correctly supported. Wing ribs, apart from those adjacent to the bellcrank, should have the holes, through which the pushrods traverse, suitably 'sleeved'; this may be achieved by using commercially available nylon bushes or by drilling pieces of 1.5mm (⅟₁₆ in.) plywood and gluing these to the side of the ribs. Supports should be aligned as true as possible to reduce friction

and wear. An alternative method with large wings is to use a low inertia (say ⅜ in.sq. balsawood) pushrod with a screwed rod at the servo connection end − if adjustment is required − and piano wire for connecting to the bellcrank.

Often used in foam-covered wings, where a bell crank system can be difficult to install, are the Bowden cable type systems. Stranded metal cable in nylon tube, nylon tube in a larger outer nylon tube or nylon rod in nylon tube may be used for this form of aileron linkage but the successful operation of the installation will depend on being able to route the tube through the wing without creating any sharp bends. It is essential that the tubing has described the full 90 degrees arc before it exits the wing, to connect with the aileron horn, otherwise a side load will be transmitted to the aileron horn during operation. By virtue of the necessity for a reasonable clearance tolerance between the outer tube and the inner cable/tube/rod there is inevitably a degree of 'play' when this form of linkage is installed with a bend. On operation of the servo the inner cable will move first to the outer or inner curvature of the internal wall of the tube before transmitting the movement to the aileron horn. A further disadvantage, when used on small wings, is the relative bulk of the adaptors used from the inner cable/tube/rod to the adjustable nylon clevis. With limited distances available, from the servo output to the edge of the servo well and from the aileron horn to the exit position in the wing, it may be a problem to fit in the adaptors and clevises. All tube/cable linkages should be checked periodically for freedom of movement as the ingress of oil or water can cause severe tightening in operation.

To reduce the friction and free play in the tube and rod systems some of the 'inners' have a fluted section so that only about 15% to 20% of the

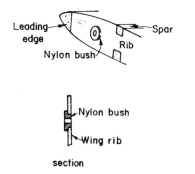

section

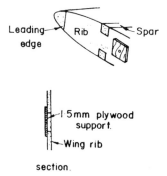

section.

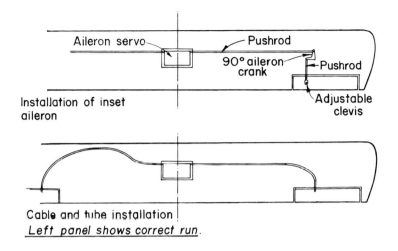

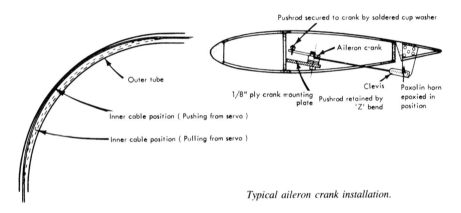

Typical aileron crank installation.

actual rod is touching the inner wall surface of the outer tube. This is certainly an improvement on the full contact systems.

INSET STRIP AILERONS

The contradiction of terms is really a combination of two types of ailerons and is suitable for small models and fast models requiring only small movements i.e. pylon racers. Note that with this form of installation the ailerons are fitted in the mid-span position; with a fully outboard aileron the 'whip' on the torque rod would be too great.

AILERON CRANK INSTALLATIONS

There are many commercially available aileron cranks, and although they vary in detail of design and manufacture they all work on the same principle of changing the direction of operation through approximately 90 degrees. One added advantage of having a bellcrank in the linkage between the servo and the aileron horn, is that the extent of movement can be adjusted at this point. With linear servos it is not possible to vary the movement from the servo, and if the full movement is transmitted to the aileron, to decrease the aileron movement to a reasonable degree may involve the use of an extra long aileron horn. By utilising the inner holes of the crank arm leading to the aileron horn the linear movement can be reduced.

Naturally, before the linkage is installed in the wing the direction of servo rotation, or travel with a linear servo, must be ascertained and pushrod connections to the aileron cranks and aileron horns designed so that the transmitter operation and aileron movements agree i.e. with the transmitter aileron sticks to the left the left aileron is up. It is all too easy to connect ailerons incorrectly, so do check carefully that they are working

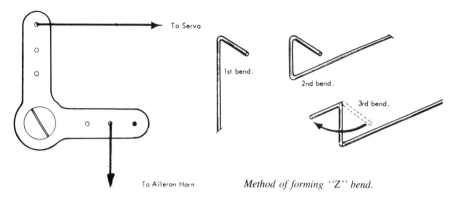

Method of forming "Z" bend.

in the right sequence and also that as one aileron goes down the opposite aileron rises.

Aileron cranks are normally mounted on ⅛in. (3mm or 4mm) plywood plates glued between two wing ribs. Where ribs are at spacings that would cause flexing in the plywood mounting plate it is advisable to insert an additional half rib to reduce the spacing. Pushrods can be secured in position in the aileron crank either by bending the end through 90 degrees, inserting through the crank and soldering with a cup washer, or by forming a 'Z' bend which is inserted through the crank before it is bolted to the plate. Methods of installing the aileron crank and forming the 'Z' bend are shown and an aileron crank installation with access for inspection and maintenance is also illustrated.

While on the subject of aileron linkages it might be as well to mention two other items connected with them, although they can be used for other installations as well. The first is the use of a ball, or double ball, connector for the take-off to the servo disc. These ball joints have many uses, as we shall see later, and allow the servo to be isolated by simply 'popping' the connector from the ball. By using two ball joint links on the servo disc, either side of neutral, we have already introduced some differential movement, but more may be required. Incidentally, it is always more up elevator than down that we require, to eliminate adverse yaw. More of that later, in aerodynamics. Adjustable bellcranks are available for varying to more or less than 90 degrees and the setting of the crank will depend on the amount of differential required and the position of the aileron horn i.e. top or bottom of the wing.

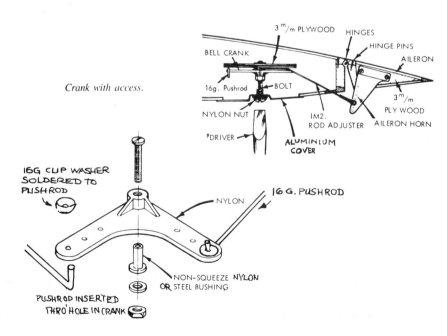

Crank with access.

Swivel socket link.

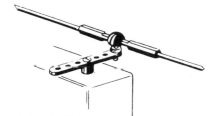

Double swivel socket link.

Heavy duty ball joint link.

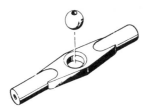

Heavy duty ball joint − double aileron link.

Ball head stud.

ribs and to ensure the epoxy grips well the top of the horn is drilled with a number of $\frac{3}{32}$ in. dia. holes to allow the adhesive to penetrate. Standard rudder horns may be used for ailerons − in the case of strip aileron they are bolted right through the aileron and for the inset ailerons a plywood plate must be installed in the underside of the aileron. It will be noted that with aileron horns installed the hinge line does not correspond with the horn/clevis pivot and this will inevitably involve a differential aileron movement. Fortunately the differential works to our advantage in this instance as the down-going aileron travels less distance than the up-going aileron. The down-going aileron provides additional lift but, if the movement is too great the additional lift is nullified by the extra drag caused by the aileron being deflected into the airflow. Should an equal movement up and down be required the horn must be raked forward to coincide with the hinge line.

A final reminder to check thoroughly that the aileron installation is completely free in operation, and that all the cranks, horns and pushrods are secure, before the wings are finally covered.

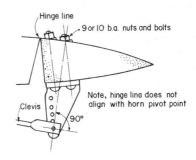

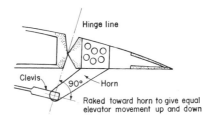

AILERON HORNS

Again a wide variety of commercial aileron horns is obtainable or you can make your own from $\frac{1}{16}$ in. thick paxolin or plastic laminates such as 'Formica' and 'Warerite'. With the thin paxolin-type horns the horn should be epoxied securely between two hard balsawood or plywood aileron

SPECIAL LINKAGES

Again, the number of 'special' linkages that are possible are legion; they may be required to operate flaps, undercarriages, wheel brakes, elevons, all moving tailplanes etc., and there is only room in this book to include some of them. I am including, however, details of differential aileron linkages, probably the only differential movement of a control surface that is of any great value in most models. Also included are details of a 'novel' aileron linkage that will be of particular use to scale modellers and coupled aileron/rudder methods allowing greater flexibility with three-function radio outfits.

'T' TAILS

'T' tails, or aircraft with high mounted tailplanes, are more prevalent on gliders than powered models − to reduce the danger of damage to the tailplane when landing on rough slope soaring sites. Flying boats are also frequently designed with a high positioned tailplane to keep it well clear of water surface and spray. Undoubtedly the main reasons for the limited number of designs using the 'T' tail feature are the more difficult linkages to the elevator and the problems in producing a sound fixing of the tailplane on top of the fin, frequently resulting in struts being used from the fuselage to the tailplane. One distinct advantage of having the tailplane at a high position is that it will probably be clear of the 'wash' and turbulence from the propeller. This consideration, however, is seldom sufficient reason alone for using a tailplane mounted on the fin, with the associated difficulties.

ALL FLYING TAILPLANES

As the title suggests, instead of having a fixed tailplane with movable elevators, with the 'all flying tailplane' the whole of the tailplane is hinged to move up and down. This form of longitudinal control is frequently associated with 'T' tails, as used with high performance full-sized sailplanes. All flying tailplanes can also be used in the conventional position i.e. on top of the fuselage, but, again, are more likely to be associated with gliders. Theoretically, the fully moving tailplane is more efficient than using separate elevators but the advantage is minimal with powered models and unworthy of consideration, except for scale models where the full-sized control has to be duplicated.

CONTROL SURFACES WITH SWEEPBACK

Sweepback on rudders and ailerons can present problems when the linkage meets the hinge line at an angle considerably more or less than 90 degrees. With an acute angle the amount of twisting of the horn and clevis would be totally unacceptable and the answer to this problem is to fit a special universal joint at the pivot point.

Swept elevators also present difficulties because it is impossible to join the elevators in the normal way, with spruce or piano wire, due to the hinge lines being at an angle. Separate linkages must be taken to each elevator or from the servo or by a twin take-off from the end of the pushrod. In most cases there will still be the problem of having to fit universal joints to each elevator horn position. A simpler answer would be to use tapered elevators to match in with the overall swept tailplane effect.

FLAPS

The purpose of flaps is to increase lift, by projecting the flaps below the rear wing surface, so that the airspeed can be lowered without the model stalling. This enables a model to be taken off the ground quicker and landed more slowly. Unless your model has a high wing loading or you have to operate from a small flying area, there does not seem any great point in fitting flaps; for a model that is very aerodynamically clean, and has a shallow gliding angle, it may be more advantageous to fit air brakes. The optimum amount of flap movement for a particular model can only be found by experience, similarly, the change of flying attitude may vary considerably from model to model but will almost always result in a nose-up pitching moment.

ELEVONS AND 'V' TAILS

Flying wing models, lacking conventional elevators, require their ailerons to act also for longitudinal control, making it necessary to incorporate both the elevator and aileron servos in the linkage. 'V' tails present a similar requirement because of absence of a fin and rudder and, in this case, the elevator and rudder servos must be combined. Commercial units are available for these purposes and are easier to install than home-made sliding

Servo mounted control mixer.

devices. Naturally the aileron and elevator function of the elevons operate in the same sense as normal.

Mechanical mixers rely on linking the two servos with a pushrod so that, in effect, the aileron, or rudder servo is moved backwards or forwards to induce the elevator movement. In the home-made mixer this is actually what is achieved, with the elevator servo being fixed, but the aileron servo fitted on sliding rails. The commercial item is a moulded fitting which is attached to the top of the aileron servo and a rocker arm is connected to the elevator servo. When the elevator servo comes into operation it pushes or pulls the rocker arm and introduces the elevator element.

Electronic mixers, for two functions i.e. aileron/elevator, rudder/elevator or flap/elevator, are still produced on a separate basis, although the mixer functions now part of the transmitter is making them obsolescent. These mixers allow the two servos to be fitted to operate one side of the elevon, or ruddervator, each without physical connections.

Full electronic mixing, through computer-controlled transmitters offers, as we have seen, all aspects of control mixing, with differential and exponential and end point adjustment, et al! What you have to remember are the directions of travel required (back to basics for this one) and how to feed the information and requirements into the transmitter.

STEERABLE NOSEWHEELS AND TAILWHEELS

To control a model accurately on the ground it is necessary to be able to steer it to a greater degree than is possible with rudder only. Steering by rudder is only usually effective as the model builds up speed for take-off. With tailwheel aircraft on grass, the additional drag and, therefore, more engine power required may give adequate control. Any form of steerable undercarriage is probably wasted if you have to fly from a rough grass field;

taxiing is virtually impossible in these conditions and the vibration transmitted from the steerable wheel to the servo is likely to damage the latter.

Nosewheels need to turn only through a small arc to be effective and connection to an outside hole in the steering arm (and an inner hole on the servo output disc) is normally sufficient. There are many different types of nosewheel gear available including single and double leg units for all sizes and weights of models. The steering arms vary in position from low mounted to high, the high position arms being suitable for internal connection of the linkage. Whether you use an internal linkage connection, or external on the underside of the nose, will depend on the available room inside the nose of the model and the accessibility. The linkage connection underside the nose is often the easiest to arrange even though the routing of the linkage from the servo to the steering arm may be more circuitous. Avoid linkages between the servo and steering arm that are too rigid, to prevent the transmission of landing and take-off loads on the nosewheel. Cable and tube linkages are most suitable for the purpose.

Steerable tailwheels can be linked directly to the rudder or by a short linkage between the rudder horn and the tailwheel support. Because the moment arm between the tailwheel and the main wheels is proportionally greater than with tricycle undercarriages the turning arc needs to be larger; although not necessarily as large as the rudder movement. Too much movement will give an erratic take-off path, even with minor rudder corrections.

DIFFERENTIAL LINKAGES

For the 'in-house' programmable transmitter we don't have to worry about setting output discs with staggered take-off holes, or raked control horns, the electronics will take care of it all. Transmitters having less advanced functions will require the introduction of differential through the mechanical side. Differential movement simply means that, for an equal servo movement in each direction, the control surface will move more in one direction than the other. For instance, we may wish to have more UP elevator than DOWN and this can be achieved by varying the position of the elevator horn connecting hole relative to the hinge line, or by modifying the location of the servo output arm take-off.

Differential control is most useful for elevator and aileron control, but more so with the latter function. Certain types of aeroplanes, notably high wing models and biplanes, suffer from 'aileron reversal' due to the high drag of the down-going aileron (in the high pressure air) being more effective than the lift from the up-going aileron i.e the drag from the movements of the ailerons is greater than the lift created for the bank. Raising both (or all four) ailerons might help by reducing the amount of movement into the high pressure, but the real answer is to introduce differential control so that the movement upwards is much greater than the downwards movement of the aileron. Although we are not considering aerodynamics at the moment it is worth stating that, even with the improved banking the differential gives, the model will also probably need an input of rudder to produce a balanced turn. With the elevator, it is simply a matter of possibly needing more UP elevator, for the landing round-out, than DOWN elevator, although for an aerobatic model it is likely that no differential at all will be required. Only test flights will determine the need, or otherwise − this is undoubtedly where the programmable transmitter has an advantage.

Serious helicopter flyers will certainly want more than just the basic five-function outfit. The fact that differential and exponential control is available on the more advanced sets makes the additional expense worthwhile.

The geometry of differential controls can be a little confusing, even when worked out from basics. Hopefully the illustrations of the various

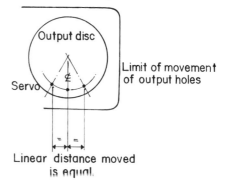

Standard arrangement.

Linear distance moved is equal.

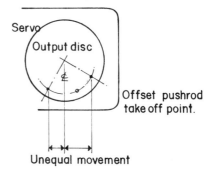

Offset arrangement

Unequal movement

methods of achieving the differential will be of assistance.

Having considered hinges and linkages it would be helpful to take a quick look at the methods of joining the two parts, before taking a look at the remainder of the installations. The simplest of connections from the servo to the pushrod (metal end) is the 'Z' bend, as previously mentioned.

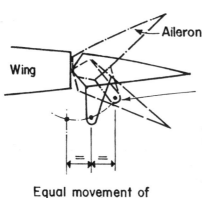

Equal movement of pushrod.

Limit of movement of horn output holes. Aileron horn offset to rear gives more movement of aileron upwards.

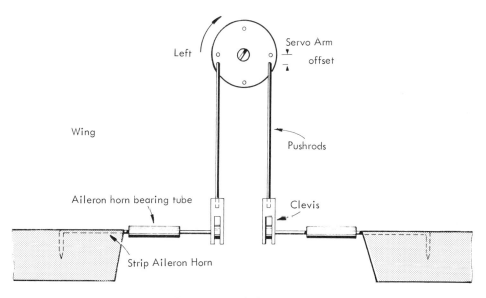

Differential by offsetting holes on rotary servo disc

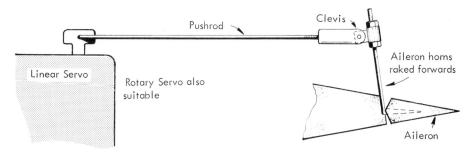

Differential movement from Linear Servo

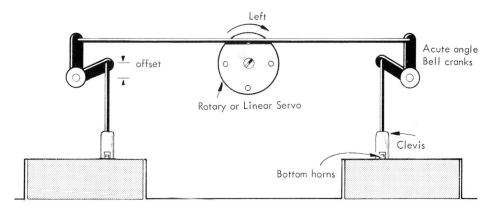

This does not, of course, offer any adjustability and nor does the 'keepers' for connecting the pushrod to the servo output. Grandaddy of these is a 90-degree bend in the pushrod wire, with a piece of thin wire soldered to the shaft and taken past the bend point — simple and still effective.

However, there are moulded keepers available that will do the job just as well and only cost a few pence — just be sure that they are the correct size for the wire — or vice versa.

For adjustable pushrod ends we have the clevis. The metal types started life as part of a typewriter,

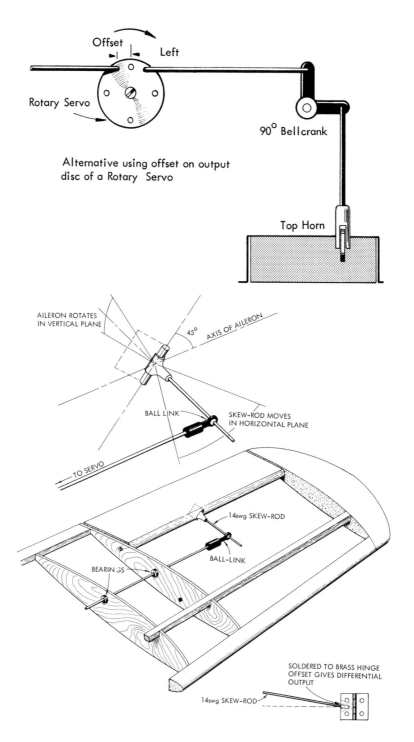

Offset

Left

Rotary Servo

Alternative using offset on output
disc of a Rotary Servo

90° Bellcrank

Top Horn

AILERON ROTATES
IN VERTICAL PLANE

45°

AXIS OF AILERON

BALL LINK

SKEW-ROD MOVES
IN HORIZONTAL PLANE

TO SERVO

14swg SKEW-ROD

BALL-LINK

BEARINGS

SOLDERED TO BRASS HINGE
OFFSET GIVES DIFFERENTIAL
OUTPUT

14swg SKEW-ROD

their function being to provide adjustment for the lengths of the letter key pushrods, not that much different to our uses. It is prudent to purchase the threaded metal rods with the metal clevises or you may find that the humble cycle spoke is not the correct gauge or thread. They certainly fit some metal clevises but not all. If you are coming from a 'snake', the tube and tube/rod/cable inners, mentioned in 'Inset ailerons' there will be special adaptors from the inner to the clevis, or keeper.

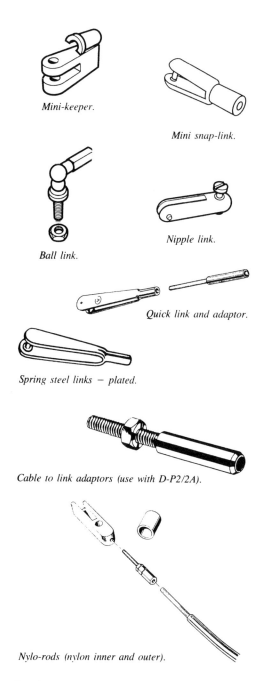

Mini-keeper.

Mini snap-link.

Ball link.

Nipple link.

Quick link and adaptor.

Spring steel links – plated.

Cable to link adaptors (use with D-P2/2A).

Nylo-rods (nylon inner and outer).

In those cases you have to ensure that metal clevises are a good screw-on fit to the threaded part of the adaptor.

Nylon clevises give you a little more tolerance with regard to the screwing onto the threaded part. If the hole in the nylon clevis is too large for the threaded rod there is nothing much you can do about it, but usually it is the other way round and the hole may need to be fractionally enlarged. It

is usually a matter of self-tapping the clevis onto the thread, so be careful to get the fit right – too small a hole and it will be very difficult to turn the clevis, too large and there will be insufficient internal thread to hold the clevis firmly onto the thread. All clevises should have keepers, small pieces of tubing, slipped over the ends after the clevis has been closed onto the control horn, or arm or servo disc. Check, also, that the pin has closed fully into its housing – it will usually 'click' home.

RADIO EQUIPMENT INSTALLATION

Now that we have considered hinges and linkages we should be able to put it all together and prepare a fully planned installation, showing the proposed positions of the radio equipment, all linkages, control horns, switch position and aerial.

Planning the complete installation (batteries, receiver, switch, servos, linkages and control horns) before you commence construction will allow you to include supports for servo rails, cut outlet positions for linkages, drill holes for pushrods or flexible tubing, fix sponge rubber packing in inaccessible areas where equipment is to be installed etc. Do not be tempted to rush ahead with a view to sorting out the radio installation at a later date – it might not fit!

Radio equipment is not only expensive but sophisticated and delicate electronic equipment that requires protection. It is in our interests to see that the equipment is efficiently installed in the model and protected, as far as possible, from accidental damage. Most manufacturers supply with their radio outfits, comprehensive instructions on the 'dos and don'ts' of installing their equipment. This information is based on practical experience and specialised knowledge and is written for your benefit. Read the instructions and adhere to them, if for no other reason than that by acting contrary to them the equipment guarantee may be made null and void.

BATTERY PACK

This is usually the heaviest item of the airborne radio equipment and is the most likely to create damage during a crash. Partially for this reason, and also to help prevent damage and reduce

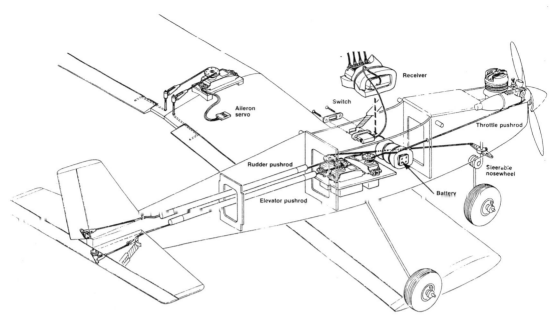

Typical R/C installation for high wing or shoulder wing model (with acknowledgements to Thunder Tiger).

vibration effects from the engine, the battery pack must be surrounded by foam material. Foam plastic, unless of very high density, does not have sufficient resistance to crushing to be suitable for battery pack protection. As an experiment try holding a piece of plastic foam — the normal lightweight variety — between thumb and fore-finger and squeeze it. Very little effort is required before the battery pack in even a minor crash exerts considerably greater pressure than this. Foam rubber, the lighter forms of rubber carpet underlay, are ideal for our purposes and the battery pack should be completely surrounded in this material, secured lightly in position with adhesive tape or rubber bands. Do not bind the foam rubber too tightly to the battery pack or some of the vibration resistance will be lost. Take care not to strain the wires leading out from the pack; a sensible precaution here is to double back the wires and tape them to the pack.

I prefer models to have separate fuel tank and battery compartments but where the batteries are

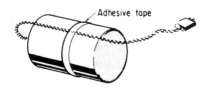

Securing the lead from the battery pack.

placed directly under the fuel tank the battery pack should, in addition to the foam rubber, be protected by wrapping in a polythene bag. This will prevent damage to the batteries should a leak occur in the fuel tank.

RECEIVER

The most delicate and most expensive part of the airborne equipment, the receiver, should be given special treatment. All too often, unfortunately, it is wedged tightly in a small area offering little or no protection from engine vibration or crash damage. The same principle of protection applies to the receiver as for the battery pack. Fortunately with less mass than the battery pack there is less inertia during a crash but, once again, foam plastic is barely enough protection for the receiver unless it is very thick and dense. The foam-wrapped receiver should be a 'loose fit' in the fuselage and should not be placed behind projec-tions, such as switches, dowels, nuts and bolts; all possible causes of damaging a receiver in a crash. Position the receiver in the fuselage so that the servo and switch leads come in a convenient place, usually at the bottom of the fuselage, and for changing or switching the frequencies if these features are fitted.

Receiver aerials are necessary evils and although

it would frequently be helpful, particularly in scale models, if we could cut them shorter or double them back on themselves this must never be done. To shorten an aerial at all will result in loss of range of the model and probably in the loss of the model too. Aerials should be routed directly out of the fuselage wherever possible and always kept clear of battery and servo wires. Taking the aerial to the tip of the fin is normally convenient and the aerial can be retained on the fin by using a small rubber band.

To prevent strain on the receiver aerial connection a 'stop' should be attached to the aerial wire where it exits through the fuselage. This can be made simply from a piece of ³⁄₁₆ in. dia. dowel.

The aerial is looped through the dowel and 'slack' left between it and the receiver when the aerial is tensioned on the fin.

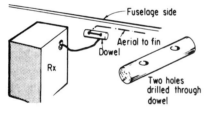

Retaining the end of the aerial at the fin.

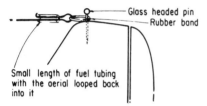

Receiver aerial restraint.

Not popular now, but very well worth considering for models where receiver reception may be poor i.e. biplanes with a multitude of rigging wires, or a fuselage covered in a metalised finish, is the vertical whip aerial. These were used in days when radio transmitters and receivers were less reliable than they are today and are still used on boats and some vehicles. Whip aerials can be purchased commercially, as used for boats, or you can make one from a length of piano wire (say 1.2mm dia. − 18 swg). The total length from receiver to end of the piano wire should be the same as the original aerial length and the tip of the

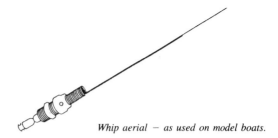

Whip aerial − as used on model boats.

aerial should be protected by forming it into a small loop, or gluing a coloured bead to the end.

PLUG SOCKETS AND SWITCHES

I was always told that plugs, sockets and switches were the most vulnerable part of any radio equipment. This may not be so true now, but we must treat them with respect, keep them clear of dirt and dust and not just take them for granted.

Receivers normally feature block connectors, for the direct plugging in of servo plugs, although some feature a fly lead for the battery plug and a fifth or sixth function (these are connected via 'Y' lead). The chances of the plugs coming adrift from the connecting block are fairly remote but the protective receiver sleeve, if a moderately snug fit over the plug leads, should hold them in place. Separate plugs and sockets, such as the ones from the battery to the switch, should have a secure fitting but if any of these start to become a little loose, they should be taped together with self-adhesive electrical tape. Although you may not believe it, initially, the position of the servo leads, battery and switch wires etc. can be planned and the usual 'rat's nest' of wires avoided. Use a piece of wing mounting tape to hold the loose wires to the fuselage side.

Where the aileron servo is fitted in a separate wing you should use an extension lead to prevent any risk of straining the lead from the servo to the receiver. You will often see modellers fitting the wing to the fuselage and desperately trying to connect the servo plug into the receiver − with the wing almost tight on the fuselage and hardly enough room to get a finger in the gap. However, with the extension lead fitted you must be careful where the surplus lead length is situated − it mustn't foul the servo outputs or the linkages. A favourite place is between the wing and fuselage wing seating, with a little loop of lead extending outside the fuselage and nicely trapped! Of course, you don't notice this until the wing bolts are all tightened and you then have to remove the wing and start again. Don't be tempted to partly undo the wing bolts and then push the loop back into the fuselage with a screwdriver − you don't know where it is going.

Dirt and oil and switches don't mix and you should never place a switch close to an IC (internal combustion) engine on the exhaust exit side. It is acceptable to install the switch on the side of the fuselage, away from the unburnt oil residues, but use the switch plate supplied and mount the switch vertically or horizontally. The plate should indicate the ON/OFF positions, have the ON positions to the rear (in case it is accidentally knocked on launch) or at the bottom (in case it vibrates downwards). Better still, install the switch internally and operate it externally. There are commercially available switch actuators, or you can make one by mounting the switch on the bulkhead with double sided servo tape and forming a wire hook to extend through the fuselage side and locate in the switch dolly.

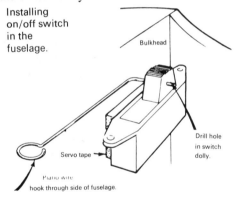

Installing on/off switch in the fuselage.

Bulkhead

Drill hole in switch dolly.

Servo tape

Piano wire hook through side of fuselage.

Installing on/off switch in the fuselage.

SERVOS

Since the time when servo reversing became an automatic feature on transmitters, we haven't needed to worry about the rotational direction of the servos supplied with the R/C outfits. That doesn't mean that we can install the servos 'willy-nilly' and then sort out the linkages to and from the control surfaces. This is a vital part of the preparation of the model and a little thought and care at this stage will certainly help to prevent control difficulties later. Servo reversing is not the perfect answer to all situations, there are just a few that cannot be answered by the flick of a switch. For instance, you may be trying to link up, via a 'Y' lead, two engine throttles or retracting undercarriage legs, where the servos have to be located with the pushrod connections working opposite to one another. With the 'Y' lead it is only possible to operate the servos in the same direction. You may find that buying from alternative sources the servos will operate in opposite directions and purchasing one of these will obviate the need to rewire the servo internally, not to be recommended for the non-electronic enthusiast.

It should be common sense that the most direct route between servo and control horn will be the most effective. Changes of direction allow for friction or unwanted bonding to occur. The ideal arrangement, for a typical trainer or sports plane is for the elevator and rudder pushrods to cross one another so that they exit in a direct line with the control horns. With pushrods you must arrange for them to be clear of one another when they cross. This calls for a little thought on how to connect at the servo outputs (one below and one above) and staggering the heights of the rudder and elevator control horn connecting points. If it remains difficult to achieve this with conventional pushrods it will be easier when using 'snake' linkages as they only have to pass one another to be OK. With these angled linkages the rudder horn connection needs the horn raking forward slightly so that a 90-degree angle between the pushrod and horn bisects the rudder hinge line. For the elevator, the pushrod connection is not at 90 degrees to the hinge line and the control horn should be angled to the same line; the fitting of a ball-link connector is good practice in this situation.

Quite frequently, the pushrod end (the metal rod part) has to exit the fuselage with a 'dog leg'. Providing it is not excessive in angles, or length, this does not give too much concern for the average size sports models but, for the faster and heavier models there is the risk of the wire pushrod ends flexing and introducing unwanted control movements. A typical example of this is with the elevator horn being on the underside and the model is divided to a high speed − no problem here because the pushrod is in the pulling mode. Control is then given for full up and, because of

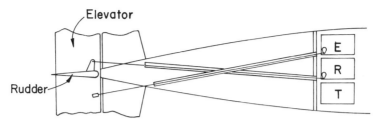

Direct linkage possible with Bowden cables and pushrods.

the bends in the wire end of the pushrod and the force exerted by the air on the elevator, the wire flexes excessively and there is insufficient up elevator available.

Place some tracing paper over the plan view of the model fuselage and sketch out the linkage routes and types. When they are finalised you can use them − and the side views − to prepare the pushrod, 'snakes', control horns and linkage connections.

SERVO INSTALLATIONS

When fitting the servos we must bear in mind the ruination of all electronic equipment − vibration. We must do all we can to prevent the vibration from the engine being transmitted to the servos, in particular, as these are electro-mechanical devices and more suspect to vibration than solid-state electronics. Achieving high levels of vibration damping is not difficult in itself, just a matter of soft mounting, but this gives too much free movement of the servo case. We have to achieve a compromise where the servo is resiliently installed but without excessive movement within its mounting.

Servos are supplied with grommets, or rubber pads, small eyelets, washers and wood screws for mounting. Beech or maple hardwood mounting rails, traversing the fuselage, are fine for servo mounting, around 8mm square (⅜ in.) to 10mm square for larger models. The ends of the servo rails must be adequately secured on the fuselage

sides and this is where our planning comes into use. There should be some horizontal supports glued on the fuselage sides to accurately position the bearer ends, gluing the ends to the sides only is not sufficient. Also with our planning arrangement we can pre-drill the servo bearers. Drill small diameter pilot holes and then a slightly larger hole in the first half depth of the bearer. We want the screw to go in and hold well but not be a struggle to tighten − that is when the screwdriver slips and goes straight through the side of the fuselage. We also need some semi-circular cut-outs in the centre of the servo locations to allow the servo leads to pass through when the servos are being positioned. A simple way of doing this, and providing alternative mounting with the output to the front or rear, is to place the two bearers together, facing the same way as they would be in the model, punching a start position at the centre of servo location and drilling through with an 8mm drill. All that is required now is for the bearers to be separated and the corners of the 'half moons' rounded off.

When fitting the bearers (use a white PVA glue or long-setting epoxy) just check that the servos fit neatly − they should do if you have done your homework correctly. There should be about a millimetre space between the ends of the servos and bearers (on no account should it be a 'wedge' fit) to allow the transmission of vibration. Fit the grommets, or pads, to the servo lugs and then insert the eyelets in the holes *from the underside*. The principle behind the fixings of the servos is that the screw will tighten onto the washer and eyelet, but will not crush the rubber cushioning. 'Nip' the screws home and leave it at that.

For any control where there is likely to be relatively heavy loads i.e. elevator, rudder and aileron, the servo should be mounted fore and aft to the direction of travel of the pushrods. Connections to the throttle and some other auxiliary

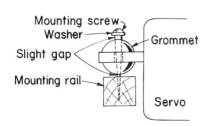

controls are less important in this respect as only light loads are involved. If a servo was positioned beamwise to the pushrod direction, for a high loading control, then the 'rocking' motion of the servo would be too great.

SERVO MOUNTING TRAYS

Many manufacturers now produce, as an additional item in some cases, servo trays or mounting brackets to take one to three servos. Should trays or brackets be available for your type of servo I strongly recommend buying them; they make installing servos so much easier and more efficient too. There are a number of different patterns but the most common are for three servos abreast and two servos with one servo in front across the tray. Using a servo tray also gives us double vibration insulation as the servos are still mounted on grommets and the servo tray itself is fixed with grommets.

The servo tray is mounted on hardwood rails fixed across the width of the fuselage; alternatively the rails may be fixed on the side of the fuselage and the tray mounted with the servos facing across the fuselage.

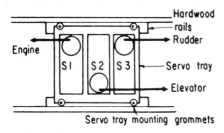

PUTTING IT ALL TOGETHER

Having described some of the equipment and components in some detail we will return to a pre-installation period.

We have now reached the stage where the pushrods and throttle linkage is made, the hinges and control horn are fitted, the servo rails installed and holes cut for the switch and pushrod exits. We are now ready to install the equipment permanently − not quite! First we make sure we remove from the inside of the fuselage all traces of balsa chippings, dust, bits of wire, old screws and any other debris which, if left in there, will do a lot

of damage to the equipment once installed. Bang the sides of the fuselage with the flat of your hand to remove the dust and, if you have it available blow compressed air from a tube through the fuselage.

I am including the following how-to-do-it description of making and installing pushrods and 'snakes' as many modellers find these a little baffling in the beginning stages.

Conventional pushrods were the earliest form of linkages between servo and control surface and, like the sewn hinges, still take a lot of beating. Firm, but light, grade balsawood of 5/16 in. or 3/8 in. square or 1/4 in. dia. dowel and 15g cycle spokes (or 16 swg piano wire) are just about ideal for the construction of the pushrods. The dowel can be from ramin wood (available from woodworkers' shops) which is lighter and cheaper than birch dowel; it is also straighter grained with less risk of warping or having weaknesses of 'cross grain'. The dowel should take up as much of the total length of the pushrods as possible, bearing in mind that the dowel must not foul the rear former or end of the fuselage inside or hit the rear of the servos. Bending the cycle spoke at the rear of the pushrod is the first job, so start by screwing on a nylon clevis to the threaded end of the spoke unit, the end of the spoke just appears in the circular cut-out in the clevis. Hold the clevis over the plan and mark the position of the first bend. Bend to the required angle by using heavy pliers, checking with the plan, and proceed to the second bend. Allow a further 1½in. from the point where the dowel starts, for fixing the spoke to the dowel, and bend the final 1/4 in. of the spoke at right angles and pointing down. The spoke for the rudder servo can also be bent; this is rather more difficult as there are complete changes of direction and not on one plane only. It may mean you have to do a bit of 'jiggery pokery' to get this right but take satisfaction from the fact that it is probably the most difficult part of the construction you will have to face. When you are satisfied that the rear end spokes have been bent accurately remove the clevises. Cut the elevator and rudder dowels to the length you have drawn on the plan and, if the two are different lengths, mark them rudder and elevator to save confusion later. At a point 1¼in. from each end of the dowels drill a 1/16 in. diameter hole; the holes at each end should follow the same line. Insert the bent-over end of the spoke

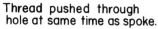

Thread pushed through
hole at same time as spoke.

Binding to push rod and
clevis spoke.

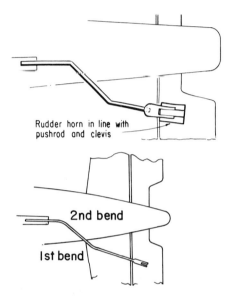

Rudder horn in line with
pushrod and clevis

2nd bend

1st bend

Pushrod fitted to elevator horn (bends exaggerated).

the spoke and the dowel. Smear white PVA glue or balsa cement over all the threaded area, rubbing it in well with your finger. The servo ends of the pushrods are treated in a similar way but with a straight piece of cycle spoke and not threaded. Leave the wire projecting about 1in. beyond the servo arms or discs at this stage. When the glue to the four bound ends of the pushrods has dried remove the clevises. If the rudder and elevator control horns have not been fitted previously they should be fixed now. Note that it is better practice to slightly angle the elevator horn to the line of the pushrod. Similarly, if not already cut, the slots for the pushrod exits should be made in each side of the rear fuselage. These slots should be about an inch long and $\frac{3}{16}$ in. wide. Remember to fuel-proof the cut edges of the slot. Slip the pushrods down the inside of the fuselage and feed the threaded ends through the respective slots for the elevator and rudder. This is easily achieved with the tailplane and elevator off. Reconnect the clevises to the rudder and elevator horns on the second hole from the outside and check for full and free movement by operating the pushrods from the approximate position of the servos. When all the movements are satisfactory, and minor adjustments made to the bends of the spokes as necessary the pushrods can be removed again.

Heat-shrink tubing (6.4mm dia. available from radio spares) can also be used on the pushrods to retain the wire ends. Firstly drill holes in the end of the pushrods — a V-block holds the dowel satisfactorily when drilling with a pillar drill — and then file a small groove from the hole to the

into the hole drilled in the dowel, at the same time inserting the end of 4–5 feet length of thread. Bind the thread tightly and closely around the dowel and spoke. To secure the opposite end of the thread, when the binding is complete, wind the thread round the spoke and pull it tight between

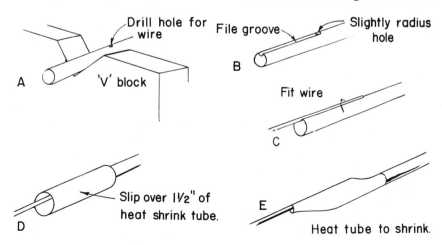

end of the dowel. Fit the wire into the hole and slip over a 1½in. length of the heat-shrink tube. Hold the tubing over an electric hot plate or a gas flame and the tube will shrink tight over the dowel and wire.

'Snakes' have their disadvantages, as we have stated before, but also have uses where it would be difficult to fit any other form of linkage, in foam wings with inset ailerons for instance.

Despite the fact that this linkage system is referred to as tube and cable (a throw-back from the Bowden cable types originally used) the more frequently used materials are nylon tube/rod and nylon tube in nylon tube (or PTFE, a similar, but possibly with lower friction, material). Apart from the tube inside a tube, where a threaded stud is screwed into the inner tube, there has to be an adaptor before the clevis can be fitted. For metal stranded cable the adaptor must be soldered to the cable and, in the case of a nylon rod inner, an adaptor is 'self tapped' onto the rod. Even the stud screwed into the tube causes the tube to 'swell' and this area must not be allowed to reach the outer tube at any control position and risk 'jamming'. With any of the adaptor arrangements there is bound to be a considerable distance between the control horn and the outer, support, tube. To try to reduce this distance to an absolute minimum i.e. so that the adaptor hits the outer tube at full deflection, will cause too much bending strain on the cable at the full opposite movement due to the non-linear movement of the control horn. Completed linkages must always be checked manually to assess the ease of operation and cause of any excess friction determined and rectified.

It is *absolutely* essential to fix the outer cable *firmly* at the extremities of its length. Without solid anchor points at these positions useful control of the function being used may be totally lost. In addition to the end anchor points the tube should also be supported through its length, with straight runs, and anchored at positions of bends. Nylon and PTFE are not the easiest of materials to glue but there are a number of methods that will give reasonable results. Contact adhesive will adhere to outer cables providing they are thoroughly roughened first with a coarse sandpaper to provide a key. Using this adhesive it is still important to 'extend' the glued anchor point by binding and

gluing a block to the tube first. This block can then be glued to the fuselage side or a bulkhead etc. Gluing can be made very much easier if the outer tube is first wrapped with drafting tape. Bind the tube tightly with drafting tape at the point where it is required to fix it − this will adhere to the tube and the paper surface of the drafting tape will equally adhere to balsa or plywood. Cyanocrylate adhesives, mentioned earlier, will glue most of the outer tubing satisfactorily providing there is a close fit between the tubing and the wood, try a test joint first though. Balsa rods, spanning from bulkhead to bulkhead can also support and anchor the tubing. Supporting the tubing, when a balsa rod is not used, can be by strips of balsawood spanning the width of the fuselage or on the fuselage side by using small saddle clips sold for the purpose.

Commence the installation by first fitting the pushrods into the fuselage, through the slots and screwing on the clevises, remembering to leave room for adjustment in both directions. Do not attach the clevises to the horns at this stage but push the rods back as far as they will go and masking tape the servo ends clear of the servo positions. Screw the servos, or servo tray with servos installed onto the bearers bringing the plugs and leads under the servos and towards the front of the fuselage. Take care not to trap any of the wires between the servo and bearer when screwing the servo down.

Connect the throttle servo first, slide the wire rod into guide tube and attach the clevis to the carburettor throttle arm. Before cutting and bending the wire, to fit the other end into the servo arm, we must plug in the servos to the receiver and the receiver to the battery pack and switch on both the transmitter and the receiver. The receiver and battery pack can lie loosely in the fuselage for this purpose. Move the throttle lever and trim lever to the fully open position and manually open the carburettor throttle by pushing, or pulling as the case may be, on the wire linkage. We now have the servo and engine throttle in compatible positions. Just make one more check; by operating the transmitter throttle lever back and then forward again. We are about to connect the linkage to the correct side of the servo arm or disc. With the wire held over the top of the hole in the servo arm (try the outside initially) mark with a soft lead or

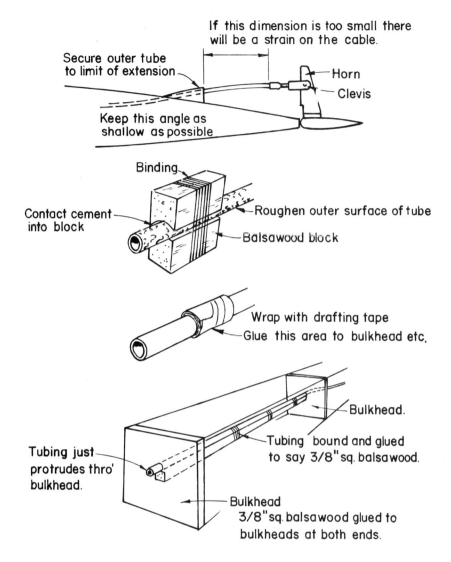

Chinagraph pencil the position for the bend.

It may now be impossible to remove the rod to bend it, otherwise, after it's bent, it would be impossible to get it back through the guide tube. We must, therefore, carefully hold the wire and, with a heavy pair of pliers bend the end of the wire vertically upwards. The end of the wire is clipped off with wire cutters, to within ¼ in. of the bend. It may be necessary to remove the arm or disc, in order to push the wire up from beneath the disc or arm through the hole. You may also find that the diameter of the hole in the arm or disc is too small to receive the wire rod. If so drill out the holes carefully with the correct size drill. Never attempt to drill these holes with the disc or arm connected to the servo; drills have a habit of

suddenly grabbing in nylon and you could easily penetrate the servo case by accident. With the servo disc or arm reconnected and the rod in position, retain the wire with a nylon keeper. Now check to see what carburettor throttle movement you are getting. If it is too small a movement, try fitting the clevis to a higher hole on the throttle arm. Should this still not do the trick you will have to obtain or make a longer servo arm, but this is very unlikely. For too large a movement, the linkage rod must be repositioned to a hole closer to the centre of the servo arm or disc. Do not forget that final bit of movement we require in slow throttle when we move the trim lever back to cut the engine. I am assuming that at this stage you have bench-run the engine and found the best slow speed settings − if not, you may have to make more adjustments to the throttle and linkage after the first flights.

It should be remembered that these descriptions are for the standard transmitters and not the 'all singing, all dancing' types where adjustments can be made electronically. Also, as previously pointed out, the throttle connection could be by a 'snake' linkage with an adjustable clevis at one end, this does make length adjustment easier − as does the spline adjustment of the servo output arm.

On to the rudder and elevator pushrod connection. The clevises may now be connected to the respective horns, and then a similar procedure is followed for marking, cutting and bending the wire as used for the engine throttle servo. The only two differences are that, this time, the sticks, trims and control surfaces want to be at neutral when marking the wire and the pushrods can be removed from the fuselage for bending. The elevator and rudder pushrods should also be retained at the servos by nylon keepers. Small adjustments to centre the control surfaces by screwing the clevises in or out are acceptable, but any appreciable miscalculation in pushrod length must be put right by binding on a new wire at the servo end and re-marking, bending and cutting. If you have followed the procedure carefully, this should not occur. Check that all the control surfaces are moving freely and in the correct directions; any serious binding will be noticed by the slowing down and 'labouring' of the servo motor. If this happens trace the fault (the pushrod exit may not be long enough for instance) and remedy it.

Aileron linkages we have mentioned before, but not specifically the mounting of the servo. Single mounting trays, either of the 'bath tub' or bracket variety are commercially produced, but most modellers opt to install the servo on hardwood or plywood bearers. Again, the installation should be preplanned, whether strip or inset ailerons are going to be used. Check on the plan view that there is space available for fitting the servo between the wing ribs (foam wing installations were dealt with separately) and also how the servo projects below − or for a low wing model, above − the wing surface. Ensure that, with the wing fitted to the fuselage, there will be no clashing of the aileron pushrods with the installations in the fuselage.

Strip aileron linkages are the easiest to install

because there is a straightforward pushrod (threaded rod) take-off from each side of the servo arm or disc. With the adjustable height of the aileron horn, the servo output arm holes closer or further away from the centre, the rake forward or backwards of the horns and the offset of the servo disc connections, there are ample methods of making adjustments for throw and differential of the ailerons.

Inset ailerons, with a central servo, have to be a little more carefully considered. Because we have a single servo take-off point we cannot allow for differential adjustment here, although we can vary the throw (even so, this is more easily done at the inset aileron horns). Remember that you have to be able to remove the linkage from the servo and the servo from the wing − the moulded bracket type mount is useful for this application. Differential may be obtained by using acute or obtuse bellcranks, but this has to be 'designed in' at the planning stage and aileron horn rake can also be employed for this purpose, but you will have to try to find horns with different rake angles.

Increasingly popular, even for the modest size models, is the installation of a separate servo to each aileron. The servos are connected to the aileron socket in the receiver via a 'Y' lead and, of course, the take-off from the servo arms arc on the opposite side for the left and right-hand ailerons. This system allows you to introduce differential and control surface movement very simply and similar to the strip aileron system.

Having reached the stage where everything is operating as it should we can permanently install the receiver battery pack and switch harness. With the foam rubber packing in place, position the battery pack and receiver as drawn on your plan, the switch can be laid loosely on top of the receiver for the moment. Rubber band the wing in position, check the balance point, not by holding your fingers under the lower wing spars − this is too inaccurate a method until you are experienced at it. Get a piece of aluminium or thin dural about 4in. long and ½in. wide, bend it at the centre to the same dihedral as the centre of the wing. Drill a small hole in the centre of the bend and attach a piece of thread through the hole, knotting it on the underside. Slip the aluminium under the wing retaining rubber bands and slide it into position at approximately the balance point.

Suspend the model by the thread and adjust the position of the metal strip until the model balances in a slightly nose-down attitude — the centre of the metal strip is the balance point. Remember, slightly forward of the designed balance point is acceptable, further aft spells disaster. Slight adjustments to the battery pack and receiver positions are possible but any gross out-of-balance condition must be remedied by adding lead weights to the nose or tail. When lead weights are used, they should be fitted to underside of the engine mount or plate, and securely bolted to it, or to the front of the stern post and secured with epoxy and a woodscrew. With the correct balance point obtained the battery pack, receiver and switch harness can

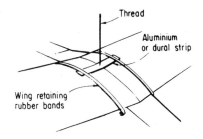

Finding the Balance Point.

be permanently positioned. The various leads from servos, receiver switch and battery pack are neatly tucked away under the receiver foam, making sure that none of them are being strained.

CHAPTER 9

Covering Methods and Finishes

Given two similar models, equally well built and equal in flying ability, the only thing that will distinguish one from the other is the type and standard of decoration. It is amazing how much difference a well thought-out and executed colour scheme can make to a model; it can make a plain model attractive and an attractive model beautiful. This difference demands only a little extra effort on the part of the modeller once he knows the methods to apply. Most modellers take a pride in constructing a model only to fall down, through lack of knowledge, when it comes to the finish. Equally, although a good finish will improve a model, the finished model will only be as good as the preparation of basic construction, and therefore, we will first consider the preparation of the airframe.

Before commencing final sanding of the airframe all fittings and equipment to be used in the finished model should be positioned to avoid having to cut and carve the airframe about during the finishing stage. These items include engines and spinners, tow hooks, linkages, hinges, holes and outlets etc. Naturally, engines, fuel tanks, radio equipment, and anything likely to be adversely affected by the finishing process must be removed again before sanding is commenced. Sandpaper, or better still garnet paper, and the elbow grease that goes with it are the simple necessities for a good preparation. It is important when sanding a model to work from a coarse sandpaper through to gradually finer grades. Try to avoid going back to a coarse sandpaper once a finer paper is being used as this will lengthen the sanding procedure considerably. Although a coarse sandpaper may be used initially for taking away bulk excess balsa, on wing tips, leading edges, fuselage cowlings etc., care must be taken not to sand too close to the proposed finished surface. Leaving the coarse sanding marks showing will, when the covering is applied, result in moisture from some covering materials entering the cuts and raising the grain of the balsa. A

variety of shapes of sanding blocks will assist in obtaining a smooth surface and prevent 'ridges' occurring with different densities of balsawood or at glue joints. Some of the best sanding tools available commercially are the 'Permagrit' selection. They are available in a variety of shapes and grades and are very hard wearing — it saves a lot of time making your own blocks, rods etc. Sanding with the sandpaper held over the fingers will almost certainly result in an unevenness of the surface of the model as the sandpaper will 'ride' over the hard surfaces and over-sand the soft spots. Continue sanding the airframe until, with the finest grade of sandpaper available, the model is as smooth as you can make it.

Inspect the airframe for any small indentations, cracks or nicks which must be removed before covering can be started. Small indentations can be removed by applying a small amount of water to the area; this will swell the grain of the balsawood sufficiently to resand the area to blend with the surrounding surface. For filling larger dents and gaps a lightweight model filler may be used, this being suitable as it sands as easily as the balsawood frame. Where a reasonable depth is to be filled it is better to build up in layers. Forced drying of each layer can be employed, rather than trying to fill in one go. A tip to remember during sanding to help avoid the annoying dents is to have a sheet of foam plastic or rubber on which to rest the parts of the airframe.

When you are satisfied that the surface of the model is as smooth as you can get it the framework must be sealed. Remove all surface dust by blowing it clear and wiping carefully with a cloth. Some materials are better than others for removing balsa dust — avoid cloths containing lint or wool.

It is at this stage a decision must be made on the type of covering and finishes to be employed on the model. One of the most significant developments — nay, revolutions — has been the introduction of heat-shrink covering films and fabrics. All but the lightest of these materials are coated, on the reverse surface, with heat-sensitive adhesive so that the material can be applied by using a heat iron and then the film or fabric tightened by further application of heat from the iron. At one time tissue and nylon, even silk, were the normal covering materials, but no longer — the heat-shrink films and fabrics now probably account for 80% of the coverings of all models. Only traditionalists and some scale modellers fight shy of these, not-so-new, materials. In fact, this is another area where techniques developed by modellers have found their way into the full-size manufacturing processes. Heat-shrink fabric, not always with adhesive backing, is used regularly on light and micro-light aeroplanes.

LET'S HEAR IT FOR PLASTIC!

Some experiments were carried out by modellers with covering using materials such as Melanex, but these only had limited success. It was not until the introduction, in America, of Monokote and, in Britain, of Solarfilm that the revolution really began. Both of these were heat-sensitive films, although the plastic used differed in specification. The high-strength plastic film is coated with the heat-sensitive adhesive which also provides the colour; the plastic sheet being clear. A protective backing is applied to the rear of the sheet and removed after the material has been cut for application.

A few of the reasons for the success of these materials include:

Ease

It requires less airframe preparation than tissue or nylon covering. Indeed, it is better not to carry out the preparation further than sanding to a fine, smooth finish and fuel-proofing the areas close to the fuel tank, engine and silencer. Being self-coloured we only need to concern ourselves with decoration on the covering and not painting the whole of the airframe.

Convenience

Compared with traditional methods there is a welcome (by non-lovers of the smell of aircraft

dopes) lack of strong smells and mess. The covering operations are now commendably clean and free of odours — pleasant or otherwise. It means that you can carry out the covering in front of the television without incurring the wrath of your partner.

Low weight

The overall weights, allowing for the fact that they are self-coloured, are good compared to the equivalent traditional covering materials and finishing techniques. So, Airspan and Litespan are lighter than doped and fuel-proofed tissue, Solarfilm, Solarkote and similar polyester and polymer films are lighter than, say, a heavyweight tissue doped, painted and fuel-proofed. Similarly, Solartex and Glosstex compare favourably with a doped, coloured nylon in the first respect and colour sprayed and fuel-proofed nylon in the latter comparison. Strength is also greater in regard to being 'puncture proof' and in tensile strength, for the films and the 'Tex' materials.

Although there are not many trade-offs in using these covering materials it must be remembered that the films do not add appreciably to the strength of the airframe in a torsional respect, probably less than is the case with tissue and nylon materials. Also, the coverings will not shrink to a drum-tight finish, which may not be good in a visual respect, but may prevent warping of the airframe components. Nylon, in particular, is very tough and resilient to scuffing and general damage, the heat-shrink fabric materials slightly less so.

Silk is rarely used as a covering material these days — it is expensive and not readily available. Scale modellers will occasionally use it, applied over tissue, to represent the fabric finishes of prototypes and, on its own, vintage enthusiasts will cover their models with silk to be authentic in appearance and actuality.

One other form of covering, only suited to fully sheeted airframes, is glass cloth and resin. This gives an extremely tough finish and if applied correctly the penalty of additional weight is not too great.

HEAT-SHRINK FILMS AND FABRICS

Preparation of the airframe for covering with

heat-shrink films or fabrics basically stops with the final sandings. You should ensure that all the particles of dust are removed, or they will show through the covering as small bumps, but the only other treatment concerns the areas where fuel and exhaust residues may be present. A fuel-proof treatment, such as Clearcoat, should be applied to the engine bay and fuel tank compartment where the covering will not reach. It is important that the Clearcoat is applied before the covering in case there is a slight seepage under the covering.

Applying the heat-shrink materials, with heat-activated adhesives, is not difficult but does require a little practice and understanding. Without any doubt the biggest problems in applying the materials result from the modeller failing to read, or to follow, the instructions. Every roll of covering contains a sheet of instructions − they have been written by the manufacturers who have put in a tremendous amount of research and development on their products, please believe them and do what they say. Solarfilm, by far the major supplier of covering films and fabrics in the world (even if they are under a different brand name) even produce a video showing you how to apply their products and to decorate them. There is much to learn from this video, even for the experienced modeller − it

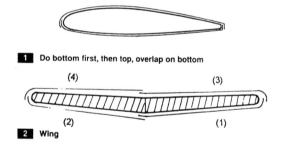

1   Do bottom first, then top, overlap on bottom

2   Wing

Covering sequence for wings.

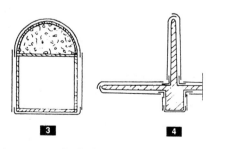

Covering sequence for fuselage and attached tail surfaces.

is the next best thing to a hands-on attempt with the various types of covering materials.

Two other worthwhile purchases are a purpose-designed modeller's covering iron and a small Coverite thermometer. You can use a domestic iron, a small thermostatically controlled travelling iron is the most suitable, but the commercial modelling iron is easier to use. Without doubt, the principal reason for covering failures where, after a period of time, the covering goes slack is because the wrong temperature has been used for shrinking. The manufacturer will instruct you on the temperatures to use for fixing the material around the edges and for tautening the covering when it is fixed. Both the films and fabrics have a natural stretch resilience but if you use all this facility up during the initial covering process there will be no 'recovery factor' for a later date. The reason for over-tautening is almost invariably due to using excessive heat to get a smooth finish. Even if you do not possess a thermometer the instructions will show you how to recognise the required iron heat.

You may find it difficult to decide, looking through the advertising material, which film or fabric you should use for a particular model. You can always write to the manufacturer and ask for literature explaining the advantages and limitations of the products. The video previously mentioned will answer most of the queries, but the following is a summary of the materials and their uses.

Although, as I have indicated, there are instructions supplied with all rolls of covering (they can be purchased in a variety of lengths) there are a number of points worth emphasising.

(1)   Marking out the material sizes to be cut is best done with a Chinagraph pencil on the reverse side of the material i.e. on the backing sheet.

(2)   It is tempting, to save money, to cut with little spare material. This is a false economy as it will make it difficult to hold and fix and where there are double curvatures you will certainly need to 'grab' the covering to pull and achieve a wrinkle-free result.

(3)   When you are cutting matched pairs of material e.g. for the left- and right-hand sides of the fuselage remember that they must be marked out as opposite pairs and not both from the same side.

(4) If it is difficult to remove the backing sheet use a pin to 'winkle' the backing away from the covering. Once a corner is released the remainder is easy to pull away.

(5) I seem to generate a lot of static electricity and it causes the backing material to stick to anything but, more of a problem, the adhesive side of the covering will attract dust. If you suffer from the same problem ensure that you work in a dust-free environment and ensure that all dust is removed from the airframe before taking it out to cover.

(6) Some modellers use heat guns for the shrinking process. I used one for many years, but you will see no mention of this implement in the instructions or shown on the video. The iron is the safest and surest way of both fixing the covering material and shrinking it; a heat gun will certainly shrink the material but not necessarily evenly. Even worse is the use of an electric bar fire to hold the covered component in front to shrink the covering. It is quite possible to burn a hole in the covering film with a heat gun, it is almost certain to happen when you use an electric fire for the shrinking.

(7) Do take trouble to work out in advance of commencing covering the procedure for overlapping the joints so that the joint is not facing the direction of flight of the model. Again, the instructions will tell you how to achieve this, but it does require advance preparation and consideration.

(8) It is not a good idea to attempt to glue items to the covering. Even if the adhesive will bond with the covering there is every chance that it will pull the covering away from the airframe and you will not have a sound fixing. For example, if a tailplane is fully covered before it is glued to the fuselage, the covering must be removed over the area of the glued surfaces before the join is made. Attempting to glue to the covering will lead to a failure and the tailplane coming adrift. It is preferable, when carrying out the initial covering to only take the material as far as the join line, you will then be sure of a good seal of the material at the edge. Cutting away the material after complete covering has two disadvantages; the knife cut — however carefully done — may weaken the balsawood and the new edge will need resealing.

If, for instance, you want to glue a 'teardrop' style canopy to a fuselage which is fully covered, you can use a small bit soldering iron to burn an outline of the canopy base. This will seal the edges of the covering and expose the airframe sufficiently to glue the canopy soundly. The edges can be trimmed with a contact adhesive style material e.g. Solartrim.

(9) When using contrasting colours in covering, say, the wing, thought must be given to the dividing line between the colours, if an open frame structure is being used. It is not a good idea to attempt to cover one film over another for large areas — it will result in airtrap bubbles being formed and the appearance will generally be disappointing. Small overlaps are acceptable, indeed they are preferable to butt joints which are liable to open slightly and allow in fuel and dirt. Where a butt joint is used it should be covered with a trim material. In working out the divisions on the airframe it must be remembered that they must occur where there is a sheeted surface (and don't work too close to the edge of the surface) and the colours must be applied so that the overlaps are facing away from the airflow. Incidentally, few models will look good with contrasting wing, tail surfaces and fuselage colours e.g. a red fuselage with yellow wings and tail. You see few full-size aircraft decorated in this way; it is generally preferable to use a base colour over the complete airframe and then to apply contrasting trim.

(10) Cleanliness is important in all stages of covering with heat-shrink materials. It is most annoying to have covered a component only, on shrinking, to find a little 'pimple' caused by a speck of dirt on the underside. Sharpness of cutting implements is also vital to ease of work; use new scalpel blades, razor blades and sharp scissors.

(11) Most of the heat-shrink coverings are airtight which means that, on a wing, you are producing a completely sealed bag. Obviously, when you come to shrink the final panel on the wing the heat will expand the air within

and cause the covering to 'bulge'. To avoid this make a couple of pinholes in the centre section, where it is covered by the fuselage, to release the excess pressure.

(12) When in doubt read the instructions again.

SHEETED AND OPEN

There are two principal methods used in covering with films and tex's: that used for open frames and the other for fully sheeted structures. Once these methods are understood and applied you will be able to cope with the covering of any airframe. For open structures the material is tacked in position around the edges of the structure and then sealed all the way round. Once sealed the material can be shrunk. For lightweight structures it is vital to cover both sides and then shrink, panel by panel, on alternate sides to ensure that no warps are introduced. Although less likely to induce warps, compared with a doped covering, they can be difficult to eradicate once they have occurred. This is one time it might be acceptable to use an open electric fire. The warped component is held in front of the fire with an opposite twist held in, and then allowed to cool with the component held straight. This, however, is a last resort and it is better to avoid the warp in the first place.

The technique for fully sheeted surfaces is to attach, with the iron, the material in the centre of the component to be covered and work outwards to avoid trapping air at any point. When you come to double curvatures the material is pulled around the curve, applying the iron at the same time. Small radius compound curves can be smoothly covered in this way. Not quite so simple are concave curvatures as there is a strong tendency for the material to pull away from the curvature as the heat is applied. For these areas it is easier (and essential for 90-degree internal corners) to cover with two separate pieces of material.

Not all the heat-shrink films have an adhesive backing, some require the airframe – and in cases of sheeted areas, the reverse side of the film – to be coated with a special adhesive. This is allowed to dry and the film is then ironed on in the normal way, using the methods previously described. With adhesive only applied where necessary, the overall weights are very low. For the traditionalists there is even a film material which can be ironed

on, shrunk and then treated with a thinned down coat of clear dope.

All of the iron-on heat-shrink materials differ a little and are used for certain applications and for particular results. It will take time to understand the reasons for the different types and finishes, also the types of decoration and paints that can be used with them. If you are unsure which product to use either ask the retailer, an experienced modelling colleague or the manufacturers – they will be *pleased* to advise.

COLOURED TISSUE

Used on small radio control models. For the small sheeted model, where maximum performance is essential, coloured tissue is an excellent covering material. It has the advantage of requiring no further colour painting but simply, in the case of powered models, of fuel-proofing. Choose contrasting colours for the different areas of the fuselage and wing. The pieces of tissue should be cut and placed as accurately as possible but narrow trim strips of contrasting tissue can be doped over the abutment to mask the joint. Banana oil can be brushed over the doped tissue to give a glossy finish to gliders.

NYLON

The beauty of nylon covering, practically speaking, is in its tremendous toughness and resilience but this is achieved at a certain increase in weight. For this reason, it is important to keep any further weight penalty down and this means limiting the amount of extra paint applied to the nylon as far as possible. Nylon can be bought in a variety of colours or white. For modelling purposes it should be light (not more than 1½oz weight/sq yd) yet close weave. If the weave is too open more dope and filler is required to give a smooth and airtight surface. Dyeing nylon to your own choice of colour is not a difficult business providing you use the correct type of dye and follow the instructions properly. An alternative to dyeing white nylon is to add an aniline dye to the clear dope to achieve a translucent coloured finish. It is important to have spraying equipment to obtain good results but there is an advantage of being able to 'fade' one colour into another and to pattern mask to

Attractively finished Veron Cardinal *shows how simple decor scheme can be effective.*

increase the potential of decoration. Coloured nylon on its own is seldom sufficient, but it is only necessary to add paint or coloured dope to a small proportion of the total area.

GLASS FIBRE AND RESIN

Sheeted structures, built-up and veneered foam can be substantially strengthened and made more rigid by the application of lightweight glass cloth (0.6oz/sq yd) and a thin coat of glass fibre resin. This method is very popular with competition glider pilots as thin section wings require to be rigid, strong (to take the stresses of fast winch launches) and have a smooth surface finish. Apply the resin sparingly (some of it will soak into the balsawood or obechi veneer), the surplus can be taken off by pressing the surface with toilet tissue. Very sharp and tough trailing edges can be formed by this method and the resistance to puncturing by thorns, stones and other sharp objects, is greatly enhanced. As with many of the covering methods the 'knack' of using the material can only be obtained by practice but, once this has been gained, the glass fibre covering system has much to commend it; the surface can be sanded to a super-smooth finish. The overall weight increase is not unreasonable if limited amounts of resin are used, the finish is well sanded and no further paint is applied − the finish is fuel-proof.

COVERING TECHNIQUES

Undoubtedly, for the reasons stated, most models will be covered with one of the heat-shrink films or fabrics. There are, however, modellers who prefer to use the more traditional covering materials such as tissue and nylon and the following information is for their benefit.

What material is used for covering will depend on the type and size of the model. Generally speaking, large models, unless wholly sheeted, are best covered in lightweight nylon for its strength and durability. Smaller models (40in. wing span and under) can be covered in heavy-weight tissue, as can the larger fully sheeted models where most of the strength is in the balsa covering. Covering techniques are similar with tissue and nylon but vary according to whether a sheeted or open framework is to be covered. For sheeted areas the covering material should be dampened and laid over the framework to be covered allowing about a ½in. overlap all the way round. While the material is still damp and slightly stretched (nylon can be pulled tighter than tissue) brush on a 50−50 dope/thinner coat over the whole of the covering, smoothing out any trapped air bubbles with the brush or a 'wad' of tissue. Make sure the thinned dope is brushed right through the covering. For a first-rate finish, the covering should be butt jointed rather than overlapped. This can be achieved by firstly overlapping the various areas covered and running a *very* sharp razor along the centre of the overlap. Aim to cut *just* through the two thicknesses of covering material and not into the balsa underneath. Lift the edge of the covering at the butt joint and remove the surplus material trapped underneath. Replace the edge, redoping where necessary, and smoothing down with the tissue 'wad'. Overlapped joints are easier than butt joints when nylon is used and are acceptable on models where a fully painted job is not to be employed; in this case pinking shears can be used to trim the edges of the nylon to prevent fraying.

When the covered frame has dried, give it a further coat of thinned dope followed, allowing drying between each coat, by two or more coats of sanding sealer. The aim of this process is to fill in all of the pores of the covering material and finish up with a completely smooth surface; hence it may take more than two coats of sealer to obtain this surface. Sand, with very fine paper such as 400 wet and dry grade, after the second and all successive coats. Check for smoothness and complete filling by holding the structure at an oblique angle. This will show up any imperfections and these must be given additional coats. With the structure filled and lightly sanded and dusted to your satisfaction, give one final coat of thinned dope, sprayed on if possible and set aside to dry thoroughly.

Open framework structures require a slightly different procedure to sheeted surfaces in as much as the covering is attached only to the outer members i.e. around the edges. With the dampened covering material spread out over the framework, start to stick one edge down by brushing thinned dope through the material. This will soften the filler previously applied to the framework and bond the covering material to it. Stretch the covering as much as possible and stick the covering to the opposite edge of the framework. Continue stretching and sticking the covering until all edges are secured. Covering a model for the first time can present a few problems due to lack of experience, but the important thing to remember is not to get flustered. Take it steadily and logically. If you make a mistake the covering can be removed by applying dope thinners to the areas that have been stuck down and, when the bonded surface with the framework has softened, the covering

can be gently pulled away.

Doping an open framework also requires a different technique to sheeted areas so let us consider, as it is the most prone to warping, doping a wing. We have already covered the model and, when it has dried out, the covering should already be quite taut. For large models a fairly wide brush (say 1½in. wide) can be used for 'filling' the pores of the covering material, but the brush should not be overcharged with dope. The reason for this is that the dope has a tendency, particularly with nylon, to penetrate the covering and, if applied too generously will form 'blobs' on the underside of the covering. For this reason, too, it is preferable to use a thinned dope (30% thinner) for all dope coats; being thinner it dries much quicker and successive coats can be applied more rapidly. Carefully brush on a coat of dope over the upper wing surface in the *open* areas, being careful not to brush over the sheeted areas and wing ribs. Do not brush in strokes using the flat of the brush but use side strokes in line with the narrow tip of the brush. Sheeted areas and ribs are avoided at this stage to reduce the dangers of warps forming due to small panels shrinking independently and unevenly. Also, to help avoid warping the wing, the underside of the wing panel should be doped immediately the top surface has been completed. Continue applying coats of thinned dope until all the pores of the covering are filled; the final coats of dope can be taken over the sheeted areas and the brush used to give full flat strokes. At this stage a decision must be made as to whether the open areas of the framework are to be 'filled' or not. Unless the model is going to be painted over these areas, and a high-gloss smooth finish is imperative, I would suggest that the open areas are not filled. When filler is applied sanding must follow and there is always the danger of weakening the covering material when sanding at the point where the covering joins the framework. A suitable filler, if it has to be used, is a 50–50 mix of sealer and dope, once again thinned down so that it will brush on smoothly. After a light and careful sanding the framework must be given one final coat of thinned dope. Before any further colouring work is contemplated an ample drying time *must* be allowed – this may be up to a week in cold conditions but a minimum of forty-eight hours is necessary.

DECORATING THE MODEL

The complexity of the decoration you employ on your model will depend on the type of model i.e. scale or sports model, and the time and patience you are prepared to spend on it. For a first model of any particular type I would certainly recommend sticking to a fairly simple decorative scheme. Inexperience in flying a particular type of model means that you are more likely to crash the model and, if the model has a superb 'showroom finish', it makes it harder to accept a crash.

Decorating a model is, for those that build from kits or plans, one of the few ways of expressing individuality with any particular design. Regrettably, many modellers decorate their model in exactly the same way as the prototype illustrated in the magazine photographs or on the kit box lid. Designers do not have a monopoly of the best ideas for decorating models and, with so many types of finishes available, practically any colour scheme can be put into practice. Indeed, this variety of materials for finishes sometimes makes it difficult to make a final choice. Before considering these finishes and the methods of applying them, though, a word of warning. Every extra coat of coloured dope or paint adds weight to the model and will affect the flying performance. As flying is the primary aim of building the model, keep the amount of decorative dope or paint to a minimum to achieve the desired results.

DOPES AND PAINTS

Take a look at the superb finishes of a group of competition scale models and the chances are that the immaculate paint jobs are a result of a sprayed application of the paint finish – the paint can be applied more evenly and thinly – and a smoother effect, with no brush marks in evidence. Aerosol sprays are available in a wide range of colours and paint types – cellulose, acrylic and enamels – but they can prove to be very expensive to use. It is surprising how many coats are required to cover a moderately sized model. For those modellers in possession of a compressor and airbrush, or spray gun, the spraying of paint finishes is advised, for general painting and decorative work. Small airbrushes, operated from CO_2 canisters, are not very suitable for R/C models but it is possible to build your own compressed air unit utilising a compressor from a disused refrigerator (articles have appeared in the modelling magazines covering this subject).

For many of us, however, spray equipment is beyond our reach and all of our painting and fuel-proofing must be applied by brush. Do not despair, the results can be highly gratifying and more than one winning model of the National Scale competitions has boasted a hand brush-painted finish.

Coloured dope, for a long time the standard finish, is not the easiest of finishes to apply over a large area with a brush. It is, of course, an ideal material for spray application but, when applied with a brush, it has a tendency to soften the previous coat. Practice is needed to learn to 'flow on' quickly and smoothly the coats of dope to achieve a good even opaque finish. A word here about brushes, which are high on the list of important items. A cheap, stiff brush will not only leave a stream of shredded hair in its flow, but will frequently not hold a sufficient quantity of dope. This will result in the dope not flowing out evenly and smoothly and the stiffness will cause 'corrugations'. Your best investment is to purchase top quality brushes (sable hair) and these, with reasonable care, should last for many years and are more economical in the long run.

Quick-drying enamel paints have increased in popularity in recent years – and deservedly so. The range of colours is excellent; colours are intermixable, and the enamels are available in small ½oz and 2oz tins or spray cans. Gloss enamels are fuel-proof against diesel and un-nitrated glofuels but, if some clear doped areas are to be left on the model, it is suggested that the whole of the model is fuel-proofed. Matt enamels have the distinct advantage of containing a high percentage of colour pigment and therefore a greater covering power and a resulting reduction of weight. Normal hot fuel-proofer can be applied over the matt enamel to produce a gloss finish or matt proofer for a scale finish. An eggshell finish can also be achieved by spraying on clear polyurethane varnish and, when it has hardened, rubbing down with steel wool; this, too, will give a fuel-proof model. Thorough stirring of tins of paint is essential to ensure all the pigment is mixed and the tin should be stirred occasionally during the progress of the painting. A number of thin coats

113

of paint on a model is preferable to one thick one as this reduces the chance of paint 'runs' and gives a smoother consistent finish. Although enamels can be applied over dopes with perfect safety, a nitrate dope should never be applied over enamels. For this reason also, dope should be allowed to dry thoroughly before enamel is used over it. This incompatibility between dopes and enamels does present a slight problem when it comes to repairing a model. With the model painted with an enamel doping a patch on to the existing covering will cause the enamel to 'pickle'; this will also happen with some fuel-proofers and other forms of paints. The answer is to mask off the area of the patch and to clean off the existing paint back to the original clear doping.

KEEPING COSTS DOWN

First the materials. Dopes and thinners are purchasable by the gallon, and are always more economical in these quantities. See if you can find a suitable purchasing source − the local airfield if they have servicing facilities. An alternative to finishes of colour dopes and enamels is the use, by spraying only, of acrylic car finishes. Again, these are more economical purchased in quantity, although quart cans should be available. Polyurethane paint is used on models and, although tough and fuel resistant, it does tend to be heavy and the surface may 'craze' even on recommended fillers. Epoxy paints, unlike adhesives, have not found great favour in Great Britain and neither have butyrate dopes which have the advantage over nitrate dopes of being fuel resistant.

DECORATING FILMS AND 'TEX'S

Heat-shrink fabrics can generally be decorated in the same way as nylon but, being self-coloured, should not normally require all-over painting. There are exceptions of course; if you are trying to emulate the finish of a WW2 camouflaged fighter then, you will need to paint the complete airframe. Whichever covering material you are using you should always test the compatibility of the paint before committing yourself to the application. Fabrics will accept most paint types without any problem but there may be the occasional aerosol type which will cause the covering

colour to bleed through.

For films the situation is rather different and not all of them will take a paint satisfactorily. Solarfilm, for instance, is not a good material to paint, but Solarkote, a polyester film, can be painted with such materials as Solarlac. Again, be advised by the manufacturers and carry out your tests first.

Quick decoration, in the form of self-adhesive Mylar decorative film, solid sheet colour, chequerboard patterns etc. means that we can produce an attractive model with a minimum of effort. These materials are especially useful for the covering films as the Mylar decal material adheres well to the gloss surfaces. There are numerous companies who can produce lettering cut to almost any size, font, extended or compacted, sloping forward or backwards − even mirrored images − in the thin self-adhesive films of many colours. Now you can personalise your model, have your 'pilot's name' under the cockpit or your own registration on the fuselage.

The adhesive on the Mylar decal material is strong and if you try to apply it in its 'off-the-sheet' form you will have to be sure to get the positioning absolutely right first time − there will be no second chances. A much safer way is to dip the material in a bowl of water, with a few drops of washing-up liquid mixed in, before applying the decal material to the model. Indeed, it is safer to separate the film from its backing under water then there will be no risk of adhesive surfaces coming together and becoming irretrievably stuck. With the soapy water barrier the Mylar can be positioned on the film covering and slid around until it is correctly positioned. Make sure that all the air is removed and pat the area dry with a clean rag and then leave for a few days to thoroughly dry and the decal will be fully adhered to the covering.

I said that when cutting the covering for matched pairs e.g. fuselage sides, you had to remember to cut opposite pairs − well, the same applies with the trim pieces. Making a card template for curved areas is a sensible idea and this must be reversed for the opposite side decal − it rarely fits in so well on the decal sheet, but that's life!

Another form of simple decoration which will brighten up a single colour model considerably is the use of self-adhesive stripe trims. These come

You do not have to spend hours or a fortune to produce an attractive model.

in a variety of colours and numbers and widths of stripe trims and they are easy to apply.

A final thought on decoration. Keep it light, keep it simple. The best results come as a result of planning rather than quantity.

If you are looking for inspiration on colour schemes you can do worse than refer to full-size types.

CHAPTER 10

Radio Control Engines and Ancillaries

Radio control engines have shown a gradual improvement since their introduction in the 1950s until, today, they represent the finest arts of engine design and precision engineering. When we talk about an R/C engine we only mean a normal miniature internal combustion engine fitted with a throttling device. Initial experiments involved the use of an exhaust baffle or variable air intake cut-off. Neither of these methods were very effective in themselves but coupled, as they later were, a reasonable speed variation was possible. The carburettor was further refined to include adjustable stops on the variable rotary air intake barrel and an adjustable air bleed. This form of throttle, although operating reasonably over the quarter to full throttle range, still lacked a method of metering the fuel supply as the throttle was varied. The new generation of carburettors incorporate this feature and give safer low idling and smoother progressive pick up throughout the entire speed range.

The gloplug (or glow plug) engine was used almost universally at one time, but the diesel has been making something of a comeback recently. Initially only to be found in the smaller capacities, the diesels are now available also in '40' and '60' (10cc) capacities. Earlier problems of poor throttle capabilities and a sometimes embarrassing lack of pick-up from a low idle position have been mainly overcome, although the latter inability to pick-up can occur if the engine is held in idle for very prolonged periods.

Starting a diesel requires a different technique to a glow engine as there are two controls to adjust − the needle valve in the carburettor and the compression lever. Quite often it will be necessary to increase the compression for starting, by about a quarter of a turn, easing back to its running position as the engine warms up. Old aeromodellers will be familiar with the 'diesel flick' used to start the engine; once you are familiar with the pro-

cedure and you avoid flooding it, you will find it quite safe to start by hand. Most engines *should* be started by hand, you get a much better feel of the engine i.e. whether it is short of fuel, or over wet, and you can tell whether it is firing as the piston passes top dead centre. It is because of the risk of the motor being flooded that we should avoid the use of electric starters, particularly for diesels, as there is the danger of bending or breaking the conrod.

Diesel fuel, it has to be admitted, is smellier than glow fuel and the exhaust residues can be dirtier (although they can be wiped easily off the airframe after the flight). So why should we bother to use this type of engine when there are perfectly good two and four stroke glow engines available? Diesel engines are extremely tractable, they can operate with a wide diversity of propellers and are excellent at pulling very large propellers at reasonable rpm. Whereas a '60' glow engine might be expected to swing a 12in. × 6in. propeller, a good '40' diesel will also swing this size of prop. and at only a few rpm less and little loss of power during the climb. Some of the diesel engines have their compact silencers tucked away behind the cylinder − very unobtrusive but efficient in noise reduction. Because the diesel tends to be operated at lower rpm, swinging a large propeller, the sound is more acceptable than many of the high revving two-stroke motors. Fuel consumption with diesels is excellent and compensates for the higher fuel costs. Although the diesels are useful for all types of R/C powered models the combination of small fuel consumption, small inconspicuous silencer, acceptable sound levels and the ability to swing large propellers make them good candidates for scale models. Standard diesel fuel will not attack cellulose and enamel paints and many of the heat-shrink coverings are not affected by the fuel.

Radio control glow engines are made in a range

from .05cu in. (.8cc) to .90cu in. (15.0cc). There are a number of throttling devices for even smaller engines but they tend to be rather ineffective. In the lower range of engines the difficulties in setting up the engines for reliable control are increased but with patience and experiment it should be possible to obtain a safe idle speed of 3–3,500 (with a top rpm of 11–12,000) with the .09 to .15cu in. engines.

Glow engines of .19cu in. and above can be purchased with the improved metering carburettors. These carburettors are not over-difficult to set up *providing* you follow the sequence recommended by the manufacturers closely. To understand better the reasons why a glow engine will, or will not, throttle it is worthwhile investigating the operation of a standard carburettor.

For a glow engine to run at all the glow plug must be glowing to a red heat. Initially this is provided for by an external starting battery but, once the engine is running properly, the starter battery can be removed and the engine will continue to run – the coil in the glow plug being kept hot by the continued 'firing' of the motor and the catalytic action of the platinum coil. When we throttle back an engine we reduce the air supply to it which considerably richens the air/fuel mixture. With the richened mixture vaporisation is incomplete and the fuel reaches the combustion chamber with droplets of the mixture in liquid form. Too much of this unatomised fuel and the liquid hitting the coil already a little less hot because of the slower engine rpm will put the glow out completely.

With the near universal adoption of silencers the exhaust 'chopper' throttle was rapidly discarded. Fortunately, the effect of fitting the silencers was to add a slight back pressure to the exhaust gases and to maintain a reasonably high temperature at the plug. As engine design advanced and fuel atomising improved, the problems regarding glow plug 'swamping' were eliminated – even with silencers designed to extract exhaust gases more efficiently – provided the correct type of glow plug is used.

Many of you may purchase a second-hand engine where the instructions have been lost – here is the basic method of setting up a 'standard' carburettor.

It is assumed that the engine is already fully run in, has the correct plug and propeller fitted and the right fuel is being used. Start the engine by sucking in fuel, with the finger over the air intake and turning the propeller two or three times, connecting the starter battery and flicking the propeller smartly in an anti-clockwise direction. When the engine has started remove the battery clip from the plug and allow the engine to fully warm up for a couple of minutes. Adjust the needle valve to a full, smooth two stroke i.e. with the engine at maximum speed but not 'leaning' it out to the point where it is 'hunting' slightly. Pull back the throttle arm on the carburettor to the low-speed position. I will remind you here, as I will again later, that a glow engine operating at many thousands of rpm is a lethal weapon. Operated on the ground it can severely damage a hand or cause the loss of an eye; in the air it, and the model, can cause death – *take care*. As the throttle is moved to the slow position the engine 'note' will change to a rough uneven beat and may be causing some vibration. Set the idle stop screw – the one that limits the rotation of the intake throttle barrel – at as 'closed' a position as possible without the engine cutting then slowly open the air bleed screw. If, as is likely, the engine speeds up a little reset the idle stop to a lower position. Try adjusting the air bleed again and allow the engine to idle for a few minutes. On opening up the throttle rapidly there should be a good responsive pick up of the engine revs. An engine that coughs and splutters, and throws out a lot of smoke and unburnt fuel is still running too rich and requires further carburettor adjustment.

Carburettor design is constantly being improved and new types i.e. slide carburettors, in-flight mixture control devices are introduced by engine manufacturers in attempts to give smoother and more reliable engine speed control through the entire rpm range. Some engines are fitted with fuel pump/regulators to give even more positive fuel supply and this becomes increasingly important as the maximum performance is extracted from a specific engine design. There may be occasions (with models fitted with a pusher engine for instance) when the fuel tank must be situated some distance away from the engine. This is far from ideal when using a standard fuel arrangement; there is insufficient suction from the engine to ensure a consistent fuel supply with the model in all attitudes. Fuel pumps and regulators are available as separate items and can be interconnected with the fuel feed, vent pipe and a pressure tapping from the engine crankcase, to ensure a consistent fuel supply to the engine at all times. The combined pump/regulators are physically very small (they utilise the positive and negative pressure fluctuations from the engine crankcase) and are reliable in operation.

TWO-STROKE, FOUR-STROKE AND PETROL

Petrol engines were the first IC motors to be used to power model aircraft, followed by diesels and, lastly, glow plug engines. As soon as efficient carburettors were fitted to two-stroke glow plug engines, petrol engines and diesels took a 'back seat'. For many years this situation continued until the enterprising Japanese O.S. company introduced a four-stroke engine version of '60' (10cc) size. Other manufacturers quickly followed their example and a variety of medium and large size four-stroke engines − including multi-cylinder designs − came onto the market. Constructional and design complexities of the four-stroke engine might suggest that the demand for these types would not be commercially successful (they are more expensive than the equivalent two-strokes) except for the fact that they are considerably quieter in operation and have a vastly improved fuel consumption. The power output is lower than two-stroke types, but not appreciably so − although the low speed torque enable them to swing a large propeller − a '70' sized engine is about equivalent to a high performance '60' two-stroke engine. Undoubtedly part of the fascination of four-stroke engines is the quality engineering involved in the overhead valve gear and the unique sound emitted from the exhaust. In times when people are becoming highly noise conscious the four-stroke has a positive advantage over most other power sources − except electric power.

Petrol engines have also made a comeback, mainly as a result of conversions of units taken from commercial chain saws, hedge trimmers and lawn mowers. Purpose-designed petrol engines are making their way onto the model market and it can be expected that there will be an increase in the numbers available, and a reduction in the capacity of the engines (most of the converted engines are in the 25cc to 80cc capacity range).

Electronic ignition does away with the necessity of having separate batteries and coils, associated with early model petrol engines and, of course, no separate battery is required to start the engine, as is the case with a glow plug motor. Large petrol engines have allowed, and encouraged, the movement for large models, some of them powered with engines up to 240cc capacity. Low fuel consumption, cheap fuel (relative to glow fuel) clean running conditions and ease of operation have all encouraged the popularity of the petrol engine and the success of this type is likely to be further enhanced as smaller and less vibratory engines are developed.

SILENCERS

An engine silencer does not silence an engine, it merely reduces the exhaust sound level to an acceptable degree. From an engine operating point of view there is no need to have a silencer fitted; in fact it is in some ways a positive disadvantage. With a silencer fitted it is difficult to 'prime' the engine with a spot or two of fuel to assist starting. The silencer is a reasonably large mass of metal and, offset from the engine centre of rotation can cause the inherent vibration of a two-stroke engine to be amplified. Silencers, except for specialised units of the tuned variety, cause a loss of power often related to the efficiency of silencing. The physical size of the silencer makes it difficult to install on the model without spoiling its appearance. Why then, if the silencer has all of these disadvantages, do we fit them to our engines? The answer is one of moral and legal obligation. When we are flying near to built-up areas we may be causing a considerable amount of noise nuisance to the people living nearby. *We* may not mind the sound of an engine, indeed we may barely notice it as we are concentrating so hard on flying the model, but to the layman it may be completely ruining his weekend's rest in the garden. To be truthful a half dozen '60' engines going at full bore can 'kick up' a terrific din and it can be wearing on the ears of the flyers too. I only wish that the engine designers could come up with a silencer that is more effective, less bulky, and allows access to the exhaust ports − perhaps I am asking for too much.

Tuned pipe silencers work on the same principle as those used on motorcycle engines and, correctly fitted and tuned, offer a useful power *increase* from high performance two-stroke engines. Where maximum power is a criterion, aerobatic models for instance, they are popular and the 'quiet' pipes offer reasonable silencing levels. Some experimenting with the length of the pipe may be necessary to obtain optimum performance and they can be temperamental and susceptible to temperature and humidity changes. For ordinary sports work where a slight loss of power is acceptable, the simple expansion chamber type of silencer is easier to fit and operate.

PLUGS

There is a bewildering variety of glow plugs available these days in both the 1½ volt and 2 volt types. With a 2 volt wet accumulator for the starting battery it is obviously sensible to use 2 volt plugs or a 'dropper' lead will have to be incorporated to bring the voltage down to 1½ volts. Dry batteries, of 1½ volts, can be used for starting; they must be of the large capacity type and do not expect them to deal efficiently with a 2 volt plug. I would certainly recommend obtaining a 2 volt accumulator as this will, providing it is kept fully charged, give much more reliable starting, particularly with a 'flooded' engine or in cold weather.

Two main types of plugs are used in R/C engines, the plain coil plug and the idle bar or shielded plug. The theory of using the latter plug is that, at idling, it protects the coil from impingement of fuel droplets and, possibly, assists in keeping the coil hot. Plain coil plugs can be obtained in a range of 'cold' to 'hot' plugs for engines of different compression ratios etc. A further variation in the types of plugs is that they are available in short, standard or long reach. Your engine is specifically designed for one of these types so check which one you need.

The variety and types of plugs may be very confusing to the beginner but start with the manufacturer's recommended plug; from there on you can experiment with different plug, fuel and propeller combinations until you find the optimum for your particular aircraft. Maximum performance is only required for the competition enthusiast so you may settle for a less than perfect set-up, but

as long as it is reliable and powerful enough for the model you have no worries.

PROPELLERS

Propellers are designated by diameter (distance from tip to tip) and pitch (the distance the propeller would move forward in a 'solid' body for one revolution). Engine manufacturers will suggest suitable propeller size for their engines but the optimum will depend on the type of the aeroplane and can only be found out by experience. As a rough guide, for sports models the following propeller sizes can be tried. Bear in mind, though, that it is a *rough guide* only; engines of comparable sizes vary tremendously in performance. Small engines like to run fast.

.09 cu in. engines	–	7in. × 4in
.15 "	"	"	8in. × 4in. or 8in. × 5in.
.19 "	"	"	9in. × 4in. or 9in. × 5in.
.21–.25 "	"	10in. × 4in. or 9in. × 6in.
.29–.35 "	"	11in. × 4in. or 10in. × 6in.
.40 "	"	"	11in. × 5in. or 10in. × 8in.
.45–.51 "	"	12in. × 4in. or 11in. × 6in.
.60 & .61	"	12in. × 6in. or
			11in. × 8/7¾ in.

Propellers are manufactured from three different materials – wood, nylon and glass fibre.

You will see all serious competition modellers using wooden propellers. They are the most efficient, are rigid and can be reworked and prepared to a high finish. They have one big disadvantage – they break easily if the model tips over on landing or in a crash. This can make learning to fly rather expensive. Nylon propellers are much more resilient and are unlikely to break on landing unless there is a severe nose-in, with the engine running, on tarmac or concrete. However, nylon propellers also have disadvantages. Being flexible the pitch (angle of the blade) tends to vary in flight and the efficiency, therefore, is lower than that of the wooden propeller. The biggest disadvantage, and danger, is that in the manufacturing process it is possible to build up internal stresses in the propeller during the moulding. The only way these stresses – and then not always completely – can be eliminated is by ageing. When you buy a propeller it is impossible to tell how much natural ageing it has had so it is safer to age it artificially. This can be done by boiling the propeller in water for a period of ten to fifteen minutes which should remove most of the internal stresses. Always treat nylon propellers with a great deal of respect; they could shatter at any moment — more so in very cold weather — and never stand in line with or in front of the spinning propeller disc when the model is on the ground. To me, it is frightening to see a modeller leaning over the top of his nylon propellered engine to make carburetter adjustments. Should the propeller disintegrate there is a fair chance that a piece of the propeller could hit him in the face.

For safety reasons the nylon propellers should not be used on high-speed (over 12,000 rpm) engines.

Glass fibre propellers and glass fibre/nylon mixtures, come in the range between the wood and nylon ones. They are more rigid than nylon, but stronger — on impact — than wood. Both nylon and, more so, glass fibre propellers may give a better engine idle due to their heavier comparable weight and the flywheel effect associated with it.

ENGINE MOUNTS

Engines can be mounted in three basic different positions, upright, side mounted or inverted. The most common of these positions is upright and this is the easiest mounting for the beginner to use. Side mounting has the advantage for some models, aerobatic and certain scale ones, of a more convenient silencer position. In other respects it is virtually as easy to start the engine in this position as with the upright engine. The inverted engine is necessary for some scale models but is not generally recommended for sports models and trainers. Not only is the inverted engine, with a two-wheel undercarriage, more prone to crash damage but it also makes the engine more difficult to start. Flooding an inverted engine results in the excess fuel being dumped into the cylinder head, soaking the plug and making it very difficult for the starter battery to make it glow. For this reason you will frequently see scale modellers, with inverted engines installed in the model, starting the engine with the model

Careful adjustment of the throttle is essential to prevent engine failures during flight.

upside down on the flight box. Once the engine has started, and is running smoothly, the model is rotated to the normal position.

Mounts for engines, as opposed to mounting positions, are either beam or radial.

Beam mounts were used exclusively, except for small engines with direct radial mounting lugs, until the advent of the aluminium cast and nylon moulded engine mounts. Beam mounting an engine can be direct to hardwood bearers or on to a paxolin engine plate and then to hardwood bearers. The plate fixing gives a greater flexibility in the different engines that can be mounted in the model and also for varying the side and downthrust of an engine. Either way it gives a rigid fixing for the engine and blind, or anchor, nuts can be used in the bolting to the hardwood bearers.

Radial engine mounts have been received by the experts with mixed feelings. Basically, opinion is divided between the engine and the radio manufacturers. Both the cast aluminium and moulded nylon engine mounts give a more flexible engine mounting than the beam type. But, the beam mountings, with their rigidity, transfer more of the engine vibration to the airframe and consequently the radio equipment. With the radial mountings it is the engine that takes the 'beating' and *may* vibrate more than on a rigid mounting but transfer less of it to the airframe. The radio manufacturers are all for using radial mounts but the producers of engines say "OK if you want to ruin your engine go ahead and use these abortions". The truth, as usual, probably lies somewhere down the middle but it does emphasise the need to use a good radio installation, to isolate vibration, and the right engine and propeller to cut down vibration at the source. Some types of engines do vibrate more than others as they are less well balanced and some vibrate more at specific speeds − use a propeller that will avoid that speed. It is most difficult to measure vibration levels of an engine but the best way to find out the good and bad engines in this respect is to read the monthly articles in numerous magazines − new engines are reviewed and mention is normally made of vibration levels.

I should have mentioned earlier one of the chief offenders in causing vibration − an unbalanced propeller. You can consider yourself extremely fortunate if you purchase a propeller that is perfectly balanced − regardless of type. Most propellers will need a certain amount of balancing and without it you could be doing a lot of damage to the engine and installation. A simple propeller balance tester can be obtained commercially. To balance a wooden propeller it is a matter of sanding down the rear tip area of the heavy blade until the correct balance is achieved − not forgetting to revarnish and fuel-proof the blade that has been sanded. Nylon and glass fibre propellers cannot easily be sanded in this way but it is possible to achieve sound results by judicious use of knife 'scraping' and 'wet and dry' abrasive paper.

Not so great an offender, but worthy of consideration is the propeller spinner. With small spinners there are normally few problems but with large diameter turned metal spinners used on large scale models of 'Spitfires' and 'Mustangs' etc. the unbalanced effect can be considerable. Balancing the spinner is really a lathe job and when the heavy side of the spinner has been located the back plate can be drilled out with lightening holes to compensate.

Going back to radial mounts, I prefer to use the nylon variety for the smaller engines (up to 35's) and cast aluminium, because they are more rigid, for large engines. Do select radial mounts that have plenty of 'meat' on them so that they can be secured solidly and do use a substantial plywood engine bulkhead for fitting the mount to. Once the mount is bolted in position it may be impossible to get at the rear of the bulkhead so it is wise to use anchor nuts in this area. Mounting the engine on the radial mount is equally important; the engine must sit on the flanges and mate accurately. File and cut the flanges if necessary. Never force the engine into the mount. With nylon material self-tapping screws should be adequate for holding the engine down but check them occasionally to make sure they have not come loose. Aluminium mounts can be drilled and tapped or drilled and the engine secured with nuts and bolts.

In an effort to reduce both transmitted noise and vibration from the engine to the airframe, manufacturers have developed radial mounts incorporating a dense synthetic rubber layer sandwiched between two back plates. This effectively isolates the front part of the engine mount, with the engine fitted to it, from the plate fixed to the model bulkhead. Similar arrangements can be devised by the modeller, shock absorbers are commonplace in the motor industry and for many other commercial applications!

FILTERS

Filters are used for keeping the dirt out of the air intake to the engine and the dirt in the fuel out of the carburettor and interior of the engine. Air intake filters are useful when models are being flown from dusty concrete or hardstanding areas. They could also be useful, in the summertime, for the grass field flyer to stop those annoying little grass seeds from dropping into the air intake. Many a time I have watched an engine 'playing up' only to find that a small grass seed is responsible for the intermittent running of the engine. Fuel filters will save a lot of frustration from the results of temporary fuel blockages. Most commercial fuels are prepared with cleanliness and care but, inevitably, a few foreign bodies will find their way into the can or bottle. The next time you have a gallon polythene bottle of fuel shake it up and observe the number of different particles floating about. Unless you filter your fuel between the bottle and the fuel tank, or the fuel tank and the engine, all of those particles are going to find their way into your engine and it doesn't do it much good. A two-part, cleanable, in-line filter is the best to use and between the fuel tank and engine is generally considered the favourite siting. Naturally, as a filter is there to collect dirt it will also require occasional cleaning. Remove the filter, dismantle it and wash it out thoroughly in petrol or methanol. If you get caught on the flying field with a clogged up filter then soak it in fuel for a few minutes and then blow through it in the opposite direction of the normal fuel flow. It is advisable to mark the direction of flow on the filter to prevent accidentally refitting it reversed, causing any particles unremoved to be sucked into the engine.

FUEL TANKS

I do not know who first thought of using a polythene bottle as the basis of the standard − as now accepted − R/C fuel tank. It was one of those strokes of luck that has become part of the radio-control scene. Surprisingly though little more has been done to develop the tank from its original

conception. Admittedly square tanks have been used and tanks with a sloping front but, essentially, the humble clunk tank remains the same. Perhaps someone will come along with a better article one day but, until then, we are stuck with it. The operation of the clunk tank is self-evident, some have a filler and vent tube and others have just the vent tube, relying on the removing of the tube feed connection to the engine as the point for refilling. Buy the former tank where possible. It saves a lot of fiddling about in removing and replacing the feed line. The flexible feed line in the fuel tank often gives trouble. It is difficult to find a material that will stand up to high nitro fuels, will not 'grow' and has just the right amount of flexibility to bend back on itself without 'kinking' and starving the engine. Keep an eye on the flexible tube and replace when necessary. Positioning the tank in relation to the needle valve on the engine is most important. First the tank should be located as close to the engine as practical. Long fuel draws do not suit some engines at all and will cause erratic running. Nor is it any good positioning the tank close to the engine and then having a long winding feed line from the tank to the carburettor − keep it short as possible but without any sharp bends. The most important factor is the height relationship between the centre line of the tank and the needle valve. Engines vary enormously on the variation of fuel head they will take; some are not over-worried about it, others are very critical. High performance engines, with large air intakes and poor suction, are the most critical.

With a tank centre line mounted above the needle valve you will have an engine that may be difficult to start because it is flooding through the gravity fuel supply and may tend to run right through the first half of the flight, leaning out as supply of fuel in the tank lowers. If, for design reasons, you have to have a tank positioned a little on the high side a tip on starting procedure is to

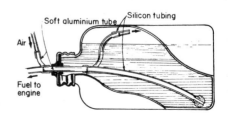

Construction of fuel tank.

Be certain the engine is running properly before releasing the plane.

keep the tail of the model well down to prevent flooding during starting. Most engines will accept a fuel suction i.e. centre line of tank below the needle valve, of about an inch, so it is safe to mount the tank centre line up to ½in. below the needle valve – this applies to side mounted engines also. With the tank a little lower than the needle valve some of the flooding problems of a full tank are overcome and it should not affect any inverted or negative 'G' manoeuvres of aerobatic models. An assistance in overcoming tank head differentials is to use a pressurised fuel system. Nearly all silencers are fitted, or supplied, with a nipple to allow tubing to be taken from it to the vent on the fuel tank. After filling the tank the pressure line is connected and the filler must be sealed off – a screw inserted in the flexible tube on the filler pipe is fine. Once the engine starts the pressure created in the silencer keeps the fuel at a slight positive pressure throughout the flight and often results in a more consistent engine run throughout the whole of the tankful of fuel.

It is possible to obtain engines fitted with fuel pumps (the pumps may also be obtained separately) and this allows the fuel tank to be fitted in virtually any position relative to the engine and still obtain satisfactory running.

If you are anticipating a fair degree of vibration from the engine it is as well to pack the fuel tank in foam 'frothing' in the tank – another cause of

engine 'surge'.

Small sports models and aerobatic models quite often have small areas available for fitting the fuel tank and a polythene clunk tank of the size needed will not fit in. A purpose-made metal (tin-plate) tank is the answer to that problem. The completed tank can be pressure tested under water by blocking of the filler and vent with rubber tube and blowing hard down another length of tubing connected to the feed.

RUNNING IN

The most important moments in an R/C engine's life are the first thirty or so minutes. Within this period the engine can be ruined or set fair for a long and reliable life. The main enemies at this period of running in an engine are lack of lubrication and overheating. Lack of lubrication is caused by using a fuel with too low an oil content, for running in, and overheating is a result of letting the engine run too lean in the initial stages.

Most commercial engines over the size of .40cu in. are now ABC or ringed engines and do not require a great deal of running in – that does not mean, though, that you can bolt it onto your model and go out and fly it at full bore right from the word go. Do that and you might as well go round to the model shop and collect another engine because your original one will not have 'bedded in', it will have been 'scratched' out of existence.

Even the ABC (aluminium piston and chromed brass cylinder liner) engines require some running in − it may only be a five minute period. Read the instructions and follow the advice, erring on the side of caution.

Smaller capacity engines, with lapped pistons, do require a little more in the way of bench running. It may be no more than half an hour but you will soon begin to feel the engine loosening up. Whether you are running in the engine in the model or, with the smaller ones, on the bench the advice is the same − keep it running rich. About 25% oil content is what we must aim for in the fuel for running in purposes, the engine will throw a lot of the oil out of the exhaust again but do not be tempted to reduce the percentage − it is needed to give the mating parts a chance to bed down. It is always preferable to bench run engines before fitting them into the models as this gives a chance to get used to the handling of them, and find any faults, before permanently installing them. It is also preferable to run the engine *without* the silencer during running in − remember what I said about the silencer keeping the engine hotter during running. That is just what we want to avoid at this point. You may not be too popular running an engine for prolonged periods in the garden shed − particularly unsilenced − but an aid here is to fill a biscuit tin, or similar receptacle with old rags and foam polystyrene and position it at the side of the exhaust outlet. This will absorb quite a bit of the noise.

Positioning the fuel tank for a bench run is as important as it is in the model so make sure it is not mounted too high or low. Whatever the manufacturers may say, open up the needle valve about four or five turns, prime the engine, and get it started. The chances are that it will take quite a bit of flicking initially before it burbles into life − and burble is just what we want it to do. Once it is running try removing the battery clip; if the engine splutters to a halt turn the needle valve down a quarter of a turn and try again. Once it is running at a stuttering four-stroke leave it to run the tankful through, keeping an eye on it in case it shows any signs of speeding up towards a two-stroke. On the following runs you can start to turn the needle valve down for a few seconds at a time so that it is just breaking between a four- and two-

stroke. For a .19 engine about a half-dozen four ounce fuel tankfuls of fuel should be sufficient to free it up; you can bring it into a two-stroke for short periods during the last two or three tankfuls. Never let the engine stop by getting to the end of the tank, and gradually leaning out the fuel mix to the engine. Put your finger over the air intake and choke it to death but take care not to put your finger in the prop instead. Another advantage in running in your engine on the bench is that you will be able to find the optimum settings of the throttle ready for fixing the engine servo linkage when it is installed in the model.

When the engine is finally installed and flying in the model continue to treat the engine with a lot of respect for the next hour or so. Have it 'singing' between a two- and four-stroke for most of the time only gradually easing it into a full-blooded two-stroke. Keep an ear open for that tell-tale slight hunting variation in the engine note when it is two-stroking − a sure sign that it is running lean. A continued lean run is no good to an engine at any stage of its life and if you see signs of discolouration on the cylinder head you know that you have been 'over-cooking' it.

Starting four-stroke engines is no more difficult than starting the two-stroke variety, but there are one or two things to watch out for. Because the four-stroke is not firing every stroke it *sounds* as though it is not performing as well as a two-stroke engine. This is deceptive. To set the main needle turn it *slowly* in until it is obviously running lean (the rpm will begin to drop off) and then open up the needle a full quarter turn. As a final check hold the model nose-up, with the engine running at full rpm to ensure that it does not start to run lean. Four-stroke engines are certainly more expensive than other types but they do have the advantages of low fuel consumption and acceptable noise levels and *quality* of sound. For the beginner this latter quality also has a beneficial effect. A two-stroke will build up speed with the model in a dive, usually inadvertent with the trainee, and it can all sound rather frenetic. The lower, slower sound of a four-stroke in similar circumstances strikes less terror into the heart.

FUELS

I have always tended to be very conservative

Multi-engined models require even more careful attention to engine adjustment. Failure of an engine can be fatal with some multi-engined models.

regarding my choice of fuels for engines. Additives may give more performance; special oils may result in less 'goo' being thrown out on to the model but it is usually at a price — a reduction in the life of the engine. When you read an advertisement in a magazine claiming that a fuel, brewed to a special secret formula, will make your engine go faster, carbon up less, be more economic or give any other special advantage, view it with suspicion.

Not all manufacturers' claims are incorrect; development of synthetic oils have resulted in fuels having certain advantages i.e. lower oil contents give better power, fuel consumption and give cleaner running — less oil sprayed down the side of the model from the exhaust. Any responsible fuel supplier will display the constituent parts of the fuel on the canister — if he is using quality materials he has nothing to fear.

Glow fuel consists of two basic ingredients and one main accepted additive, i.e. methanol, castor oil and nitro methane, and if you use only these ingredients, in the right proportions you will not go very far wrong. Castor-based oils are used because they mix well with the methanol and have a good film strength which prevents the oil from breaking down at high temperatures. Nitro methane really does increase the 'performance' of the fuel, not in direct proportion to the percentage used in the fuel but there is a gradual increase as the nitro content is increased. Nitro methane also has the advantages of making the engine easier to start and will give you a more reliable idle. Small engines in particular benefit from nitro in the fuel

and the smallest (.020 — .049cu in.) will only perform properly with a minimum of 20% of nitro methane. Commercial fuels are available, in a straight mix or with varying percentage of nitro, in cans from half pints to gallon cans. It is much more economical to buy your fuel in gallon cans.

CHOOSING YOUR ENGINE

We must look for an engine that is easy to start, has smooth running and good idle characteristics, is not over-sensitive to needle valve setting and is robust with a long operating life. What is not required at the beginner's stage is an engine with maximum output — this is often achieved at the expense of some of the other desirable features. The 'beginner's' engine will often have a greater stroke to bore ratio than racing engines and this gives a greater degree of flexibility.

STARTERS AND TACHOMETERS

Electric starters are a common sight at the flying fields. They save a lot of time and hard work in flicking a propeller — they also keep your fingers in better shape for flying and building. You can always recognise an 'old' aeromodeller by his battered forefinger with a broken nail. Properly used the starter will not damage the engine and will frequently start an otherwise 'reluctant' engine. Do not expect it to do miracles with an engine that is obviously flooded solid. This should be cleared by holding the engine on its side, with the exhaust outlet facing downwards, and turning the engine over by hand to get some of the excess fuel out through the exhaust ports. If possible start the engine in this position as it will get rid of the fuel build-up in the crankcase quicker. Apply the starter to the engine in short bursts and if you do not get a fire after a short time check the engine for another fault − perhaps the plug has burnt out.

To attempt to start a flooded engine by holding the starter continuously on the engine will only aggravate the situation; it will cause more fuel to be drawn into the engine and may result in serious damage to the engine. If you are unsure whether the engine is flooded or not (a meter fitted to the glow plug battery should give an indication) turn the engine over by hand − with a finger guard fitted. The engine should either 'kick' as soon as it comes up to 'top dead-centre', or, if it is excessively flooded, it will be hard to turn over and neat fuel will be ejected from the exhaust.

A near foolproof way to start a two-stroke glow engine (fitted in the model) is to open the needle valve, put your finger over the air intake, turn the propeller over until the fuel reaches the carburettor, turn over another two or three times and then turn the model slowly over in a clockwise direction (viewed from the front) until the engine is inverted. This will have allowed the fuel to go down the transfer ports to the head of the cylinder in the combustion chamber. Return the engine to the upright position, attach the glow plug starter lead and pull the propeller (holding it firmly) over top dead centre. You should feel the firing 'kick' as it passes the top of the compression. With the throttle opened about a quarter turn flick the propeller smartly over (you can wear a finger guard for safety). The engine should fire immediately and, within a few flicks be running. If this fails, go through the procedure again and if there is still no luck you will have to go through a routine of checks of the glow plug, battery, fuel and engine (check bolts for tightness) blocked carburettor and

fuel tank and pipe plumbing. If the engine ran before, obviously there has to be some logical reason why it is not operating now!

A tachometer is an electronic or mechanical device with which you measure the rpm of the engine by holding it in front of the propeller. The problem with checking the engine speed is that it can only be done on the ground and the maximum rpm setting there will not necessarily be the setting that will give maximum rpm in the air. The probabilities are that, if you lean the engine out on the ground to give a maximum rpm reading, the engine will lean out further in the air and the engine will cut. An easy check, to see whether the engine is likely to lean out when airborne, is to hold the model with the nose vertical before contemplating launching. If it starts to lean out too much push the nose forward quickly, to prevent it cutting altogether, and open up the needle valve another notch or two.

A tachometer is useful for comparative readings i.e. if the engine was doing 10,500 rpm on a Groupner 11in. × 8in. propeller six months ago, it should be doing just about the same now. If it is not there must be a reason for the deterioration and the fault needs correction − it may just be that the engine needs a 'decoke'! Setting up engines on a multi-engined model is made easier with a tachometer. We are not necessarily trying to get absolutely the same rpm from the engines on the port and starboard sides, we are looking for absolute reliability. Therefore, each engine is run-up independently and set to give a reliable top end and idle performance. The rpm are noted for each of these settings on each engine. When more than one engine is running it can be difficult to check, by ear, whether the engines are running perfectly − this is where the tachometer comes in useful. A check with the tachometer on the doubtful engine will confirm whether it is performing correctly, simply by checking with the previous figures obtained.

CHAPTER 11

Electric Power

Undoubtedly, as a nation, we are becoming increasingly noise conscious and attempts to reduce extraneous high noise levels have, quite rightly, affected IC engines as used for R/C model aircraft. Model glow engines can now be silenced to a legally acceptable level but are still relatively noisy and, as noise criteria is such a personal thing, can be objectionable to some people. To many modellers the optimum power source would be totally silent, giving the combined advantages of the silence of a glider with the flight flexibility of a power model. Electric powered model aircraft must come, in theory at least, the closest to this ideal as the only noise discernible is the 'air' noise from the rotating propeller. Under no circumstances could that *sound* be called objectionable although it is audible with no other power model operating. Any less noise could make the model dangerous in the same way as an electric milk float is dangerous — too much silence makes one unaware of the approach of the model. Electric power is not used commercially on full-size aircraft and it certainly looks (or rather sounds) wrong with a scale model of a 'Spitfire' or Sopwith 'Camel' powered by an electric motor. One could argue equally that a small two-stroke IC engine, turning at 10,000 rpm does not have the scale sound of a 'Merlin' or 'Gnome Rotary' engine but at least it *has* an engine sound of some sort. Scale models apart, what does electric power have to offer?

Electric powered models are certainly not a new innovation; round the pole models were flown regularly at exhibitions in the 1940s; free flight models followed not long after. A small number of radio-controlled models featuring electric power have also been flown successfully but not on any large scale basis. It is only relatively recently that electric power has been developed into an acceptable commercial proposition. Why? Two principal reasons. First, the introduction of sintered cell construction, nickel cadmium cells with high permissible discharge rates and high capacity ratio for size/weight. Secondly, these cells are also capable of being totally recharged in periods varying from 15–30 minutes, making a reasonable number of flights during one visit to the flying

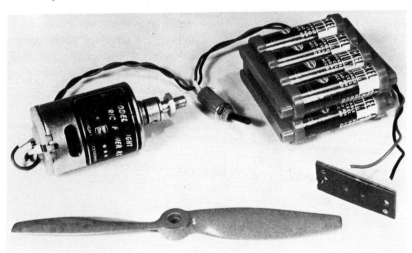

The motive power: surprisingly powerful electric motor, neat battery box, on/off switch and prop, ready for assembly in the aircraft.

field a possibility.

Complete airborne electric power units, i.e. batteries, switch, electric motor, charging socket, wiring, etc., range from a small system with an all up weight of 14oz (using 600MAh rechargeable cells 9.6v) suitable for lightweight sports models of 40–45in. wing span. Powered gliders can be of larger wing spans.

Quick recharging is achieved from a 12-volt car battery, the larger systems require a 20 amp hour lead acid accumulator to ensure a reasonable number of full charges of the flight pack. Some systems are supplied with charging monitors that can be set to give a specific charging time and an ammeter indicates the charging rate. It is important to have some positive form of timing or cut-out for the quick charge rate as it is easy to damage the cells by overcharging at the high rate used. With certain higher voltage (over 12-volt) systems it was impossible to rapid charge from a single 12-volt car battery but most systems now have 'split' battery packs to allow this to be achieved.

All of this may seem to be remarkably attractive and easy for the 'average' modeller. No fuel, no mess, no starter, virtually no noise – almost too good to be true. In common with most 'ideals' electric power has its limitations and more than one modeller has found, to his considerable cost, that theory and practice do not always go hand in hand. Knowing the limitations of electric power units and batteries, the types of model best suited to this form of power and the pit-falls to avoid will certainly help you towards successful electric flight, but you should not expect miracles. To achieve the present 'state of the art' many modellers have put in hours of experimental work on the bench and with practical tests on a variety of models, and I am sure that they would be the first to admit that they have not come up with totally straightforward answers. There are conflicts and compromises to be resolved in electric powered R/C aircraft to a greater degree than in most branches of the hobby, for example: the powerful (and expensive) motors are often only superior when more nicad cells are used to supply a higher voltage. More cells equate to increased model weights, higher wing loadings and faster models (with a greater risk of damaging the model during landing). Experiments may show that a model with a 'standard' motor and battery pack will only just remain airborne, but changing the motor to one of the more 'exotic' types and using specially selected nicad batteries improves the flight performance appreciably. However, by using an improved motor and more expensive battery cells the overall effect is to reduce the operating time. Only by having a specific aim for the type of electric powered model you wish to fly can you work towards obtaining reasonable goals in flight quality. A fast aerobatic model will require a totally different approach to a powered glider style aircraft or a scale model.

Quite a measure of space is allocated in magazines (*Radio Control Models and Electronics* and *Radio Modeller*) to electric model flight, for the subject does have a great fascination, and much useful information may be gleaned from reading of the experiences of these experimenters. There are also specialist books available on the subject of electric flight. To attempt to start from basics can be very expensive and frustrating, good motors and batteries are costly and can be easily damaged through ignorance. For those of you who are 'hooked' on the idea of electric power I

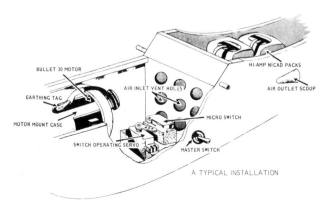

A typical installation.

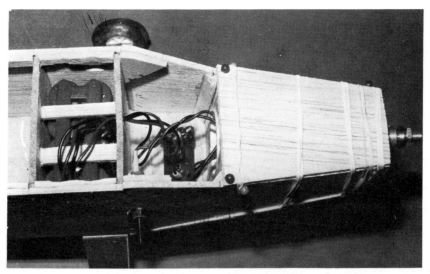

Nicads take up space but there is still room in the fuselage for R/C gear.

Charging up for another flight. This ability to recharge 'while you wait' is one of the attractions of electric flying.

would strongly suggest buying a fully matched outfit, i.e. motor, batteries and model kit; at least you will know that this system is compatible and has been flight proven. Demonstrations by the trade may look very convincing and whet your appetite for this novel form of flying; remember that they have a choice of the very best of the motors and batteries! If you think that all motors and batteries are of roughly equal standard, ask some of the electric car racing fraternity and obtain their views. There are *very* considerable differences in the power of the motors and capacity of the batteries, even those from the same production batch.

MOTORS

Electric motor costs vary from a few pounds to approaching a hundred pounds. To a large extent you tend to get what you pay for but the high cost motors are expensive because of the engineering required to achieve that extra few percent efficiency (it will also result in a higher quality product). Because electric flight can be somewhat marginal as regards power/weight ratios *any* increase of efficiency is more than welcome. This does not mean that the cheaper motors are a total waste of time, merely that the type of model and construction

Small ARTF models are available and practical, but not suitable for beginners.

bining a motor/reducer unit with a lightweight airframe perfectly adequate flight times can be obtained, sufficient to satisfy the modeller who enjoys a summer's evening trip to the local park (if flying is allowed there) and to have four or five minute gentle flights. Perhaps we are wrong in trying to compare the performance of electric motors to conventional IC engines, they are totally different and, because of these differences, will probably appeal to modellers with a different outlook. Electric flight is certainly more popular in some European countries than it is in Britain and this may well be due to a different mental attitude.

BATTERIES

Nicads of 104MAh capacity (sub-cells) are the standard battery used for electric powered aircraft models — and cars. These must be of the vented type to allow rapid charging; if you don't have this facility you have only one flight per session, followed by a 14 hour charging period. Buying 'selected' batteries i.e. batteries that have been checked and found to have a better than average capacity, will cost you a little more initially but should prove to be a good investment. Correct charging, with the fast charge methods, is impera-

of the airframe must be tailored to the motor performance. Reducer units (gearing down the motor to the prop. driver) allows the motor to turn larger, and more efficient, propellers and produce sensible power from inexpensive motors. By com-

Light structure, light wing loading models are excellent for powering with low-cost electric units.

tive if you hope to make use of the full capacity of the battery, without risking damage to the cells. There are a number of recommended methods of charging to obtain the best performance; a common claim is that you should charge at a constant current until the voltage stops rising and then switch off. Using this method you will either have to invest in some expensive equipment, to safely achieve this effect automatically, or you must be prepared to keep an eagle eye on a voltmeter over lengthy periods of time. Fortunately, fully regulated chargers have now come down in price and are well worth the investment, they will give you peace of mind and prevent damage to the battery cells.

Charging at a constant rate for a 'safe' period followed by a trickle charge, will not damage the cells but may not give you absolutely maximum efficiency and connecting a battery pack (8 cells) direct to a car battery must be undertaken with caution and on no account must the charging time (20 minutes) be exceeded. Battery packs do need 'running-in' and you will almost certainly find an improvement in performance after they have been cycled a few times. Consistent rapid charging will also result in a deterioration of the potential capacity of the batteries. To overcome this 'quirk' of nicads the pack should be given a normal rate charge (14 hours) after each flying session, to keep them in trim. At the termination of fast charging a nicad cell will probably have a nominal voltage in excess of 1.5 volt (normal rated voltage is 1.2 volt) and it is, therefore, only possible to charge a maximum of eight cells from a standard 12 volt car battery − the nicads are wired in series and they should never be charged in parallel. Any battery packs with a total voltage exceeding 9.6 volts nominal must be subdivided so that they can be independently charged. As the higher cost, more efficient, motors seem to be happier operating on ten, twelve or more battery packs you must be prepared for this additional complication.

Nicads are not only damaged by overcharging, they can also be ruined if a motor is stalled and some form of power cut-off switch should be incorporated in the circuitry so that it can be actuated in the event of an emergency. The switch can be operated from a separate servo or from, say, full down elevator position (this must be a positive action as you may wish to cut the motor in the air). With eight or twelve nicad cells fitted into a medium-sized model there is not an abundance of room remaining for the R/C equipment. Using the motor battery to power the receiver and servos, through a voltage regulator, has obvious advantages − and some disadvantages. Because we wish to use all of the battery capacity to prolong our flight time we run the risk of having insufficient power left to operate the R/C equipment for the landing!

BECs (Battery Eliminator Circuits) are now commonly used for combined motor and receiver nicad supplies. When the battery voltage drops to a pre-selected figure the battery will only supply the receiver and this allows time for the model to be landed before the voltage drops too low. This system is perfectly adequate for sports models and it is only when the models get into the specialist and competition classes that a separate, small capacity, nicad is needed for the receiver and servos.

Electronic speed controllers are also in common use for electric powered models, these are in effect the carburettor throttles of the electric motor. Although used more in electric powered cars and boats, where they are virtually essential, they still have a place in R/C aeroplanes. Powered glider type models may be perfectly adequate when fitted with an ON/OFF motor switch, full power is used for the climb to height, the motor switched off, the model glides down and the performance repeated. For a scale model, or a waterplane, the take-off needs to be a gradual affair with a steady acceleration. It is also more acceptable if the model is landed with power on, and that entails reductions of power round the circuit and on the approach and the use of a speed controller.

MODELS

It is not true that you have to build flimsy, insubstantial airframes to effect a practical flying electric model aircraft. If you are looking for a fast aerobatic model with a limited duration you can use a strong GRP and foam structure − you will probably need it to withstand the flying and landing stresses! Having unnecessary weight in the airframe will entail having a smaller pay-load of batteries or poorer flight performance and, to this extent, the lighter and more efficient the air-

Some of the older, built-up structure, designs make good subjects for electric R/C.

frame the better the model will fly. Electric models seem to be divided into three types.

1. Duration models, where the power is used to obtain height and the flight extended by thermal activity and/or the efficient glide ratio of the model.
2. Aerobatic models, using airframes that are a compromise between standard forms of construction and lightweight techniques used in gliders and some older types of model aircraft designs – before the introduction of high powered IC engines did away with the need to design efficient structures!
3. Scale models, where the flight time is not the critical factor and the appearance of the model in flight is the most important consideration. One enormous advantage with electric power is the instant starting of the motors – at the flick of a switch – and the reliability of

operation. Multi-engined scale models do not hold the same terrors when fitted with electric motors as it is most unlikely that an engine will fail, the loss of power on the engines being contemporaneous.

All of the electric power units available commercially have very complete instructions included that deal with the installation, charging and operation of the equipment. The dos and don'ts are well covered – and there are quite a lot of them – and there is no point in repeating all of this information in this chapter. There does not seem to be very much to be gained by trying to make up your own electric power system as the individual costs of the batteries, motor, switch and fuse are likely to cost as much, if not more, than the complete units. The manufacturers have carried out many experiments to ascertain the best combinations of motors and batteries and it is only in the field of models and propeller sizes that you are likely to obtain substantial advantages. Whether or not you find that electric power models suit you will depend on a number of factors, not the least being where you fly from, and a summary of advantages and disadvantages may assist you to reach a decision.

ADVANTAGES

No problems with engine starting, just flick a switch at the point of launching the model and instant start. No damaged fingers − no starter required. A simple on/off switch can be fitted operating from a heavy duty microswitch or, for larger models, a proportional speed controller can be incorporated.

Noise levels are exceptionally low allowing models to be flown from sites where normal power models would be banned. The lack of noise makes the R/C electric powered model as socially accepted as a glider.

Power costs are low compared with diesel and glow fuels.

Maintenance costs, except for possible damage to the rechargeable batteries, are low.

'Refuelling' or rather recharging, is a totally clean operation as is the whole of the flying operation. Models, assuming no crashes, should last longer as there is no fuel penetration into the airframes. Finishes to the models can be more simple for the same reason. Vibration levels are very much lower than is common with normal power models; this being beneficial to the airborne radio control equipment.

DISADVANTAGES

The power/weight ratio is inferior to that of the conventional small diesel or glow motor and the practical duration is more limited by battery capacity/weight considerations.

Design of the airframe and selection of materials has to be carefully considered to maintain minimum weight. A model finishing with a heavy wing loading is likely to be both difficult to fly and more prone to damage. The heat produced by the batteries and motors must be dissipated.

Charging times, at the rapid rate, are critical and batteries can be damaged by relatively short overcharge periods.

The weight of the lead acid recharging batteries can be considerable, particularly if you have a long distance to travel from your car to the flying area.

Stalling the motor, when no R/C on/off switch is fitted, can easily result in damaged batteries as can over-discharging them following a flight with the motor 'windmilling' during a prolonged glide.

Propeller selection is critical for good perfor-

Typical fast, powered glider approach favoured by the Europeans for electric flight.

Electric power is also suited to unconventional models, such as this simplified helicopter.

mance relative to both the motor and the model. It may be that a wooden propeller gives the best results but that the flying area you use is unsuitable for flying with such easily breakable items.

The initial cost, bearing in mind the additional cost of recharging batteries and timer, is high.

CONCLUSIONS

There is no possible doubt that electric flight is here to stay and that its popularity will increase. Every little improvement in rechargeable battery efficiencies − and they are gradually improving all the time − helps to improve the viability of this form of power. If there was ever a major break-through in battery output, say a 300% increase in efficiency, then it would revolutionise this power basis. But then, it would probably change much more important forms of power users i.e. the automobile and other vehicles.

In our environmentally sensitive areas − and that seems to be the larger proportions of highly populated countries − it may help us to continue flying and where the use of internal combustion engines in models might be banned. Personally I believe we should fight for our rights in respect of noise levels − we have already voluntarily reduced noise levels by very considerable amounts and we

Multi-engined models benefit hugely from the use of electric power. It is extremely rare to have an engine fail!

should not be hounded from flying sites simply because people believe the countryside has to be perfectly quiet. But that is another story — and another soap box. If electric power gets us back to flying in some of the more properly noise-sensitive areas, such as parks and other open areas in urban areas, then great — it is certainly worthwhile using this form of motor.

Providing modellers do not view the use of electric power as the answer to all problems there will be much to gain by using batteries and electric motors. From indoor models to FAI style aerobatic models, all can be efficiently powered by electric but, and it is a big but, you will have to work hard to achieve the results and probably have to pay quite handsomely too.

Electric powered, gas filled airships are highly suitable for flying in large indoor halls — and as advertising media.

CHAPTER 12

Batteries

Batteries could be described as one of the most important 'accessories' for radio control equipment. They are essential for the operation of the equipment and will be with us until someone can devise an alternative and superior source of power. Despite the importance of batteries they are frequently ignored, abused or taken for granted by modellers. They are a necessary evil that occasionally need replacing or recharging — when one remembers to. It says a lot for the quality and construction of modern batteries that, even with this misuse they rarely let us down. When a battery or rechargeable cell does fail it is more likely to be as a result of our malpractices than a manufacturer's or design fault.

Technically speaking a battery comprises a series of linked cells — a single cell, such as an HP7 pen cell, is not a battery. The two types of cells used for our purposes are classified as Primary cells and Secondary cells. Primary cells are normally known as 'dry cells' and are capable of generating power within themselves and, once they are exhausted, must be discarded. These 'dry cell' batteries are the common flashlight and transistor portable radio types available in many shops and stores throughout the country.

Secondary cells have the distinction of being able to be recharged; they act as electrical storage vessels. The most common of this type is the lead acid accumulator which, because of its bulk and weight, is used only for ground equipment, i.e. for the power source to electric starters and fuel pumps and for starter batteries for the engine glow plug.

DRY BATTERIES

Dry batteries were once the most used form of battery for radio control work but these have now been largely superseded by the small efficient rechargeable nickel cadmium cells. They have the advantage of being relatively cheap to buy and are readily available; for this reason they are still used in some of the cheaper proportional outfits in addition to single channel equipment. Some transmitters in three and four function proportional control outfits also use dry batteries but the use of nickel cadmium cells is more and more likely to become the norm for both receivers and transmitters.

One of the big disadvantages with dry batteries is that the inexperienced modeller is always doubtful of the state of the battery and whether it needs replacing. The result of this uncertainty is that batteries are often discarded a long time before they are exhausted. This is a natural worry and if it is a case of spending a few more pence on a new set of batteries instead of crashing a model it must be a good form of insurance. Where you have an alternative use for the batteries, in portable radios, record players, flash lamps etc., they can be removed from the radio control equipment and re-used without any concern over the economics. Dry batteries, mostly of the alkaline type for our purposes, have a limited 'shelf' or storage life and it is essential that, when we purchase them, they are fresh. Choose a shop or store that has a good turnover of sales or at least a shop where there is a stocking system that ensures that the batteries cannot be left on the shelves for many months. Storage should also be in as cool a position as possible — the hotter they are the more rapid the chemical reaction taking place inside the battery. The domestic refrigerator is a good place to store the batteries, if your wife will let you, but never leave your spares in a cupboard or on a shelf close to a radiator or the fire. When batteries have been kept in a cold place they should be brought up to ambient temperature before use — cold cells may have a limited output and this may also affect your equipment's capability when flying on a very cold winter's day.

Checking the voltage of dry batteries can present a number of problems. The cells will recuperate

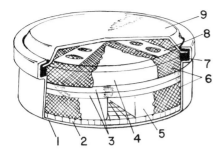

Section of disc type cell:
1. Cell cup; 2. Bottom insert;
3. Separate; 4. Negative electrode;
5. Positive electrode;
6. Nickel wire gauze;
7. Sealing washer;
8. Contact spring; 9. Cell cover.

considerably when 'rested' and may give a good reading, when tested initially, only to fail shortly afterwards during use. Testing *must* always be carried out on load otherwise the readings are worthless.

Leakproof batteries should be used for all air-borne battery packs but bear in mind that 'leak-proof' is only a general term. Although this type of cell has an extra protective case it is still possible, if the battery is left in its exhausted state long enough, for the cell to be corroded through. Batteries should never be left in equipment for long periods — particularly throughout the winter period with no flying activity. The alkaline dry battery is capable of continuous duty but will have a much longer working life if it is used in short periods with a rest in between. Avoid leaving the transmitter and receivers switched on for longer than is necessary. It is possible to purchase a 'dud' battery, either one that has discharged through excessive storage time or one, that, as a result of manufacture, has a high internal resistance. Batteries should be checked before they are purchased.

The range of dry batteries is quite extensive but, for radio control work, is usually limited to 1.5v pen cells (HP7). Soldering wires to pen cell terminals is not generally recommended by the manufacturers as the heat from the iron can be detrimental to the cell. From the electrical safety point, though, it is preferable to solder a number of cells together to form a battery — it is a safe method providing it is undertaken correctly. The terminals must be cleaned thoroughly and slightly 'roughed up', this applies especially to the base, negative, terminal. A large hot iron is used for making the soldered joint and the iron should only be in contact with the terminal long enough for the solder to flow smoothly on to it. Leads coming away from the terminals should be taped to battery sides to prevent straining the soldered joints. Taping four pen cell batteries together can be somewhat tricky as they tend to move around relative to one another as the taping proceeds. A

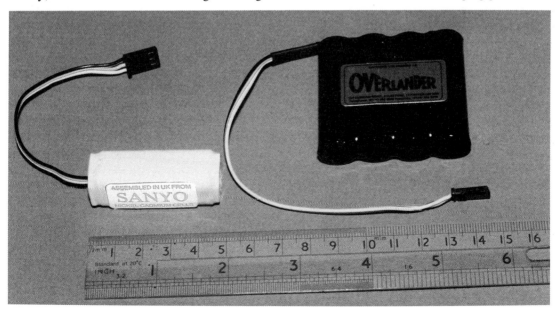

Battery packs are available in a very wide range of capacities and sizes, from 50mAh to 4.0Ah capacities and above.

simple tip for overcoming this is to insert a piece of ¼ in.sq. balsa in the centre.

In addition to the leakproof alkaline cells it is also possible to obtain mercury and manganese/alkaline cells. Both of these types of dry cell have advantages of higher capacities − particularly in continuous use − and better shelf life. However they have the disadvantages of greater costs, non standard sizes and are less easily available. Problems may also occur in soldering to the terminals where steel cases are used. Neither of these battery types has become very popular.

BATTERY BOXES

There are good and bad battery boxes and clips, bad, that is, because of the poor standard of electrical contact made. Soldering pen cells together is greatly to be preferred but some of the enclosed nylon battery boxes, secured through the centre by a long screw, are perfectly acceptable. Contacts should be robust and not likely to lose their 'spring' and the contacts must be regularly cleaned with some fine sand or emery paper. Do not use battery boxes that easily allow the batteries to 'spring' out of position or ones of flimsy construction.

LEAD ACID BATTERIES

The lead acid cell has a nominal voltage of 2 volts

and, as previously stated, is mainly used for engine starting procedures. It is a vented rechargeable cell that, with reasonable maintenance, will give a number of years' service. Lead acid accumulators will need occasional topping up, to the level stated by the manufacturers, with clean distilled water. Instructions regarding the maintenance and charging are usually included on the battery but always maintain the battery in a fully charged state.

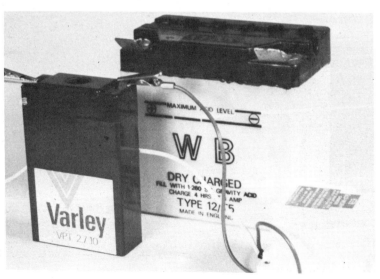

Both colloidal and standard lead acid accumulators are popular for glow plug starting and operating ancillary equipment such as engine starters and fuel pumps.

Watch out for signs of corrosion. There is usually some leakage around the terminals. When this is evident scrape and wash, in warm water under the tap, the terminals and surrounding area followed by an application of vaseline for protection. When flying has finished for the day disconnect the lead to one of the terminals on the accumulator to avoid the risk of a short.

The modern generation of sealed, colloidal, batteries do not require any topping-up with distilled water or acid but they must be more carefully recharged. Over-charging (at too high a rate or for too long a period) can damage the battery or cause it to 'blow' − accompanied by a distinctly unpleasant smell! Rechargeable lead-acid 'cyclon' batteries (2 volt) have also become popular for glow plug energising. These cells − a 5 Ah is sufficient for a normal day's flying − are conveniently small, leak proof and the glo-clip can be attached direct to the battery instead of via an extension lead, as is normal with the larger lead-acid batteries.

SEALED NICKEL CADMIUM CELLS

These rechargeable 'button' and dry battery shaped nickel cadmium cells are now used extensively in radio control model aircraft and the transmitters.

They are sealed, or automatic, non reverse, venting cells with metal cases and are available as individual cells or in welded batches to various total voltages. Their useful life, and the number of recharges before eventual breakdown, is very considerable and a battery life of three of four years is not unusual. Good maintenance is again an important factor in longevity. It is possible to get the odd 'dead' cell in a pack but this happens very infrequently. Although the cells have a nominal voltage of 1.2 volts it is possible for them to hold a voltage as high as 1.5 volts immediately after charging and the combined excess voltage of a battery pack may be sufficient to affect the radio equipment initially. For this reason it is advisable to operate the equipment for a few minutes before the first flight after charging − the excess voltage is rapidly discharged and the cells will then hold their nominal voltage steadily for most of their discharge period.

The charge rate for nickel cadmium cells is normally accepted at one tenth of the rated cell capacity i.e. a 500 mA cell or pack should be charged at 50 mA, and it should be charged for about a 50% overcharge period compared with the discharge. This will mean that the battery will require a full 14−16 hours charging from the full discharge point. In fact it is quite safe and will not

A heavy scale model with operating retracting undercarriage (including, in this case, tail wheel) together with flaps and normal functions will cause a considerable drain on the batteries and due allowance must be made for this.

harm the cells if this charging period is considerably exceeded − it is advisable to err on the side of over-charging than under-charging. Rarely does one reach the stage of completely discharging the receiver or transmitter packs through excessive flying on one day, but it can be harmful to *completely* discharge nickel cadmium cells. When this occurs in a battery pack one cell usually reaches its discharged state first and there is a risk then of that cell becoming 'reverse charged' when the pack is charged. To remedy this condition the pack must be 'cycled' i.e. charged, discharged, charged, discharged etc. over four or five times. A lower limit of 1.1 volts per cell should not be exceeded if at all possible.

A final reminder on charging nickel cadmium cells. Some built in, and some separate, chargers require the receiver and transmitter switches to be in the on or off positions. Check that you have them switched in the correct position and that the charging indicator light or meter is operating. Should the battery not have been charged there is still a strong temptation to go out and fly − don't!

In addition to standard chargers it is now possible to obtain 'rapid' chargers − normally operating from a 12 volt car outlet − that will recharge transmitter and receiver batteries in about one hour. These should only be used with vented nickel cadmium cells. Battery 'conditioners' capable of automatically redischarging and recharging batteries, i.e. cycling, are also available and will keep you informed of battery state and condition.

Powered gliders can have IC engines or electric motors for their power source.

CHAPTER 13

First Flights

The most exciting, and traumatic, day of your modelling life is likely to be the one when you, or a colleague, flies your first model. It is a day of tensions and doubts; it can be a day of elation but it can also be a day of despair. Whether you finish up a 'winner' or a 'loser' will depend a lot on how you approach and prepare for this memorable day. All too often it becomes a time of rush and battling against time to get the model ready for a deadline – probably your own imposed deadline. This is no way to tackle such an important moment. It has taken many weeks, perhaps months, to get the model this far – plus a fair capital investment – it would be ridiculous to jeopardise our chances now. What we *must* do is to sit back and work out logically, as we have done for the previous phases, our progress towards the first flight.

I have stated, in magazine articles and previous books, that I would not put the chance of a 'lone'

flyer achieving success with his first R/C models higher than 20–25%. Nothing that I have seen or heard since making these assessments has changed my opinion. A one in four or one in five chance of success does not, to me, seem reasonable odds bearing in mind the time, effort and money spent. The chance of success if you go along and let one of the qualified members of your local club test fly the model is much greater. Have one of the members teach you to fly and the chances of the model flying *and* you learning to fly are excellent. I know that there *are* some modellers stuck out in the wilds of nowhere with the nearest club 'light years' away. To them I would wish every heartfelt good wish – I learned that way – and refer you to the end of this chapter where as much detail, as is possible, is given for your situation. For the remainder of you it is a question of swallowing your pride and, if necessary, begging the services

The first flight of any model is fraught with the unknown.

It certainly helps if you have a calm and qualified helper to assist you with all preparatory work, as is shown in this sequence of photographs. (See also opposite.)

of a competent pilot to put the model and yourself through your paces. Not that that means you can sit back and take it easy; there is still some homework to do.

One of the biggest problems with flying, as we shall certainly find out, is disorientation. Disorientation simply explained, is being unsure of which way the model is going and, when we do know which way it is going, which control to apply i.e., is it left rudder or right that is required? Our

homework consists of suspending the model from the ceiling, switching the receiver and transmitter on, viewing the model from all angles and finding the correct signals to give to make the model take certain actions.

You can use the same metal bar, that we used for balancing the model previously, for suspending the model but do ensure that the cord is firmly attached to the ceiling or light. A second line can be taped to one wing tip and tied to a convenient

All's well.

point to steady the model to one angle. Alternatively, if you have a cooling fan handy, it may be possible to produce enough airflow over the control surfaces to allow them to function to some degree (as in a wind tunnel). With this system the second line should not be fitted as the single suspension point will allow the model a certain degree of 'freedom'.

With everything switched on, view the model from behind and watch the controls move as you move the control levers. Consciously think of giving left or up or slow motor etc., don't just sit there waggling the sticks. Do the same from the front of the model, noting that the model turning to the left is turning to your right. Get used to realising this factor so you won't be caught out when you are actually flying the model. Keep viewing the model from all directions, so you are sure you will recognise which way it is flying when you are out at the flying field on your own. Get used to operating all the controls on the transmitter, including the trims, without having to look for them; in fact so that it is automatic. In other words, keep at it until you feel really comfortable with the transmitter in your hands and you know at a glance which way the model is flying.

There is another 'computer age' product which can certainly help us prepare for the first flight and this is the computer 'flight training' system. These programmes are devised to teach the flying of standard powered R/C models (trainer type), aerobatic aircraft, ducted fan jets, helicopters and gliders. It is possible to programme in different wind strengths and directions, even turbulence factors with some systems. I would only recommend the systems that are operated by a transmitter similar to the ones we normally use, those using the computer keyboard, or basic joy-stick, are only glorified games.

What the computer flight training course can do is to show you cause and effect of operating the transmitter controls and to help with orientation – one of the main bugbears of learning to fly. Let me give you an example. I was taking a weekend course for trainee R/C pilots and part of the course involved hands-on experience with a large training model and a buddy box system. One of the pupils was given the buddy-box, after showing him the controls, and the result was total non-reaction – he couldn't relate to the model and the transmitter and was unable to control the model in any sense. That evening he spent a half hour on the computer with the flight trainer and the next day had a further attempt with the buddy-box and real trainer. The difference was remarkable. This time he was immediately able to co-ordinate the controls on the transmitter, relate them to the model in flight and he didn't become disorientated. Yes, he made errors, we all do when we are learning and the computer is not a substitute for practical flying experience. It is, though, a real help in those first phases, of becoming used to handling the transmitter, without having to look down to see what you are doing or where the various controls

are, and knowing which way the model is heading.

The computer programme comes into its own again when you want to practise aerobatic manoeuvres, the beauty of the system being that you can crash the model without having any costs or repair work to do.

Before arriving at the airfield with the completed model, and hopeful look of expectation, make at least one visit to the club to see what the general arrangements are, to find out the flying procedures and to introduce yourself. Find out whether the club uses a transmitter pound i.e., all transmitters, except the ones used for flight, are kept at a central point; where the pegboard is kept and any local rules and regulations that apply. (There may be limited flying times for instance.) Get a knowledge of the general 'etiquette' of the flying field. You will, I am sure, find the modellers friendly and helpful and don't be afraid to ask questions – although *not* when a pilot is flying a model and concentrating very hard to make it do what he wants it to do. One reason, probably the main one, that you are visiting the flying field is to find yourself an instructor and this should be approached carefully. Avoid rushing up to the first person you see and asking him to assist you. He may well agree but he may also be the club 'knowall' (yes they all have them) and the last person suited to teach you to fly. Watch carefully the modellers flying and, if you have no other information to go on, look for the fairly quiet competent pilot. A man (or maybe woman one of these days) that starts his engine with a minimum of fuss, takes his model out on to the flight line well away from the public, takes off and flies in a sensible manner (although he may well be doing aerobatics). On landing he will switch off, return his model to the pits area, replace the frequency peg and, probably, clean his model down. He may not appear to be quite as 'spectacular' as some of the other flyers but he is probably a sound competent flyer of quiet temperament – just the sort for a mentor. When he has obviously completed his chores, introduce yourself and ask him if he would be able to assist you or if not whether he could suggest someone that may be able to give you some tuition. You may think that this is a bit of an imposition on your part but believe me this is not the case. Any modeller, who truly loves flying R/C aircraft, will be only too delighted to assist a fellow modeller and club-member in attaining the same degree of satisfaction from his hobby that he does. It would be surprising if you left the flying field without someone having agreed to take you under his wing. Check with your newly found instructor what time he would like you to be at the flying field for the test flight and first lesson and ask him if there is a club 'buddy box' lead available (if not you will have to purchase one, to suit your needs). If you are really lucky, he will have a transmitter that is compatible with yours for 'buddy box' flying. Explain to your instructor the type of model that you have, how many functions are fitted and all of the relevant information and ask him if there is anything, in addition to the normal field box equipment, that you should bring. Don't monopolise the poor man too long, he may wish to do some more flying, but take a good look round and see if you can spot the poor flyers, and those that fly dangerously and without consideration. When you have said your farewells and returned home you still have one duty to do. The model has been checked out for warps and balance etc., and the radio has been checked out for operation of it and the linkages *but*, not with the engine running. If it is possible to run the engine at home, without annoyance to the neighbours, to check the operation of the radio, and for setting up the engine throttle, do so. Should the conditions be unsuitable then you will have to make these checks on the flying field and to do that it would be as well to get down to the flying field *really* early before the others arrive and start flying. It can be very infuriating to be waiting to fly when a fellow modeller, on the same frequency, is busy for ages making adjustments to his linkages and engine. Having assured ourselves that all control surfaces are residing at neutral — with transmitter trims central, that all controls move in the correct directions and the engine reduces to low throttle plus cut off with the trim, now is the time to admire our efforts and, for the records to take a photograph of it and perhaps to revise on Chapter 7 Basic Aerodynamics. Much better to go for our first lesson understanding the principal terms used in flying.

DAY OF THE TEST FLIGHT

A final check before you leave for the flying field

that you have *everything* you need. The field box should be well stocked, the batteries charged and the model in first rate order. Don't overlook the personal things such as sunglasses, protective clothing if it is needed, cigarettes — if you smoke *or* if your instructor smokes.

After greeting your instructor I have no doubt that he will explain to you that, although he is only too willing to test fly the model, there is no guarantee that it will fly and that he may not crash it. Obviously this is something that must be accepted and you will know full well that the chances of it flying successfully are much greater in his hands than they ever would be in yours. Despite the fact that you have checked, and double checked, the model over he will probably want to carry out his own pre-flight check. He will also probably find something that is wrong, very galling, but do not despair — you are among good company and remember that it is often easier for a 'stranger' to spot a mistake than you with your close association with it. Your instructor will also probably explain the flying etiquette (frequency peg system, aircraft landing have priority, no flying over certain area etc.) and safety. For this first flight he will not want the worry of having the 'buddy box' connected as he may have his hands full trimming out the model. With the engine running he will check that it is not likely to lean out in flight (by holding the model vertically, nose up) that the throttle is correctly set and that all of the control surfaces are moving freely and in the correct 'sense'. He may also carry out a protracted range check although it is to be hoped that you have been able to do this at home prior to coming to the field. Assuming that the model is to be taken off the ground the instructor will want to carry out a taxi check and when he is satisfied that the model is tracking straight and there is sufficient power he will lift off the model with ample speed reserve. After the climb out and tentative turns in each direction he will be moving the stick trims until the model is flying straight and level 'hands off'. Should the trim of the model be too far out he will land and make immediate adjustments. Providing the model is behaving itself he may well climb to a safe height and hand over the transmitter to you. Almost certainly you will be feeling too 'churned up' to do anything with the transmitter sticks but it is nice to be able to say

Big or small...

...low wing or high wing...

that you 'flew' the model on its maiden flight. After landing, and a period for recovery, comes the debriefing and the correction of control surfaces so that the transmitter trims can be centralised again. Transmitter trims are *not* for permanent trimming; this *must* be corrected on the model itself.

Having recovered from the elation of the first flight it is time to get down to the serious business of learning to fly the model until you reach the stage where it goes where *you* want it to, rather than trying to correct it after it has been allowed to wander away from the desired course. It is vital that there should be a good understanding between you and your instructor regarding the operation of

...sports or aerobatic...

...all can be hand launched, provided the launcher is proficient.

the 'buddy box' system and the commands for handing over. Let him explain the movements of the control sticks and the trim levers. Get him to check the way that you hold the transmitter to make sure that it is at least one of the two 'standard' ways – you will probably have decided previously at home which way suits you. Disorientation, as 99 out of 100 will find out, is the biggest initial problem and there are two agreements that you

can sort out with your instructor, prior to flying, that may make learning a little easier. Left and right are accepted terms that normally are fully understood and commands using these words are readily obeyed. In times of stress and concentration the order 'turn left' may not become automatic and may take a second or so before the direction is realised. This is particularly so when the model is coming towards you and you have to

A new model, built to a new design, is ready for its first flight...

...it's a time of tension for modeller and assistants as they make a pre-flight check of engine and flying controls...

'reverse' your position relative to it. The odd second or so solving this directional, or disorientation, problem can be disastrous as far as the model itself is concerned. Rather than using the terms left and right the pupil will find it easier if his instructor uses 'in' or 'out' i.e., the model to be flown towards the pilot or further away. This term is relative to the pupil regardless of the direction or attitude of the model. With the model flying towards the pupil, despite the use of 'in' or 'out' there will remain the problem of which way to move the stick when the model starts to deviate from its course. No such problem occurs with the aircraft flying away from us because it is in the correct and logical 'sense' comparative to the transmitter stick movements, i.e. if you want the model to turn to one side you move the stick in that direction. The easiest way I know of teaching people the action required to *correct* a model flying towards the pilot is that the stick should be moved towards the low wing. Once you have learned to fly these corrections become automatic but there are odd moments when even the most experienced pilots have that momentary — and it is only a fraction of a second — disorientation problem.

For the second flight the instructor will take the model off, climb out, fly in steady circles, making final trim adjustments as he goes. Once he is

...an ROG take-off...

...climbing...

satisfied that the model is behaving as it should he will fly overhead, at a reasonable height, aim the model into wind and hand over with words like 'all right you can take it now'. The more positive the words of command the better so that there can be no doubt about who is flying the model. Your instructor will probably ask you to carry on flying upwind, maintaining height and maintaining direction. At a suitable distance away, before the model becomes too small visually, he will ask you to perform a 180° turn. The chances are that somewhere through this manoeuvre, if not before, you will 'lose' the model and it will finish in a nose down attitude with you totally unsure which way it is turning and what remedial action should be taken. This is where the 'buddy box' system is such an advantage. No need for undignified snatching of the transmitter away from the pupil, just a quiet 'OK I've got it now' and a potential disaster merely becomes a phase of learning. Don't be afraid to tell your instructor when you have had enough. It is quite a strain when you are concen-

...Success...

...and a happy 'dead-stick' landing.

trating very hard on the initial flights and there is no point in carrying on once you have reached that 'numb' stage.

And so you will carry on your training sessions. Try to get three or four flights per session or it will be long drawn out, until confidence gradually builds up. From flying around and practising straight and level, climbing and diving and turns in both directions you will advance to practising 'circuits and landings'. At this point you may well find a slowing up of the *apparent* rate of progress.

This is simply because you now have to coordinate all of your newly acquired skills and it is *only* when you get all of these 'movements' in the correct sequence and timing that your circuits, landings and take-offs become proficient. The moment will come when the instructor will decide that you are sufficiently qualified to go solo. Going solo means just that − you are on your own. No more asking your instructor to take over − if he hadn't already. You are the one, and only one, with the transmitter and you *must* be the one in charge of the model. It will *only* do what you command it to − or allow it to − and you must 'show' it that you are firmly, but gently, in charge of the situation at all times. Of course, it is still possible to thrust the transmitter into somebody's hand if the model gets temporarily out of control but it is essential that, having reached this stage of competence, you accept the responsibility that goes with it. There is no need to panic; the instructor has already proved to you that you can cope with any problem that you are likely to come across. It is a matter of keeping a cool head and remembering the lessons that you have been learning. By all means let your hair down a bit after your first solo!

With the excitement of the first solo over it will not take you long to realise that you are still far from being a *fully* proficient pilot and there is still an awful lot to learn and a lot of practice to be done. Never, in these early training days, simply go up for a flight around. Always fly with a posi-

tive purpose and aim to carry out some specific manoeuvres i.e., figure of eight, right hand circuit, simulated engine failure etc. More clubs are introducing training schedules and classes of flight proficiency. These are excellent schemes as they give a goal for the budding pilot to aim for *and* they give the club an indication of the proficiency of that member. Some clubs are fortunate in having more than one flying field but there may be restrictions on one field, because of the surroundings, and only members attaining certain flight level abilities would be able to use it.

When you have completed the basic stage of flying you will want to progress to a more advanced model and flying. Go back to your instructor and ask him to test fly the model for you − you won't have reached *that* stage yet − and to instruct you in basic aerobatic manoeuvres. From there on the limits of flying are your limits only, but remember, you *never* stop learning.

'Buddy-box' systems are ideal for training sessions and for first flights of a model when an experienced pilot is to carry out the initial trimming.

CHAPTER 14

Safety

It may seem peculiar to include a chapter regarding flight safety at this point in the book when flight testing has yet to be covered. I make no apologies for including a list of factors that may lead to an accident, or for the fact that many of these factors will be duplicated in the later chapter on flight testing. Any written word that can assist in preventing an accident is worthwhile and may also help to emphasise the dangers of flying at, over or too near to spectators. Do remember that even a low powered training model can produce very severe injuries if it hits a spectator at flying speed with the engine running; a fast aerobatic aircraft is a potentially lethal missile.

PILOT ERROR PLUS

During my training as a pilot in the RAF, part of my 'duties' was the reading of the monthly accident report bulletins which investigated in detail the various flying accidents. These reports examined the reasons and causes of the accidents and apportioned the responsibility. I can remember being rather incensed at the time that in the vast majority of cases, well over 90 per cent, the cause of the accident was attributed to pilot error. It seemed to me that the government officials who prepared these reports, when short of a satisfactory explanation, found it all too easy to simply blame it on to the poor, unfortunate pilot.

On sober reflection, over the years since then, I have come to the conclusion that, perhaps, the investigation branch of the RAF was not so far wrong after all. No one, including pilots, likes to admit he makes mistakes, particularly the ones that should be easily avoidable, but the truth is that the most fallible part of flying is the human factor. Certainly, the 'incidents' I was concerned with during my RAF services were all attributed to pilot error either due to inexperience or, I must shamefully admit, due to not following the correct

procedures and sometimes through sheer carelessness. Only one accident I can remember could be said to be positively beyond the control of the pilot.

By now you are probably wondering what on earth this has to do with radio control model flying! Well, what is true for full-size accidents is also true for models; the vast number of crashes are due to personal or pilot error. Admittedly, there are the occasions when the radio equipment will fail during a flight and the failure could in no way have been anticipated or forestalled. No radio equipment, regardless of cost or manufacture, is perfect, and must fail at some time. The exact moment it fails is largely a matter of luck, but we can take certain precautions to minimise the risks of it happening during flight. One of the obvious precautions is to ensure that the installation of the equipment in the model is as perfect as possible. Virtually all manufacturers of radio control equipment include in their instructions precise information regarding the methods of installation. They are written for your benefit, so follow them carefully. Should a set of equipment have a weak, and to the manufacturer, undetectable, component, there is likely to be a failure fairly quickly. It makes sense, therefore, to test the equipment thoroughly on the ground before fitting it in an aircraft and flying it. Do give a new set of gear a thorough check out before contemplating a flight test. Three or four complete cycles of operation, from full battery state to the time when the servos or actuators are no longer functioning reliably, should be sufficient to show any initial faults. It will also give you a good indication of the total operation time you can expect from a full battery charge. Simulate a servo load by tensioning the outputs with a rubber band or spring. Obviously the drain on the battery will be less under 'no load' conditions. Applying a load to servos may also help to indicate faults and weaknesses that may not be otherwise apparent. Consult the manufacturers' literature regarding outputs and apply about half the maximum load.

Back to the human error factor. For the purposes of considering some of the causes of accidents during flight I shall assume that the model itself has been accurately built, is suitable for its purpose and is correctly trimmed. The following list of pilot and/or assistants' errors is not comprehensive but should cover most of the causes of crashes.

1. Insufficient checking of equipment before launch or take-off.

Operate all control functions, with the engine running, and check that they operate in the correct sense, i.e. left rudder on the transmitter is left rudder on the model, etc. Check transmitter trims are set in the right positions. Again, it is assumed that the installation of the equipment and the linkages is 100 per cent satisfactory and that a range check has been carried out.

2. Interference.

Either from an outside source or from another modeller on the same frequency or an adjacent frequency with sufficient 'splatter' to cause interference.

In these days of plug-in crystals for transmitters and receivers, the risk of flying, or trying to fly, two models on the same frequency is greatly increased. It is easy to change the frequency of the outfit and forget to change the frequency pennant on the transmitter so a cursory check of the other transmitters being used is barely good enough. At the expense of receiving a few hurt looks it is worth asking the other modellers if their frequency pennant is correct.

A well-designed transmitter pennant bracket will assist in changing over frequency colours. The bracket should hold the colour ribbon firmly and should be easy to clip on and off the transmitter aerial and yet be secure on it.

Interference from outside sources is still a problem at some flying sites and may be more prevalent on one particular spot frequency. The best insurance is to have a monitor on the site to check out for interference, but remember that even this, situated at ground level, may not detect interference at flying heights.

3. Hand launch or take-off too slow or not into wind.

Without sufficient flying speed any model will stall and crash. A hand launch must be smooth, straight and level and at sufficient speed to give the model flying speed when it leaves the hand. Obviously, a model with a low wing loading and good slow flying characteristics will need less of a 'push' than a heavily loaded aerobatic type model. For rise-off-ground operation it is imperative to allow the model to have built up sufficient speed before trying to lift it off by the application of up elevator. Too soon and the model will lurch into the air, stagger, probably drop one wing and crash back into the ground. Launching or taking-off out of wind will cause the wing on the windward side to rise and cause the model to bank away from the wind. Unless our reactions are very quick and the model has sufficient reserve of speed, a crash is the inevitable outcome.

4. Engine failure after the take-off/hand launch.

Usually caused by setting the engine too lean. Check the engine for the correct needle valve setting by holding the model vertically, with the nose pointing upwards, before launching. If the engine starts to fade, open up the needle valve a little. Some motors are rather subject to cutting when the model is hand launched rather violently. These can be very difficult to cure but try experimenting with different fuel tank positions and various combinations of fuel and plugs for the engine. Changing to manifold pressure feed, where possible may also cure the trouble.

5. Over correction of the model after take-off.

For safe flying you need one of two factors, or better still both, height and speed. With plenty of height, the reserve of altitude can be converted into speed, or gliding distance should the engine cut. Conversely, with a reserve of speed the model can be pulled up from a close proximity to the ground without fear of the model stalling. When you are short of both ingredients you will probably also be fresh out of luck. This condition is most frequent immediately after launch/take-off and also again during landing. With the model just in the air it has had no time to build up a safety margin of speed and, unless it was launched off a cliff, it is also very close to the ground. Any sudden movements of the elevator or rudder/aileron will almost certainly result in an increase in drag and reduction in speed or loss of speed by climbing too quickly. Either way that loss of speed can result in disaster.

When flying near the public it is important always to keep yourself between the crowd and the model. This will ensure the model never flies over the public.

6. Inexperience.

That one word covers just about all the problems we are likely to come across in flying. It is also a title that can be applied to every R/C modeller because there is always another little problem waiting round the corner that we haven't come across before. However, to be more specific, one of the main 'inexperience' problems the new modeller is likely to come across is that of disorientation, i.e. being unsure of the model's relative position to the ground and to himself. Disorientation is a major factor contributing to crashed models. Perhaps, surprisingly, full-size pilots, when trying R/C model flying, seem to suffer from the problem just as much as any other type.

The other main factor, and it is related to disorientation, is allowing the model to drift too far downwind. When the model disappears in the distance it is difficult to tell which control is required and also the effect of the control when it is given. A model will obviously travel, groundwise, much faster downwind that it will upwind and the answer, therefore, is to concentrate on keeping the model upwind at all times until plenty of experience has been gained. When the model does get inadvertently downwind your first action should be to close the engine throttle, and try to regain directional control as soon as possible.

Over-correction of controls is another of the pitfalls designed to trap the inexperienced. A stable training model will virtually fly itself,

The use of a protective helmet is to be encouraged, particularly for pylon racing. It would also help to have some body protection.

requiring only minor corrections from the pilot. It is when it is over controlled that the problems occur. A steady turn is changed to a screaming spiral dive in the opposite direction by a fierce movement of the transmitter stick by the learner or a steady climb is suddenly changed to a vertical dive by a 'thumb breaking' push to the limits of

Take a good look around before your model is launched to see where the other modellers are situated.

the elevator stick. With the model gyrating around every conceivable axis the next phase of torment awaits the inexperienced — PANIC.

The obvious thing to do when the model is not responding in the manner that you consider any decent model should, is to close the throttle to give the model a chance to settle down and you a chance to do the same. Unfortunately, when panic sets in, anything can happen. Some pilots 'freeze' on the sticks and seem incapable of taking any action, others look round for the nearest person to thrust the transmitter at, but the ones that I admire (if that's the right word) are the ones who fight all the way down to the inevitable. They are not quite sure what they are doing, but if the transmitter was, instead, an electronic organ it would sound as if they are playing one of Bach's Toccata and Fugues with all the stops out.

Panic is one of the most difficult problems to help a modeller overcome, as he quite frequently does not realise the problems he is faced with. It requires a lot of patience from his tutor, who must be close at hand to give calm instructive advice until the learner has achieved the required stage of proficiency. He may still make mistakes and be unable to correct them, but providing he realises his mistakes, and the preventative action required, he is less likely to panic.

7. Landings.

Having launched the model safely into the air and flown it around we inevitably finish up with the problems of getting it down again, preferably in one piece. One of the chief causes of bad landings is the lack of a planned landing circuit. By executing a planned circuit, whether under power or on the glide, with a defined downwind and crosswind leg and final approach we can avoid those last-minute steep turns near the ground. Sudden movements near the ground, as with take-offs, frequently end in disaster and we must aim to have a steady straightforward approach to the landing point with only minor corrections and a shallow landing flare-out. This does not mean that you must go miles downwind to make your final approach, if you do, you will have those disorientation problems again. It means that you must make positive turns at the downwind and final approach points so that you are nicely lined up after the final turn. Watching model flyers carrying out these landing circuits I have constantly noticed a fault that many full-size pilots will immediately recognise — that of 'crabbing-in' on the downwind leg. This means that instead of flying your downwind leg parallel to the landing approach the tendency is to come in at an angle, virtually eliminating the crosswind leg, and leaving a very sharp turn on to the final approach. Another full-size practice that may be of assistance during the final approach, and providing you have throttle available, is that one should adjust the speed of the model by increasing or decreasing the dive angle and adjust the rate of descent, i.e. the distance to be covered, by use of throttle. Another common fault is to see a model coming in too high and the pilot push the stick forward to get the model down. This will only result in a build-up of

Never take your eyes from another pilot's model that 'sounds' as though it is in difficulties.

speed which will extend the glide, a better answer is to overshoot or to land the model further upwind, keeping on its original descent path.

The actual touchdown is something that will only improve with experience, but as a general rule, it is better to allow the model to settle on the ground from a steady descent rather than to over-control on the flare-out. Over-zealous use of the up elevator just before touchdown can result in a stall, a wing dropping and no effectual control left to correct it.

8. Over-confidence.

This is a stage at the opposite end of the scale to inexperience but no less dangerous. It is a phase that we nearly all go through. Only the very wise, well-balanced and intelligent modellers manage to avoid this stage. The over-confident stage follows on fairly quickly after reaching the proficient stage. From believing at one point that you will never be able to master 'these damned aeroplanes' one eventually realises that the model will do precisely what you command it to – or so you think! The radio equipment has never been working better and you feel so relaxed in your flying that there is a danger of you dropping off to sleep if

you just cruise the model around at altitude. Now is the time to do a few really low aerobatic manoeuvres; quite a few spectators on the field today – great – we'll show them just what R/C flying is all about. A nice low inverted run over the tops of their heads should impress them! Of course, you were not to know that the R/C gear was going to fail at that precise moment or that a fly would get into your eye then, or even that Fred would forget that you were flying on 'orange' and that it was not the right time for him to range-check his gear that was also on 'orange'! The lucky ones get over this phase with nothing more than a scare, with the model brushing the ground and the heart palpitating as it climbs to gain the safety of height. Maybe we were not quite the brilliant expert pilots that we thought we were!

9. Lack of concentration.

Lack of concentration problems usually occur between the learning and over-confident stages. We have probably reached the time when we can safely take the model off, fly it around and land it again and are generally feeling a little more relaxed about the whole thing. Time, in fact, as our model flies sedately around at a safe height, to have a

TV star Paul Daniels took to flying R/C models like the proverbial duck to water and was conscious of the safety element in using a dual control system.

look round to see what the other fellows are doing.

Having read through this chapter I am beginning to wonder how we ever get away with flying R/C models at all! Seriously though, I hope it will not put off prospective fliers and beginners, as I firmly believe that by recognising problems, we are more likely to overcome them.

CHAPTER 15

Field Equipment

With all the excitement of preparing for flying the model we must not overlook the preparation of the tools and spares that may be needed once we are at the flying field. Nothing is more annoying than arriving at the flying field and finding you have forgotten one vital piece of equipment.

Ideally one should have an inventory written out, and covered in clear polythene, pinned on the side of the field box. A quick check of the contents before you set off will ensure that you will be missing nothing, unless it is a major disaster on the flying field.

A well established and stocked field box is of primary importance.

Here are some of the items of equipment and tools *you* will require.

1. The *complete* model, transmitter, aerial and frequency flag.
2. Pliers, wire cutters, screwdrivers, plug spanner, adjustable spanner, small box spanners, small file, knife, razor blades, cement, five minute epoxy and cyanocrylate glue, cleaning rag or paper towels, detergent squeeze bottle (for cleaning down the model), nuts, bolts, washers, pins, thread and clips, pencil and paper (both sorts).
3. Clean fuel, fuel filling bottle, fuel 'squirt' primer bottle, fully charged battery, glow clip and cable with plug test facility built in, spare glow plugs, fuel tubing, alternative and spare propellers. Starter or finger stall guard.
4. Rubber bands, plasticine and lead for weight adjustment, aluminium sheet for trim tabs.
5. For simple models only − .8mm, .1mm and $\frac{1}{16}$ in. plywood packing for wing and tailplane incidence changes. Spare batteries for the receiver and transmitter.
6. If your club or group do not supply it, a small first aid tin should be carried. It only needs to

contain basic items sufficient to deal with cuts and abrasions etc.
7. You may also wish to allow room for carrying liquid refreshments − of any type you fancy.

Field boxes seem to come in two types, one being fairly small and compact and without the facility for resting the model on top for starting purposes. The other is a fairly large affair, not quite so elaborate and 'compartmented' but capable of being sat upon − not a consideration to be ignored − and for the model to be rested upon. An alternative to the purpose made field box are containers, designed for other purposes, that can be readily adapted to our use. The metal tool box, with the hinged lids and collapsible tool trays is an example. Another container that is most suitable for a field box is the 'baby box' designed to carry all the impedimenta required for nursing a young baby. These plastic boxes with metal carrying handles, have trays that open in a similar manner to that of a tool box and require little adaptation to our needs.

Ready made field boxes, complete with control panels, fuel pump and voltage reducers, are available (see the adverts in the model magazines) as are kits with all of the wood parts pre-cut.

FIELD BOX

Construction is, in fact, so simple that all that needs to be said is that all the plywood parts are pinned (1in. and ¾ in. panel pins) and glued together. PVA glue or one of the synthetic resin glues are perfectly satisfactory, but it is recommended that the whole of the unit is varnished or painted on completion. Here is an ideal way of using up those tins of 'thickened' fuel-proofer. When this is used instead of varnish, you can at least be sure that it will stand up to any leakage of fuel.

Naturally the model box can be made more

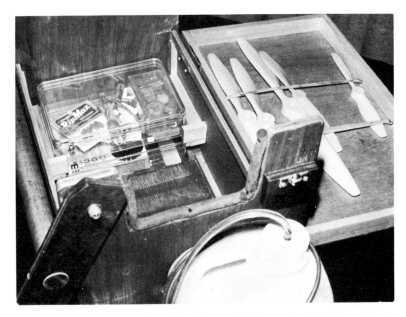

This field box is compact but strong enough to use for the occasional sit down.

sophisticated than is shown above with separate compartments for tools, fuel, etc. and a lid. Do not forget to add the plastic strip to the cut-outs in the end plates, they are ideal for supporting the model when it is being started.

CAR TRAILER FOR MODELS

The transportation of models always presents a number of problems. Judging from experience I would consider that virtually as much damage is done to models during transportation as during actual flying.

A good stock of blocks and sheets of foam plastic, to pack *all* around the model, will alleviate most of the damage and give the model a 'soft' ride in the vehicle. Keep heavy objects such as field boxes, accumulators, large fuel bottles etc. away from the model or, if they have to be in the vicinity, make sure they cannot move about or tip

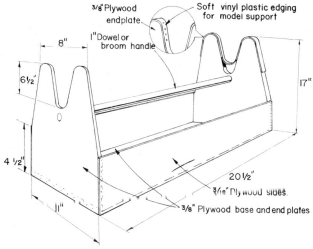

Drawing for a very simple field box.

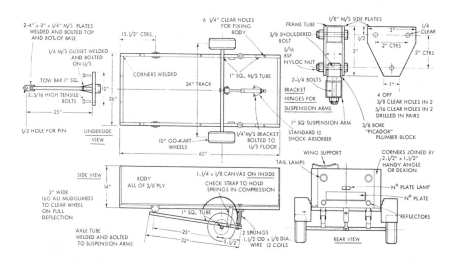

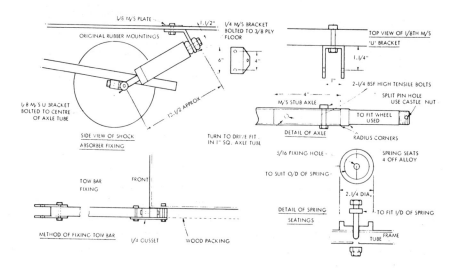

The photograph and the drawings (on facing page) show the ingenious small trailer which enables the builder to transport models and bits and pieces behind his open MG car.

Large vans can be equally useful!

over. For transporting large wings inside a car a useful tip is to have a length of light bungee cord stretched across the rear at the top of the window level. The bungee can be secured by tying the ends to picture rail hooks and fitting these hooks on to the rainwater channels outside the car. The bungee is then taken through the tops of the windows to the opposite side.

The biggest problem, however, remains the limited space available in the car. I am sure many modellers, particularly the married ones with families, will have that embarrassing problem of wanting to take both models and people to the flying field and have room only for one or the other in the car.

The trailer described here was designed to be

towed by an MG Midget car and is suitable for virtually any type of car. Sizes dimensioned on the drawings need not be followed faithfully, adjust them to suit your requirements within reason. Some of the dimensions, i.e. the plywood sides, are related to commercial sizes but they could be extended by making a suitable joint. The original trailer did not have a 'lid' to it but it would be a simple matter to make up and fit a top with a curved roof and hinged to the side of the trailer. A final word of warning, the trailer, probably because of the short distance from its wheels to the car's rear wheels, is very difficult to back accurately. On occasions it definitely goes in the direction it wants to regardless of what action you take; for this reason it is necessary to have a strong wife, girl friend or fellow modeller to 'hoick' the trailer around occasionally.

CHAPTER 16

Model Selection

In the chapter on the trainer model (Chapter 3) I emphasised the importance of having a positively stable model for the learning phase, also the civilised way of using a buddy-box system for dual control between the instructor and pupil. It doesn't automatically follow, once the pupil has gone solo, that the buddy-box will be of no further use. We may become proficient with flying a trainer-style model, but what about when we advance to other, more difficult to fly, model types. As we have seen from the chapter advising how we can extend our flying skills, there is very much more to this R/C hobby than taking-off, flying around and coming back into land. When we want to develop, build and fly more exotic types, we may be glad of a little assistance from a more qualified pilot – and out will come the buddy-box lead again. Never think that you are so experienced that you have nothing more to learn – if you do the gods will surely find you out and you will realise the truth of that old adage that 'gravity sucks'!

Before moving on to a brief look at some of the various aircraft configurations a further word regarding maiden flights might not come amiss. When we have spent many, many hours building and finishing a model we are the least ideal person to carry out the first test flight. We have been involved with the preparation of the model to such a high degree and know how much of ourselves has gone into the model that it is difficult to totally divorce ourselves from these memories and feelings. The maiden flight of any aeroplane calls for 100% focused concentration relating only to getting the model safely airborne, checking its flying qualities and returning it safely to the ground again. It is difficult, with our connections to the model, to be that single minded. It may be difficult, it might even hurt our pride a little, but it is probably worthwhile asking a proficient, calm and independent colleague to carry out that very first flight. You will also be able to watch your

model more objectively – it is very difficult to appreciate the actual look of the model when you are flying it yourself.

HIGH WING CABIN MODELS

High wing models normally feature good slow flying characteristics but may be more prone, when a flat-bottom wing section is used, to 'ballooning' when pulling out of a dive. Flat-bottom wings with a Clark Y type aerofoil create a lot of lift, hence the slow flight characteristics but, also, the excess of lift when the speed is built up as a result of a dive. When this concept is recognised it can be easily corrected by the application of down elevator and a reduction of throttle – it is a matter of anticipation and taking corrective action before the situation gets out of hand. High wing designs, with generous dihedral will not turn very well with the application of aileron alone; the dihedral is trying to counteract the banking control. If excessive amounts of aileron control are given this will probably only result in some adverse yaw, where the drag effects are greater than the lift and a yawing turn in the opposite direction to the control given, results. For such occasions it is necessary to introduce some rudder input, in the direction of the turn required, in addition to the aileron control. How much will depend on the model, but it can be introduced automatically with transmitters featuring aileron/rudder mixing – providing the degree of mix is variable and it is possible to operate the rudder independently of the ailerons i.e. the rudder comes in automatically when aileron control is given but the rudder can be moved without it bringing the aileron into operation.

When moving from sports R/C aeroplane designs to scale types the high wing monoplane is a good subject for a first scale design. It is generally not difficult to fly and will allow you to concentrate

High wing cabin models are still the most popular designs for training and sports flying.

Cabin models don't have to be slow and sluggish. The WOT 4 is quite a performer with a larger engine and ample control movements – or a 'pussycat' with less power and control movement.

on making a good job of the scale finish without sacrificing the flying characteristics.

PARASOL WING DESIGNS

These are essentially high wing cabin models with the cabin removed; the flying surfaces remain in the same relative positions, but the wing is supported by struts fitted to the fuselage and wing underside. Because the wing is in a clear airflow and does not suffer the drag interference of a join with the fuselage, it is an efficient layout. With modest amounts of dihedral it remains an easy model to fly, reasonably responsive to aileron control and a limited aerobatic potential. It also makes a good load carrier and is suited to photographic work, glider towing and use as a 'toffee bomber'.

Struttery is not difficult and can take the form of faired piano wire struts for small models, or bent flat dural plate for larger designs.

BIPLANES

We all have our favourite types of aeroplanes and I have to admit that biplanes are among my favourite aeroplanes. Some modellers would go so far as to say "unless it has two wings and a round cowl, it is not a true aeroplane", but that is a somewhat extreme view!

Visit a fly-in-style model meeting and you may be surprised at the high proportion of biplanes on view. Perhaps one of the reasons for the popularity of the 'double-deckers' is that they are not competitive types, if you discount the scale biplanes. They are mostly sports, or sports scale, types built and flown simply for the fun element and because they have a lot of character. Obviously, with the extra wing and the attendant struttery, there is more building to do with a biplane, but this doesn't deter the two-wing enthusiast. For the non-purist biplane lover it is possible to build a cabin model biplane, eliminating the centre section struts.

Flying characteristics of the biplane can encompass the advantages of the monoplane low and high wing designs. Because there is high drag the model can have higher power to size ratios and the additional wing area will provide a good speed range. The higher drag can be used to good effect, combined with the additional lift, for short take-offs and landings, making it suitable for small flying field work. The low aspect ratio wings and compact features of sports aerobatic models provide an exciting aerobatic performance, when allied to suitable wing sections and we only have to look at the full size 'Pitts' biplanes to realise why this is so. However, biplanes do not feature very often in the pure aerobatic competitions, only the large scale aerobatic contests.

In the final analysis, it is the 'character' of the biplane which makes it either loved or hated by the modeller.

SHOULDER WING MODELS

These represent the half-way position between the high wing and low wing types and the flying characteristics represent this intermediate situation. Less aerobatic than a low wing design, but more

Follow on from the solo phase on a high wing trainer — a simple low wing aileron trainer is a good choice.

Sailplanes (gliders) are not confined to slopes and can give good account of themselves when bungee-launched from flat fields.

stable, the shoulder, or mid-wing, model makes a suitable trainer for ab-initio (with a little help from a friend) or as a second model. With generous dihedral they can be flown without ailerons, but are generally more effective and enjoyable with a 'full-house', four-function radio system. Their layout also makes them good candidates for float plane and ski installations

LOW WING MODELS

The 'standard' layout for fully aerobatic and sports aerobatic models fitted with elevator, aileron, engine and rudder control. Except for some of the older designs they tend to be fast flying and manoeuvrable models with responsive controls and neutral stability (or only slight positive stability). With this arrangement it is necessary to fly the model i.e. be operating the controls, for most of the flight as the model will continue in the direction of the last control and will not right itself. Such models feature little wing dihedral and no, or near to no incidence on the wings or tailplane.

Whether or not you intend to go on to fly just sports models, scale, gliders or any other form of radio control aircraft it is important that the R/C trainee should, at some point, learn to fly one of these aerobatic type models. Until a pilot has learned to recover from every conceivable position a model can enter he cannot truly be said to have conquered flying and to be a 100% competent pilot. It may be vital, when flying a superbly built scale model, to recognise an insipient spin and how to recover from it. If your training has not reached these stages the results could be rather dire. When you are completely happy with a model inverted, carrying out snap rolls, spinning off the

top of a loop or performing a high speed stall, you will be a more relaxed flyer. You may still have the occasional 'whoopsy', but they will be fewer and you will probably be able to analyse the reason for the accident.

MULTI-ENGINED MODELS

At one time multi-engined models were feared and few modellers had the courage to build and fly these designs. That was at a time when radio equipment and engines were less reliable than they are today. Now, with the advantage of programmable computer transmitters, to automatically feed in rudder correction for varying throttle settings, gyro stabilising devices and electronic systems to co-ordinate the speeds of the engines, we have a much greater chance of continued success with multis.

Our main enemy with a multi-engined model is

Semi-scale biplanes, such as the 'Moth', are suitable for second or third models to build and fly.

the asymmetric thrust caused by the failure of an engine on one side only. If we consider a twin-engined model of, for example, a De Havilland 'Mosquito', here we have a design where the engines are reasonably outboard of the fuselage and a wing planform that has a fairly sharp taper towards the tip. This tells us two things, that there *will* be quite a strong yaw in the direction of a failed engine and that the stall is likely to be quite sharp and may be accompanied by a sudden wing drop. At least we are forewarned of the possible consequences of an engine failure and our first action must be to reduce the risks of one engine

Four-stroke engines are popular and team up well with light, open structure airframes.

stopping to an absolute minimum. If we can fit some type of gyro instrument to automatically feed in opposite rudder when an engine quits, this will also aid our chances of survival (the gyros will react much faster than we could by watching the model and then taking the corrective action). As far as the stall and potential wing drop is concerned, building in some washout (where the wing tip is at less positive incidence than the wing roof) will help to delay the onset of the stall and reduce the tendency for a wing drop.

If we were looking for a scale model with more gentle twin-engined characteristics we would find it hard to better the Consolidated 'Catalina' layout. With the high mounted parasol wing, a stable layout in its own right, and close-coupled engines we have the basis for a forgiving twin-engined design. Combine these features with generous wing and tailplane areas and modest dihedral and you have near ideal layout. In fact, the biggest problem with the 'Catalina' as a model relates to its performance as a flying boat. With a fairly short stubby nose it does not readily rise onto the planing hull to allow it to build up speed for a safe take-off.

You can, of course, go one better and build a model with the two engines on the same thrust line, similar to the Cessna 'Sky Master', push-pull

On to the slightly 'heavier' flying of aerobatic models. Start with a moderately powered model and restrict movements until you are familiar with the flying characteristics.

design. The sound of the two engines will still be thrilling but the twin effect will be lost to a large extent — the challenge factor will be missing. There is little doubt that the sound of multi-engined models contributes much to the enjoyment, the beat of two, or preferably four, four-stroke engines takes some beating. The sound of the two Laser 100 four-stroke engines in the Vickers Vimy (built by colleague Gerry Rathband) or the Zenoah 22 petrol engines on the De Havilland 'Comet' (the constructional work of David Toyer) never failed to give me a deep thrill when I was flying these designs of mine. For this reason the use of the 'obvious' power, electric motors, where it is most unlikely that you will suffer an engine failure, does not do justice to the concept of multi-engined models. But you may disagree!

Size of models, a subject mentioned at the end of the chapter, is important. I have built and enjoyed the challenge of small twin-engined R/C models but, for realistic and consistent flying it is really a case of the larger the better. Scale models in particular both perform better and look more impressive in the larger sizes and scales. A model of a Handley Page 'Halifax' will have a much greater 'feel good' factor with a wing span of 24 feet than it will with a span of eight feet, where it is impossible to fly at a scale speed.

ALL SHAPES AND LAYOUTS

The variety of aircraft models is almost infinite. In addition to the fixed-wing types we have rotary wing (helicopters and autogyros) flexi-wing (as in microlight aircraft) and — although I can only remember seeing one example — a rotary wing device where the wing rotated axially. Fixed-wing layouts include multi-wing types (triplanes and quadraplanes) canards (with the main wing at the rear and a foreplane) swept back and swept forward wings, 'T' tailplanes, 'V' tailplanes, tailless, flying wing etc. etc. And then we have the seaplane, flying boat, sailplanes, ski-planes, pylon racers and a great variety of engines to power these different classes.

In the first edition of this book I stated that if I spent the time until the year 2000 designing R/C models I would still be unable to include all the types, variations and permutations that were on my mental list of potential R/C models. Sadly,

that year will soon be upon us and my prophesy was only too true. I think I must add a further 25 years to that date and it will still prove to be an accurate forecast!

SIZE OF MODELS

Before moving onto the fascination of designing your own models a word about the size of R/C model aeroplanes. Earlier I commented that my ideal trainer would be quite a sizeable model and this philosophy would carry through to all types of models — were it not for the fact that I enjoy diversity and variety. So, I will build, or design (I never have time to build all the models I design) a giant scale model and my next venture will be a miniature indoor model.

Your choice of model size may be dictated by cost, space restrictions or flying site conditions, but there are a number of facts to be borne in mind when making a choice. Assuming that you are going to use standard radio-control equipment i.e. standard size servos, 600mAh battery etc, it should be remembered that this equipment will be the same weight irrespective of the type of model in which it is installed. Remembering, too, that we are generally looking for light wing loadings for pleasant flying it follows that the larger model,

What's good enough for the World champion should be good enough for you! Not difficult to fly — except with the precision of Hanno Prettner.

all other things being equal, will be able to disperse that R/C load over a larger wing area. Engines, too, do not increase in weight in direct relation to the capacity or power of the engine. A '60' sized engine will not weigh twice as much as a '30', but it may have twice the power.

Is there a price to pay for going larger? Only in one or two respects. The airframe and engine will cost you more and, once over certain sizes, the structure of the airframe will break away from conventional and traditional methods. However, for models up to about 8 feet (2.5m) wing span the standard built-up or veneered foam structures will probably suffice and the criteria then becomes storage, transport and flying facilities.

The choice is yours!

With the experience of a few different R/C types, you can branch out into the experimental designs – such as this small canard model.

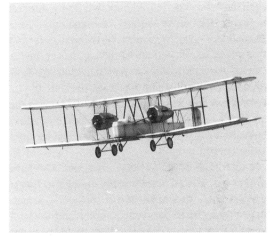

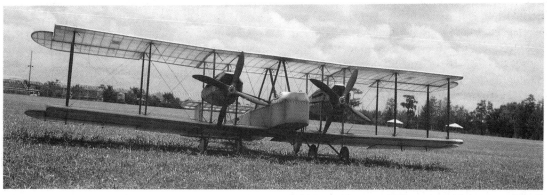

Although a 'large' model the Vickers Viny powered by two Laser 100 (16.5cc) engines, would dismantle and fit into a small family saloon.

CHAPTER 17

Small Field Flying

It is obviously desirable to have a large flying site with hard tarmac runways, or better still smooth close cropped grass, and no obstructions regardless of the take-off and landing direction. Disused airfields are absolutely ideal but, although there are still quite a few scattered around the country, very few are available to radio control modellers. Next on the list of desirable areas are large grass fields preferably without too many large trees in the immediate vicinity and preferably too without livestock in the field. Cows and bullocks are regrettably not house − or field − trained and even the most experienced pilot will find it difficult to avoid the 'obstructions' on landing. These animals are also by nature very inquisitive and you may take off, with all of the animals at the far end of the field, only to find that you are surrounded by them when you want to land. If you have to put down some distance away to avoid the creatures I advise you retrieve the model quickly, bullocks will try to eat most things and that includes radio control models.

Large grass fields, in many areas, are also hard to find but, should you be lucky enough to locate one ask the owner if he would consider you cutting a grass strip for your landing and take-off area. Perhaps your club or group could purchase a field for their own personal use. It may sound rather like a pipe dream but it has been done and purchasing land is always a good investment. Keep your eyes open in the local press and estate agents offices and if a suitable parcel of land is coming up for sale have a word with your bank manager and discuss the possibilities of obtaining a loan, repayments and sub-letting for cattle or sheep grazing. Where cattle are to share a flying field with you it is advisable to install an electric fence to protect the take-off/landing square.

There are many more average and small fields all over the country that are quite adequate for flying certain types of models from but are often overlooked by radio control enthusiasts. One of my ambitions, even before buying my first radio control outfit, was to be able to stand in the garden, launch the model over the fence and land it back on the lawn. This ambition was eventually achieved with a 32in. wing span model featuring single channel pulse proportional rudder control and powered by a half cc diesel engine. I did not make a habit of this adventure because I was lucky enough to have a small field just at the back of the house, but it did prove that it was a possibility. Flying from small areas must only be practised by experienced flyers; it is not going to help the learner if, on his landing approach, he is intimidated by the closeness of obstacles and the shortness of the landing area. When you have searched for and selected a possible site approach the owner and ask his permission to use it. Explain sensibly what our hobby is all about and offer to pay him for the use of the field. Should you be fortunate enough to be allowed to use the field, always treat it with the greatest respect; never leave litter around, never leave gates open. It may be necessary to discourage spectators to avoid too many people congesting a small area. Invite the owner along one fine afternoon to show him that you *are* a responsible group of people − let him have a 'twiddle' with the sticks to get him actively interested. With a field near to a built up area it is essential to use efficient silencers otherwise you will lose the use of the field pretty well as soon as you have got it. Be considerate to any neighbours and do not fly too early in the morning or late at night. If it is *anywhere* near the vicinity of a church do not fly during services. Generally these sites are not a substitute for the main flying field, they should be considered as an alternative to it and for limited flying only. As an alternative to the main field you must also make sure that it is not too close (minimum of 1½ miles) to ensure that there is no radio interference between the two.

The types of model that can be used from restricted sites are very variable, ranging from lightly-loaded powered sailplane variety to small faster flying aerobatic models. Of prime importance with this form of flying is having absolutely reliable radio equipment with no doubts as to the range or of obtaining the correct command required. Naturally, it is also advisable to check the model out, and to trim it correctly, at your normal flying site. Lastly always bear in mind the limitations of your own flying abilities; if you normally land the model about 200 yards away from you there is no point in attempting to fly from a field of, say, 150 yards by 250 yards – sooner or later you are going to hit something. I know one modeller who regularly puts his model in the boot of the car when taking his wife out to do the Saturday morning shopping. He drops his wife off at the shops, and carries on with his young son for an hour or so's pleasurable flying at some nearby sports field – much better than tramping around the stores!

The technique for flying from these mini flying sites is quickly learnt but does require some pre-planning for the safest results. Let us assume we have a field of 200 yards by 100 yards with the wind blowing towards the longest side of the field.

We will also assume that there are some obstructions around the perimeter of the field, i.e. hedges and trees. The launch should be made from point A (see diagram below), reasonably close to the rear and left-hand boundaries to give as much distance as possible for the model to climb before the left turn is made. Commence the turn at point B. The tightness of the turn will depend on the width of

the site and you should aim to complete the 180° turn with about 10 yards clear of the right-hand boundary on the downwind leg at point C.

Continue to make these 180° left-hand turns within the perimeter of the site until the model is clear of all adjacent obstructions; it can then be flown as from a normal flying field. The landing, as always, is the most difficult part of the flight and the result will, to a large extent depend on your ability to judge the height and rate of descent of the model. Obviously, a throttle equipped engine is an advantage in these conditions provided (a) the engine has a slow enough idle to obtain a reasonable rate of descent or (b), the throttle stops the engine completely. Procedure for the landing is very similar to the climb away of the model, only in reverse. When the model is descending to near the height of the surrounding obstacles, fly overhead of the site and carry out left-hand circuits. On the final landing circuit you may vary the position of your upwind 180° turn according to the height of the model with a view to putting it down at point E. Should you find that you are still short of height as you come along the downwind leg cut the corner of the final turn and come in towards the landing spot diagonally. Conversely, if you find you have too much height during the final turn keep the model turning left towards the centre of the field followed by a sharp right and left again to 'slip' off some of the unwanted height. The reason for aiming to land further upwind of the site than the launch area is to avoid carrying out the final turn too near the ground.

It is surprising how small field flying increases

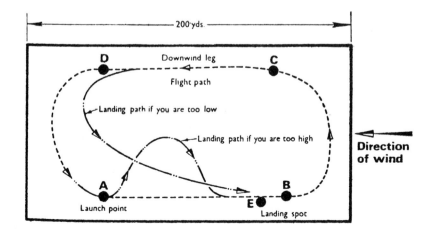

your flying accuracy (the larger the field the further away are your landings). This is largely brought about by having to plan your landing approach positively instead of aimlessly meandering around the sky followed by a 'dirty dart' for the ground. Part of the reason for the more accurate landing is probably also due to one's natural desire for safety of the model and, with the close proximity of obstructions, one concentrates harder on the flying.

Small scale models can be suitable for flying from confined sites providing they have light wing loadings.

CHAPTER 18

Gliders

Gliders are virtually a subject on their own and could fill another book explaining the various radio control techniques used to fly them. Indeed, there are specialist books on the subject and the modeller who is primarily interested in this branch of R/C modelling is advised to purchase one of these publications. As with powered models, there is a variety of models including sports designs, scale, aerobatic pylon racers and thermal soarers. It is impossible to detail all of these but I hope I can give you sufficient information to whet your appetite and that you will look further into this fascinating branch of the hobby. For the purpose of this chapter I shall divide the gliders into two classes, slope soaring and thermal soaring, and also tell you a little bit about the novelty of aerial towing, and air launches.

SLOPE SOARING

There are many areas in the British Isles highly suitable for the sport of slope soaring − from the highlands of Scotland to the southern downs and the Isle of Wight. One of the delights of slope soaring is that it is completely free from noise and smell and it gives an excellent opportunity for the family man to take his wife and children out to a pleasant spot and still manage to pursue his hobby. What could be more delightful than sitting on top of a hill, with a magnificent view all around, a warm breeze blowing and watching your pride and joy − the model that is − floating to and fro in front of you. I have heard some power R/C modellers say that there is no challenge in slope soaring − this is complete nonsense. Certainly on a good slope with a favourable wind blowing the model will have no difficulty in keeping up in the air − but nor will any powered model with the engine running. The art comes in when the conditions are marginal; then it is a real challenge to keep the model airborne − and very rewarding

when the other flyers are having to land and you are still airborne. Once you have satisfied yourself that you can fly, *and* land, a slope soarer proficiently then you have the opportunity to specialise on a particular aspect of slope soaring, i.e. aerobatic or scale models. Many slope soaring enthusiasts, however, never get to this stage as the fascination of just flying a sports model is sufficient satisfaction.

Slope soaring can be a good way of learning to fly a radio control model, providing you have a slope with good even lift and a model that is stable and forgiving. It may mean, in calmer conditions, that you have to occasionally land at the bottom of the hill but the exercise will do you good when you have to retrieve it and walk up the hill again. There are many suitable slope soaring model plans, and kits, available so, if you have a suitable slope near to your home, it may be worth considering it as an alternative method of learning R/C flying.

SLOPE REQUIREMENTS

Examine your local quarter inch to the mile map for suitable sites indicated by the closeness of the contours. It is possible to work out, if you are mathematically minded, from the map, the angle of the slope. We are looking for a slope that is somewhere in the region of 45° to 60°. You may get away with a little less but only under ideal wind conditions. When you have marked the possibilities, take a drive round and have a look at them. Some will be impossible because the tops are covered with trees and some may be ruled out because of inaccessibility. I remember taking a slope soarer with me on holiday to North Wales on one occasion, as I knew there would be plenty of hills about. The only suitable hills near our holiday area had the roads running right in the valley and to get to the top of the hills meant scampering up more than 1000 feet through heather and ferns. I eventually managed it on my own but never with the model as well. So, if you are the non-walking type of radio control modeller pick a site where the road runs over the top of the hill.

Illustrated below are some of the site features to look out for.

MODEL REQUIREMENTS

For a first model pick one that is easy to build, strong and stable. Do not go for too small a model, around about 6 foot wing span gives a model that is not too expensive to build, but can be strong enough to take the inevitable thumps. Whether conventional balsa and plywood construction, or fibreglass and foam is used does not matter — both can be made strong enough to withstand the knocks. The basic aerodynamics, considered earlier, apply equally to gliders as they do to powered models; obviously we cannot make take-offs, the glider is always hand launched, and the landing has to be carried out fairly precisely within a given area.

FLYING

Before flying the model straight off the slope, choose a suitable site for test gliding. This can be done from very much lower down the slope or it can be an entirely different site. The object of test gliding is to find out whether the model is correctly trimmed or not. Once you are satisfied with the general trim of the model, and the weather conditions are suitable, then is the time to proceed to the peak. Do not fly the model if the wind is more than 15° 'off' the ridge, or if the wind is blowing more than 20mph — not until you have more experience anyway. With the wind near to the maximum suggested speed, launch the model

from lower down the hill where the lift will be less. You may also find that, at high wind speeds, it is an advantage to add lead ballast under the C of G position; this increases the wing loading of the model and it has to fly faster to keep airborne, giving more effective penetration.

For first flights get a helper to give you a launch, making all the recommended radio and model checks first of course. Allow the model to fly straight out from the slope for a hundred feet or so, correcting with rudder if necessary. If the model tends to be nose high and blowing back towards the ridge feed in a little down elevator to build up the forward speed. In marginal conditions the model may fly out from the slope barely maintaining height. In these conditions it is necessary to 'tack' the model up and down, parallel with the slope to make the most of the standing wave lift. Never fly the model downwind towards the hill and make *all* turns away from the hill.

With the model flying away from you and climbing, keep it straight for a hundred yards or so — don't worry, it will not suddenly fall out of the sky when it gets away from the hill — and start to tack the model gradually back until it is behind you. Now you are ready for landing. The approach will vary considerably depending on the hill you are flying from. With a fairly narrow ridge, i.e. the downwind slope starts fairly soon behind you, there can be a strong downdraught immediately behind the pilot, and this must be watched out for. If you make your approach too high, don't worry — you can always fly out from the ridge again, gain height, and do another circuit. Initially, a gradual approach to landing, doing a few overshoots and coming lower each time, is preferable.

Slope soaring must be the cheapest form of radio control flying — no fuel, no batteries, no

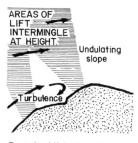

Remarks: Lift is always 'patchy'. Get model high, where lift areas intermingle—don't try low passes here.

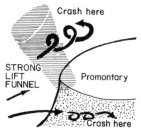

Remarks: Dangerous—if you risk it. Keep in figure eight turns all the time to keep in lift areas.

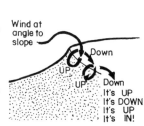

Remarks: Give up it's too hard. Move to another slope.

Something of the variety of models can be seen in this turnout for a slope soaring pylon event.

engine, no props − but is also one of the most exhilarating and, at times, demanding. Should you be lucky enough to have a site 'standing by' I certainly recommend it as a very pleasant pastime.

THERMAL SOARING

Although thermal soaring tends to be associated with competition events it is also a 'sports' event in its own right. There are many parts of the country where slope sites are unavailable, or too far distant to be a practical proposition, but there are plenty of flat sites. I feel that the attraction for this type of flying is the silence and cleanliness and this is understandable − not all modellers enjoy getting oily, or having their ears rent assunder by high revving engines. This being the case, it is not surprising that electric flight has tended to usurp the pure thermal soarer. The models are similar, many of the electric model designs being essentially a glider with an electric motor and propeller fitted on the nose. With the folding propeller neatly faired back onto the fuselage the model is, to all

intents and purposes a glider with ballast. The quiet operation is still there, but it is no longer necessary to reel out the tow line, or bungee, or to find someone to tow up the model. Also, the model can be flown in flat calm conditions, when it becomes impossible to tow up a glider.

There are, though, those modellers who prefer to stick with a simple glider system, no electric motors and no propellers.

Thermal soarers can be got to height by four different methods, tow-line, bungee, aero-tow or 'piggyback'. The bungee has the advantage that it can be a single handed system allowing the pilot to release the model and to control it as it climbs away. The disadvantage is that, of the four systems, it gives the least potential height from the launch. The 'bungee' portion of the system is from elastic cord from ¼ in. to ⅜ in. in diameter, depending on the models to be launched, to which is attached a length of nylon monofilament line. Silicone rubber may be used together with 40lb to 50lb breaking strain monofilament line about three times the length of the rubber. One soon gets the feel of how hard to pull back on the line before launching and to find the ultimate stretch for maximum launch height. If possible, the bungee and line should be held clear of the ground for the launch as the ground drag adds considerably to the feel of the stretch. However, the end of the bungee must be firmly secured, whether it is to a stake in the ground, fence post or car roof-rack.

Models used for bungee launching must be capable of withstanding the not inconsiderable initial surge when released, the fuselage must also be strong enough not to be crushed when pulling back against the resistance of the rubber. When launching, the model should be held with the nose at about 15 degrees high and the wings quite level. Avoid holding in too much up elevator at the moment of launch as the initial speed is high and the climb will be excessive, probably resulting in the model releasing from its hook. Elevator can be increased as the initial speed surge diminishes and, finally, a little down is given at the apex of the climb to release the ring on the line. A small parachute on the line, near to the ring, will help to keep the line tension and also allow the line to float downwind and avoid landing in a heap.

TOW-LINE LAUNCH METHODS

The simplest and oldest of the towing systems is hand towing. For this you will need the co-operation of a runner, or tower, since it is virtually impossible to tow the model with one hand, hold the transmitter with the other and look over your shoulder as you run along and gauge how fast to pull the model airborne. The runner has to decide how fast to run into wind to give a safe speed of climb for the model — too fast and the stresses on the glider may cause a structural failure of the wing. On some occasions, when the wind is very strong, it will be necessary for the runner to go towards the model to keep the climb rate reasonable. First, however, the model must be launched by the pilot. At an agreed signal the runner will move forward and the pilot will allow the slack to be taken up and then move forward and release the model. The desire to launch the model forward must be resisted, or it will free itself from the hook and it is also important not to release too nose-high. A good launch will result in the model ascending gradually, giving the pilot time to adjust

the hold of the transmitter and commence controlling the climb direction and angle. Once at the summit the model is released by slackening the line so that the hook will slip off the hook attached to the fuselage underside. Which all sounds very easy but may not be quite so straightforward in conditions of strong wind or a thermal. In these situations it may be necessary for the tower to run very fast downwind to slacken the line and, in sheer exasperation, the tower has been seen to throw the tow winch at the model in an effort to release the ring.

Two other forms of towing can be used, using a series of geared pulleys, or a power winch, but these are normally only employed in competitions — unless you are a member of a thermal glider only club and there are not too many of those about. Power launches are certainly effective, are one-man operation and save the legs, but they (and the batteries to power the winch) are heavy, have to be positioned and with the long line lengths used, take up quite a lot of space. What, at first glance, may seem to be a lazy man's way of getting a slope soarer airborne, can take quite a lot of effort. It is certainly not worth considering for a one-off operation.

TOW-LINE TECHNICALITIES

The siting of the hook on the glider or sailplane is quite important, as is the shape of the hook. With the hook too far rearwards the model becomes over-sensitive on directional control during the towing phase and, under extreme circumstances, will cause the model to arc right over to the ground. An over-forward mounting of the hook and height of launch will be lost due to the release being premature. A good starting point is to position the hook at about 25 degrees forward from the balance point under the wing (assuming a high mounted wing) and where this strikes the lower edge of the fuselage the hook is fixed on the centre underside. Because the exact location is rather 'hit and miss' and will only be found from experience, it is prudent to make provision for an adjustable hook position. Commercial moulded nylon hooks are available. They should be bolted to plywood on the fuselage underside, with a series of holes drilled to allow for adjusting the hook location. Alternatively a hook can be made

Another gliding scene with thermals clearly to be had. Towline launching will be used on terrain such as this.

from piano wire (12 swg to 16 swg, depending on the model size) and this can be shaped so that there is a slight upward curve for the final inch or so — this will help to avoid premature releases. There are also hooks available with positive locks, operated by a separate servo, but these are best avoided by the sports flyer where it might be necessary to make a rapid model release from the line to avoid a crash. The reactions may not be sufficiently quick to operate the switch to release the hook.

For the tow-line itself we require the line, a hook, a pennant or small parachute and a hand winch. Taking the last item first, the winch is to allow the line to be reeled in as soon as the model is released, to prevent it getting tangled as it lands, or tripped on by another modeller. Remember, the nylon monofilament line is almost invisible and it should not be left out on the ground between flights. The hand winch can be bought as a purpose-made modellers' item, or it can be made from a small hand drill or grinder. Naturally, it needs to be geared and a ratio of 5:1 or 6:1 is

suitable. A drum for the line is fitted to the geared output, this can be made from plywood or aluminium. Naturally, some of the commercial winches are more sophisticated, but our interest is only in being able to play out and wind in the line without it being tangled or broken.

Our pennant or chute will show us where the tow-line has landed and will help to take it down-wind rather than fall in a heap; by reducing the descent speed it also gives a chance for the operator to wind in the line before it reaches the ground. The pennant/chute serves one other purpose, by adding to the drag at the top of the line it helps to ensure a clean release of the hook from the model. Nothing very special is required for the hook, a curtain ring of about ½in. diameter will suffice and it is helpful to incorporate a small fishing swivel between the ring and the pennant/chute (which should be made of lightweight nylon) so that the tow-line does not form into loops. I am sure that we have all experienced nylon line, and other materials, forming loops as it is unrolled, the swivel will help to prevent this by eliminating the twist in the line.

Nylon monofilament fishing line is used for the tow-line and there is a temptation to go for the high breaking strain type, on the assumption that it will be suitable for any size of model and will not easily break. This is wrong as the tow-line weight and drag is counter productive to achieving maximum height in a tow. Take a look — if you can see it — at a long, heavy tow line and you will notice a very considerable 'bow' in the line caused by the drag. Unless the lift from the glider is sufficient to overcome that drag the model will not reach its maximum potential height. For average sized gliders a nylon line of 20lb to 35lb should be quite adequate; for a 6lb model you are going to have to pull around 6g to break the higher strength line! Tying knots in nylon line requires practice, if you are unsure of the types of knots to use, ask a fisherman for advice.

Towing — and the control of the model on the tow — needs understanding between the pilot and the runner. There is no more terrifying sight than seeing the tower tearing hell-bent into wind and the model climbing at an horrific angle, wings flexing and the end very near. The tower must constantly look at the glider and judge the speed of the ascent head directly into wind and the pilot must do all he can to make the climb as smooth and straight as possible. It must be decided beforehand whether the responsibility for the release is to be the tower, by making the line slack, or the pilot, by diving the model. In strong lift conditions it may require the combined efforts.

THERMALS

When giving talks to groups of young people one of my favourite 'catch' questions used to be "What makes an aeroplane fly"? The answer would often be that the propeller was pulling the aeroplane, or that the jet engine was pushing it through the air. My follow-up question would then be "But how does a glider manage to fly then"? This was normally greeted by silence. In still air a glider has a limited time to be airborne depending on the height above ground, the efficiency of the model and the skill of the pilot. We aim to fly the glider at its minimum rate of sink to achieve a maximum flight time and this will depend on the best combination of speed and

glide path. However, we rarely fly in absolute still air conditions and we will be hoping to 'hook' one of these magical thermals to keep our model aloft for longer periods.

Due to solar radiation during the day the ground becomes heated and, in turn this heats the air in the vicinity. This heated air will rise, as a large bubble, into the atmosphere and if we can position our glider in this column, or bubble, of rising warm air, the glider will also ascend (again, depending on the efficiency of the glider and the strength of the thermal). Unfortunately, thermals are invisible to the naked eye so how are we going to locate them, bearing in mind that for every rising current of air there must be a descending one (or all of our air would disappear upwards!)? Well, we know that certain features will 'trigger off' a thermal, such as a road, or spinney, or factory roof, so we can fly the model in those regions. We also know that birds are good at finding and making use of thermals and they can be seen whirling and turning in a thermal, gaining height all the time. Without having these pointers towards the thermal we must fly steadily around watching the model very carefully for any suggestion of it rising or, more likely, seeing its flight disturbed slightly with the wings being wobbled about. At these signs the model should be banked into a reasonably tight turn and observed to see if it continues to gain height. Thermals will drift with the wind and we mustn't become so engrossed that the model gets so far downwind that we can't get it back. Thermal soaring certainly offers plenty of challenges and only experience will help you to make most use of these, sometimes frustrating, invisible bubbles of rising air on which we can 'hitch' a free ride.

Competition flying is very strong with thermal soaring enthusiasts and each country has associations to organise the contests. The tasks include a combination of duration, speed and spot landing and the models — and launch gear — become highly sophisticated.

Competitions are popular, too, for slope soarers and these take the form of cross-country contests, aerobatics and pylon racing. Scale models have become much more popular on the slope, with PSS (power slope soarers) and with scale sailplanes representing full-size aeroplanes, particularly jets, leading the way.

AERIAL GLIDER TOWING

Not all radio control enthusiasts are fortunate enough to have a suitable slope soaring site within easy reach of them and perhaps the more special-ised form of thermal soaring does not appeal to them. An alternative launch method is to tow the glider, behind a powered model, by a towline. The traditional method of towing the glider up on a line may be fine for the fit and healthy, for 'old uns' it represents sheer hard work. Bungee launches seem to work quite well but are limited in the height that can be obtained with a glider without risk of using an over-powerful bungee and too high initial rate of climb and control problems. Power-assisted gliders I have always enjoyed, and these can represent a good compromise between a glider and power model. However, they may not suit the purist to whom the glider must have no auxiliary form of power.

Glider towing by tug aircraft is an accepted method for full-size aircraft and is used increas-ingly compared with powered winch tows. It is true, though, that aerial towing with full-size air-craft has certain advantages over radio controlled models.

For one thing the glider pilot can position him-self exactly where he wants to be relative to the tug aircraft. This is more difficult to achieve with a model as there is always one 'dimension' that is difficult to assess, depending on the attitude of the models. The full-size glider pilot will keep slightly lower than the tug aircraft to allow the tug to adjust his climb to the most efficient rate of climb. To fly the glider considerably higher than the tug can be dangerous as this will tend to lift the tail of the tug and force it into a dive – not to be recommended near the ground.

The glider, providing it is anything but a primary trainer, will be fitted with air brakes and these can be useful to prevent the towline from becoming slack by reducing the speed of the glider (increase of drag) without affecting the attitude of it. If that sounds rather complicated it simply means that, should the glider start to catch up on the tug, it can put its brakes on and slow down.

SUMMARY OF REQUIREMENTS AND TECHNIQUES

1. Compatibility of models. It is difficult to be dictatorial with regard to suitability of models and some experiment will be necessary. The tug aircraft should have ample power and a good speed range, i.e. between stalling speed and maximum speed. A reasonably large glider seems to be indicated and should not have excessive dihedral. Experimentation with air brakes may prove to be very rewarding. Colours and decoration of the models is not important as at the higher altitudes, they will only appear as dark silhouettes.

2. Compatibility of radio outfits. Test the radio outfits together carefully before committing to flight.

3. Check the operation of the release mechanisms thoroughly, both with and without towline tension.

4. A towline length of 140–150ft, works well but different lengths down to 100ft can be tried. Tie a brightly coloured piece of nylon cloth to the 'glider' end of the tow rope so that it shows up well if an emergency release is necessary. 'Non' stretch twine or cord is preferable to monofilament fishing line.

5. Get familiar with the launch technique and make sure the models are correctly trimmed before towing. As soon as the glider is safely airborne the glider pilot should move up to the tug pilot so that normal conversation is possible.

6. Do not over-control with either model; if you get into a position where gross control is essential it is probably better to release and start again.

7. Fly steady left- or right-hand wide circuits and, if the glider is sufficiently stable, leave it to fly itself. Try to avoid a slack towline.

8. The glider is normally released first, warning the tug pilot beforehand, but in an emergency either plane should release – quick reactions are important. It is not recommended that you land the tug with the line attached in case the line snags on some obstruction during the landing approach.

'PIGGYBACK' COMPOSITE

Yet another method of getting a glider airborne is to 'piggyback' it on a large powered model. The idea of composite 'piggyback' or ('pick-a-back' as they were called) aircraft is far from new. Many

Basic release mechanism

Towline release mechanism on 'Tug' aircraft should be on balance point.

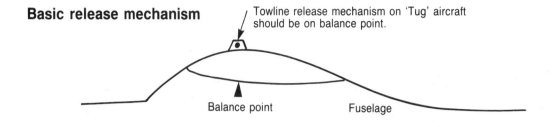

Balance point   Fuselage

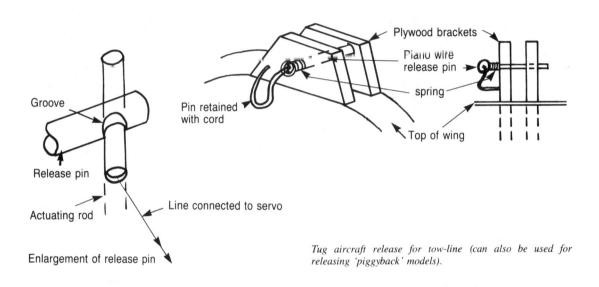

Groove

Release pin

Actuating rod

Enlargement of release pin

Pin retained with cord

Plywood brackets

Piano wire release pin

spring

Top of wing

Line connected to servo

Tug aircraft release for tow-line (can also be used for releasing 'piggyback' models).

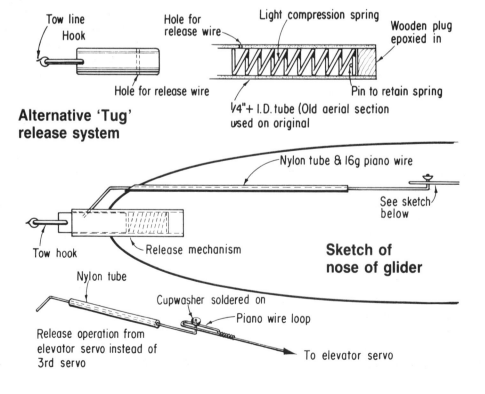

Tow line Hook

Hole for release wire

Light compression spring

Wooden plug epoxied in

Hole for release wire

Pin to retain spring

Alternative 'Tug' release system

¼"+ I.D. tube (Old aerial section used on original

Nylon tube & 16g piano wire

See sketch below

Tow hook

Release mechanism

Sketch of nose of glider

Nylon tube

Cupwasher soldered on

Piano wire loop

Release operation from elevator servo instead of 3rd servo

To elevator servo

'Piggyback' is a convenient method of obtaining a high launch with a glider.

modellers will be familiar with the Short-Mayo combination of 1938 in which the four-engine light aircraft Mercury took off from the back of the flying boat Maia. A composite full-size aircraft arrangement was first successfully flown as long ago as 1916 when a Bristol Scout was carried on a three-engine Porte flying boat. The principal reason for developing the Mayo composite was to enable the machine being carried to hold a greater load than would be feasible if it had to lift off the ground or water under its own power. Due to the development of long range anti-submarine patrol aircraft, in the first instance, and freight aeroplanes capable of carrying heavy loads, in the case of the Mayo, neither experiment was developed into commercial aircraft.

Model aircraft composites are far from new also, dating back about forty years, when rubber models were successfully flown. Methods of release varied from tensioned thread holding the parasite model to the carrier (touch paper attached to the thread released the model by burning through the thread), to release mechanisms relying on the tension reducing on the rubber motor of the carrier. The introduction of radio control for model aircraft made the operation of composites much more practical. Releases can be made as and when required and both models are, of course, fully controllable throughout the whole flight. A number

of combinations of models have been tried throughout the world, but most have featured gliders as the parasite aircraft. My first effort was a somewhat ambitious affair consisting of Mighty Barnstormer of some 90in. wing span carrying two parasite powered models, of 32in. wing span, under the wings. The carrier aircraft was fitted with a Super Tigre 60 engine and five function radio was installed — the fifth function being for releasing the two parasites. During the take-off, and flight before release, the .09 Enya engines of the small models were kept at about one third power and only opened up after release. Somewhat to our surprise the whole system worked, with no hitches, and many successful demonstrations were given before the arrangement was discontinued (the biggest disadvantage with this composite was that it tied up three sets of radio equipment). When thinking of new ideas David Toyer and I decided to have a go at a 'piggyback' composite with a conventional glider on top — I was designing an intermediate glider in any case and this seemed a good way of getting it to height for test flying. Because of a fondness for the Super Sixty model, an enlarged version of this design was used as the basis for the carrier aircraft. The one and a half times Super 60 gave us a model with a wing span of 95in. and, because of the additional load of the glider, an O.S. 80 was used for power. No ailerons are used on the model and therefore, four function radio is quite adequate for the flying and release mechanism. Construction of the Maxi Super follows, very much, the construction of the original, with wood sizes increased accordingly. Nylon covering was used for the whole of the model, the only 'beefing up' carried out was the addition of wing struts and I doubt, on reflection, that these were strictly necessary. The Tern glider – or does sailplane sound better – is also fairly conventional in appearance and construction with rudder and elevator control.

The O.S. 80 pulls the composite along without any difficulty and I suspect that a 'hot' 61 would be perfectly adequate too. Altitudes of up to one thousand feet can be achieved in a few minutes with the larger motor giving a flight time for the glider, after release, of nine to ten minutes. Most of our flights were of shorter duration as they were purely for demonstration purposes; a low fly past would normally be undertaken to give the public a chance to see the relationship of the two models. No malfunctions occurred with the release system although the separation was sometimes delayed for a few seconds, possibly as a result of applying too much differential elevator movement between the two models and applying too much pressure to the release pin.

Construction of the release mechanism, and cradle arrangements for the glider, is very simple and could be adapted to suit most gliders. We used a retract servo for operating the release as this type of servo is geared to give greater thrust at slower transit speeds. Speed, relative to normal control operations, is not required for these purposes and the additional 'pulling' power is useful. A standard servo would probably work satisfactorily providing the release mechanism is smooth in operation and the glider not too large. It would also be important to aim to keep the glider in neutral elevator trim when operating the release servo. When not in use as a 'mother' aircraft the cradle attachments are quickly removable from the model for normal flying.

Large models, such as the 100 inch wing span Centurion *shown here, are very suitable as glider tug aircraft.*

CHAPTER 19

Fun Flying

All types of radio control flying should be fun —
when you stop enjoying flying it must be time to
pack up and start another pastime. When you have
gone through all of the stages of learning to fly,
flying sports models and aerobatic types, you may
be looking for an extra dimension of fun to add to
your flying.

Three types of parachute release are illustrated.
Call them gimmicks if you like but they are, for
all that, a lot of fun to make and operate. The first
system does not rely on any radio function at all
and only costs a few coppers to make.

First make the snuffer tube from an empty tin
can and contact cement this to the side of fuselage
as near to the C of G as possible. Then drill holes
and insert a piece of ⅛in. dowel through the
fuselage as shown in Fig. 1. Make a parachute,
about the size of a gent's handkerchief from nylon
or silk, with one string (I used control line nylon
thread) to each corner and weighted with a small
piece of lead, or better still, a lead toy soldier.

Roll the parachute up as small as possible and
attach to underside of the fuselage restrained with
a thin rubber band. Place a small length of D/T
fuse in the snuffer tube and underneath the rubber
band. (See Fig. 1.)

Just before launching the model, light the fuse.
After the launching gain height and keep up wind.

The second system is for low-wing multi-
models and operates off the engine throttle servo.
The diagrams should be self-explanatory for this
device. (See Fig. 2.)

In the third method, used on a 'Barnstormer'
model, the release mechanism can be used for
dropping objects other than parachutes, including
small chuck gliders, and the aileron servo is used
for actuation in this case. Although the Barnstormer
is a parasol wing design there is no reason why
this method should not be used on a low-wing
multi-model or, with a little modification on a
shoulder wing model; the one proviso is that full

application of aileron control is not used during
normal flight until release is required.

The drawings (see Fig. 3) showing the arrangement used should be self-explanatory, but a few
points should be watched. Because of the limited
amount of servo travel available it is necessary to
cut the length of piano wire accurately to ensure
that the bomb or parachute falls freely without
fouling the wire. Movement of the linkage to the
aileron servo should always be free without undue
strain on the servo. This particularly applies when
parachutes are fitted and there may be a considerable pressure applied between the wire and the
Mylar bracket. Mylar or nylon is recommended
for the bracket rather than brass or dural, to avoid
metal to metal connection which may cause
receiver interference.

The plastic cap bomb and the parachutist can
readily be obtained from toy shops and cost only
a few pennies each. For a more exotic and realistic
parachutist one could use the excellent Action
Man parachute, but this should only be used on
the largest models as it is quite big. Modification

Fig. 1

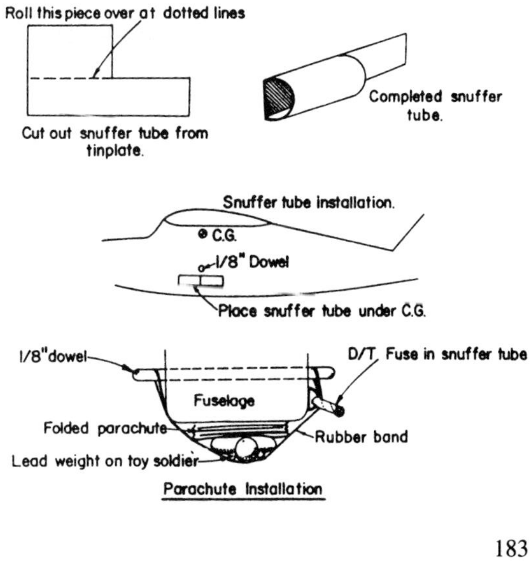

Parachute Installation

Fig. 2   PARACHUTE INSTALLATION FOR LOW WING MODELS

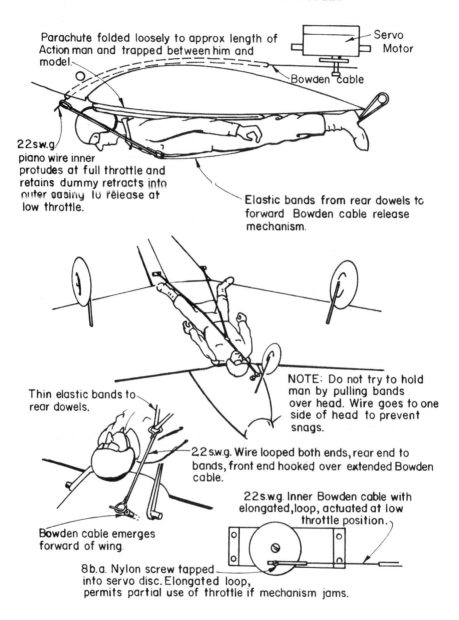

Parachute folded loosely to approx length of Action man and trapped between him and model.

Servo Motor

Bowden cable

22 sw.g. piano wire inner protudes at full throttle and retains dummy retracts into outer casing to release at low throttle.

Elastic bands from rear dowels to forward Bowden cable release mechanism.

Thin elastic bands to rear dowels.

NOTE: Do not try to hold man by pulling bands over head. Wire goes to one side of head to prevent snags.

22 s.w.g. Wire looped both ends, rear end to bands, front end hooked over extended Bowden cable.

22 s.w.g. Inner Bowden cable with elongated, loop, actuated at low throttle position.

Bowden cable emerges forward of wing.

8 b.a. Nylon screw tapped into servo disc. Elongated loop, permits partial use of throttle if mechanism jams.

of the cap bomb should be made as, flying over grass, there would be no chance of it exploding. If you fly over tarmac runways the exploding mechanism could be retained. The interior of the body was fitted with a balsa plug to give a better key for the Mylar bracket. Make a narrow slit in the case of the bomb with a sharp thin bladed knife and epoxy the bracket into position; for further security a steel pin can be pushed through the case and bracket. A more effective bomb could be made by using a .22 calibre blank for the 'warhead' and a simple percussion pin arrangement to detonate it on impact. By incorporating a whistle into the bomb one could guarantee respect and attention from fellow modellers. As an alternative to conventional bombs, flour bombs can be used. These are simply paper bags filled with a few ounces of flour and they have a much greater visual effect on impact. Why not organise a bombing competition in your club? It will make a

Fig. 3

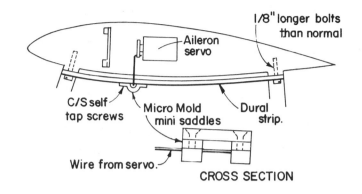

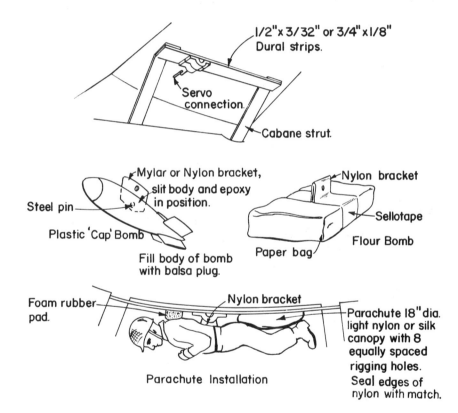

change from the aerobatic and spot landing competitions. You will be surprised at the accuracy obtainable after a little practice.

The parachutist is attached to the aircraft in a similar way to the bomb with a small Mylar or nylon bracket. Dropping of the parachute or bombs is achieved by a rapid movement of the aileron stick in the required direction. To drop one from each wing a quick movement of the stick from one extreme to the other and back to neutral will barely alter the flying attitude of the Barnstormer. By luck, or was it good judgement, the parachutist we used had a knees bent attitude that gave a suitable space between the legs and the wing for stowing the parachute. It was feared initially that the parachute might have deployed during normal flight but this didn't prove to be the case. By compressing the 'chute' slightly between the wing and the 'man' a clean release is achieved and gives the best chance of the parachute deploying.

Incidentally, we changed the small inferior poly-thene canopy for a larger, and more colourful, lightweight nylon one. Nylon of about 1−1½oz./sq.yd is about right, alternatively close weave silk could be used. Refinements on the parachute theme can be achieved by incorporating a small clockwork timer to the parachutist to release the canopy. The procedure would then be to drop the parachutist 'free fall' with a static line to activate the timer device. This would take the form of a small wooden wedge attached to the strut with a nylon line; as the parachutist falls the wedge is pulled out from the timer and starts it operating. Following the timed delay the parachute opens. Obviously the timed delay must be calculated in conjunction with the height of release. Another variable that must be allowed for is the velocity of the wind, it is surprising how much drift there is even in a light breeze.

PHOTOGRAPHY

Aerial photography, using still and video cameras, is not only possible but simple to achieve and the results can be surprisingly good − the system has been used semi-commercially. The model selected must be capable of coping with the pay load to be attached and this will depend on the type of camera to be fitted. Good results will only be obtained if we can defeat two enemies, vibra-tion and oil contamination. The latter problem can be overcome by extending the engine exhaust past the camera position, fitting the camera where it is

well away from any exhaust effluence or by using a pusher engine behind the camera. Avoiding vibration is easier than trying to cure it and for this reason, gliders and electric powered models are suitable for camera work − providing they can carry the additional load. With the conven-tionally powered aircraft it is always possible to climb to height and then cut the engine before commencing the photographic session. Whether vibration from the engine will be sufficient to affect the clarity and quality of the photographs or video film will depend on many factors.

1. The amount of vibration produced by the engine − use one with known low levels of vibration, make sure that the propeller is well balanced and operates in the rpm band that gives the lowest levels of vibration. A simple check for vibration is to operate the engine through the full speed range and place a finger on the tip of the fin to compare the levels at various engine speeds.
2. The amount of vibration transmitted to the fuselage − using an insulated engine mount or, for larger engines, commercial shock absorbers, will greatly assist in minimising the amount of vibration being passed from the engine to the airframe.
3. The position of the camera relative to the engine, the greater the distance between these two items the less chance of vibration bridging the gap.
4. Speed of camera shutter (still camera). The

A 'Carrier deck' competition can be a great fun event and easy for a club to organise. Models are fitted with arrester hooks to contact weighted lines laid at intervals across the landing area.

This Barnstormer 63 *was fitted with electrically fired rockets. Great caution must be taken when firing rockets from models to ensure there is no risk to surrounding property or persons.*

An ambitious attempt to drop two radio control 'parasite' models from a Mighty Barnstormer *mother aircraft. Despite the ambitious nature of the project it proved to be entirely practical and many demonstrations were given with this threesome (see also Chapter 18).*

faster the shutter speed the less the effects of any vibration that will show on the film. Available light, the type of film used (use the fast speed film) and the camera shutter speeds incorporated in the camera will all influence this decision.

5. The quality of camera insulation included in the installation in the model. Experimenting with insulation of different standards of resilience is the only way of finding the optimum arrangement. A fully floating system (suspended by heavy rubber bands) may be tried, or packing the camera in foam.

Having made it all sound very technical I must admit that some of our best results have come from fitting a cheap Kodak Super 8 camera, simply banded onto a pad of high density foam, onto a number of models without taking any additional precautions.

Still cameras should be of the automatic rewind type, or motorised so that the servo (operated by an auxiliary transmitter function) only has to trigger the shutter button. It does not require too much imagination to devise a simple switching device operated by a cam cut into a servo output disc, for example.

Video cameras give even less to worry about in the way of control settings, a fixed focus camera is quite satisfactory for aerial work. You will not believe the frenetic quality of the take-offs and landings until you see them from a pilot's eye view! Cameras can be mounted to face straight ahead, straight down or obliquely. If possible arrange for the installation of the camera to use all of these attitudes.

Do remember that there is always the risk of crashing the model, particularly when doing some low flying around trees and hedges to create 'atmosphere' on the film. On one occasion, when we were attempting to get some air to air shots of models, I pressed home an attack on the camera aircraft all too enthusiastically — the results were quite spectacular.

Many other forms of fun 'gimmicks' can be tried — the computer tape edges (pulled away from continuous sheets of computer paper) make excellent streamers. These can be obtained in enormous lengths and when attached to a sports model can extend so far that it is possible to produce a loop of paper and fly through it — magically it never seems to tie into a knot. You can try egg dropping by making a small cradle for the egg which is released to drop the egg. Using a normal raw egg it is possible, with the correct height and speed, to drop the egg and watch it bounce to a standstill without breaking. How is it done? It's all to do with the fact that the egg rotates as it drops and the shape of the eggshell is a very strong form.

Simple competitions are easy to organise in a club and the skill element can be adjusted according to the competence of the pilots. Easiest of all is the nominated time and spot landing where the contestant has to declare a time and land, after cutting the engine at least 30 seconds earlier, as near to that time as possible. He must also bring the model to a standstill as near to a marked spot as possible. The usual marking system is to allow one point for every foot away from the spot and one point for every second early or late. The flyer with the lowest score wins.

Competitions based on timed climbs, followed by tasks, are also easy to organise. Allow, say, a 40-second climb time, when the engine must then be cut, and aim for the maximum glide time. Alternatively, climb for height and then see the maximum number of spins that can be achieved before the nerve breaks and you recover straight and level flight. Limbo is another popular club competition, where the model must be flown under a streamer held between two poles — the most passes in a given time wins. If you want to add spice

Combat models can be flying wing types or semi-scale WW2 types where mock dogfights (with streamers attached) can provide great fun and excitement.

you can give double points for inverted passes!

More serious combat requires aerobatic models and consistent streamer lengths, plus a few ground rules, to make for a good competition — but it is worth the effort.

Although these are fun events they do serve another purpose: they will improve your flying skills because, in effect, you are carrying out specific training exercises. To fly aimlessly around the sky and then, as the fuel is used up, come into land will not improve your flying. Always plan some specific manoeuvres during any flight, whether it is aerobatics touch and goes or accurate figures of eight. The more precise your flying the more satisfying it will be.

One word of warning about competitions, even the most simple types. They can bring out the best in some modellers, by sharpening their skills and encouraging them to attempt manoeuvres they would not otherwise consider. On the other hand they can bring out the worst of characteristics in other flyers. I have seen mature men, reasonably experienced and steady, calm pilots, when confronted with a spot landing competition go completely bananas! They might find themselves high on the approach to the spot and instead of thinking 'it's only a game' they are transformed into a 'must win at all costs' mentality and push full down elevator in, to virtually crash onto the spot. If competition gets you that way, stick with normal flying.

CHAPTER 20

Floats and Skis

FLOATPLANES

There can be few areas in Great Britain that are more than a few miles away from reasonably sized stretches of water, and yet the fact remains that these possible flying sites have so far been ignored by the radio control flying fraternity. Even with the complaints of overcrowded flying fields, few modellers have 'taken the plunge' into the deserted waters.

Why? — I don't know, but I can promise that for anyone who is prepared to convert their old land-based 'bus' to float work there are some wonderful experiences in store. The sight of the model taxi-ing out and then, as you open up the engine, rising up on to the rear step; and on to the front step as speed builds up with the twin wakes getting smaller; finally — the moment when she actually breaks away and points her nose skywards is really exhilarating. Landings can be equally exciting and the satisfaction of skimming the model on to the water and barely disturbing the surface is ample reward for the work involved. Naturally, as with most worthwhile undertakings, a little patience and practice will be required to achieve the best results. It is not intended that this chapter should give all the facts and figures relating to flying boat and float design, but merely sufficient to rouse your enthusiasm and enable you to get started with the thrills of float planes. There are, from time to time, articles in the hobby magazines covering technical details and describing some of the specialist events held for floatplanes. Schneider Trophy meetings, with scale models of Schneider trophy racing seaplanes (1913–1931) offer one of the most exciting and fascinating experiences in R/C model flying. To watch these machines, the epitome of speed and aerodynamic advancements of their period, taxi out, rise onto the step of the float and fight their way into the air is a sight not to miss. Once air-borne, the models fly a triangular course for five or ten laps before lining up hopefully, to come into a long approach and gentle touch down on the water.

CHOOSING THE SITE

A preliminary inspection of a quarter inch scale map of your local area will help to locate suitable lakes, reservoirs, disused gravel pits, etc., for possible flying sites. I would suggest that the minimum size stretch of water is in the region of 100 yards square but much will depend on your own flying skill and also the features of the surrounding areas. When you have selected the most promising areas from the map, pay a visit to them to gain first hand knowledge of their possibilities.

Find out who owns them, or holds the various 'rights' of the waters and whether flying R/C model aircraft in the area would be permissible. For instance you may not be at all welcome on a reservoir where fishing and sailing are allowed or where part of it is set aside as a wildfowl sanctuary. Few sites will be completely clear of trees and other obstacles, but providing they are not too numerous and close, they do not present any greater hazard than on normal flying sites.

One obvious disadvantage in flying off water is the method of retrieving the model should it finish up with a 'dead' engine somewhere in the middle of a large expanse of water. The use of some sort of boat or dinghy is a big advantage but not absolutely essential. There are a number of ways that the model can be retrieved from varying distances from the land without having to get even your big toe wet. Because a model always takes off and lands into wind, it stands to reason that the model, when it gets marooned, will be upwind of the bank from which you are operating. Providing there is a reasonable wind blowing (at least 3 knots), the model will gradually drift back in your general direction and it is surprising how, even without water rudders fitted, the model can be 'persuaded' left or right by operating the rudder. The problems arise when one is flying in those, normally, idyllic conditions of no wind when, on a lake or waterway without any current, the model just stays put. With relatively narrow strips of water, and two accessible banks, a piece of thread or thin string can be stretched across the water and moved along until the model is caught up and so dragged to the bank. A fishing rod is also a useful instrument to have handy for retrieving; a good fly fisherman should have no trouble in casting a line over a model at considerable distances – so take a rod with you.

DESIGN

The primary consideration is that the floats shall support the model on the water, the second that it shall allow the model to take-off and land back on the water. We know that water weighs just over 60lb per cubic foot (1728cu.in.) and from this we can calculate the size of floats required to displace a given weight of model (including float weight).

Example: Model weighs 5lb.

$$\text{Float volume} = \frac{5 \times 1728}{60} = 144\text{cu.in.}$$

$$\text{or } 72\text{cu.in. per float}$$

With this size of float, however, the floats will be submerged and only just keeping the model buoyant, and it will be very embarrassing trying to take-off. We must multiply the displacement figure by a factor, to increase the amount of float that is not submerged, and a minimum factor of 2

should be applied. Thus, in our example *each* float would have a total volume of 144–150cu.in. Depths of floats should be related to the above formulae. As a rule of thumb, the length of float can be taken as 80% of the length of the fuselage. It is essential that a reasonable amount of the float is forward of the propeller to prevent nosing under. This means that the length of float forward and rear of the step is roughly between 45/55% to equal lengths respectively. The floats must be spaced sufficiently far apart to prevent the model tipping over. With a high wing model, and the C of G relatively high above the water level a wider spacing may be required compared with a low wing model. A spacing of 25% of the wing span seems to be a reasonable compromise.

The rigging angle of the floats, comparative to the datum line of the fuselage, can be critical and it is sensible to have adjustment to one of the anchor points of the floats – the rear fixing point normally being the most practical. Most models seem to fly well with 0°–0° incidence setting (datum line top of float) so aim for that initially. The C of G of the model should be a little way in front of the float step.

To understand the reason for this setting let us examine the relation of the floats to the water throughout a take-off: refer to graph and diagram on page 191.

FLOAT, DRAG/SPEED RELATIONSHIP

In *Fig. 1* the model is at rest in the water. With full power applied the model will start to accelerate and the float tips will rise out of the water as in

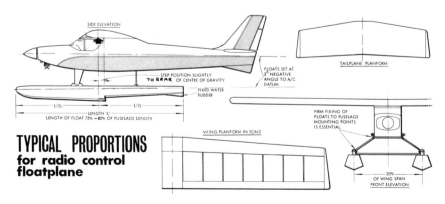

TYPICAL PROPORTIONS
for radio control floatplane

Spacing of floats may with advantage be increased from 20% of wing span to 25%.

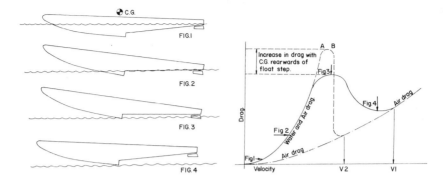

Fig. 1

Fig. 2

Fig. 3

Fig. 4

Fig. 2. During the take-off run the floats will continue to rise until they reach the maximum at the *Fig. 3* position with only the step and aft part in contact with the water. Finally, providing the C of G and step positions are correctly located the model will tip forward to position as in *Fig. 4* when the water resistance will decrease considerably and the model will quickly accelerate to flying speed and achieve this with a final small rotation on the application of elevator.

With the C of G located aft of the step the model tends to become airborne from the *Fig. 3* position.

In order to help the understanding of the four float positions, and their significance to the take-off, a graph can be plotted of drag relative to speed. Note how the drag is reduced (due to the rapid decrease of skin friction of the floats) during the transition from *Fig. 3* to *Fig. 4*. From this point on, the speed increase is rapid to take-off speed V1. We can also see from this graph what is likely to happen to the model with the step forward of the C of G. This is indicated by the

broken line showing the increase of drag to the floats remaining in a position as in *Fig. 3*. The model in fact becomes airborne from this position (point B) after accelerating to point A, providing sufficient power is available. Speed at V2 is very close to the stalling speed and will result in many models 'flipping over' on their backs before a safe flying speed is built up.

CONSTRUCTION

Rigid fixings are essential for float supports; unlike wheeled undercarriages we do not want any 'give' or springing. For this reason the dural U/C can be bolted direct to the fuselage ply plate, using anchor nuts mounted on the internal face of the ply. As a precautionary measure, nylon bolts may be used for this purpose instead of steel or brass bolts although the latter would also shear in a collision. The rear float struts are from 10swg piano wire retained to the fuselage by means of 10swg piano wire saddles. The 3/16 in. or 1/4 in.

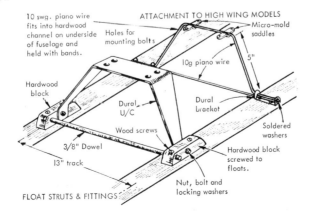

FLOAT STRUTS & FITTINGS

plywood insert on the fuselage bottom should be wide enough to allow moving the rear strut fore and aft about 2in. This movement will effectively change the incidence angle of the floats, allowing the optimum to be achieved.

Construction of the floats can be by conventional methods using balsa and ply bulkheads, but I prefer to use expanded polystyrene as a core material. This core is covered with obechi, mahogany or plywood veneer and the underside of the floats reinforced with nylon covering or fibreglass. An alternative is to use 0.8mm plywood on the underside. The cores are cut on a vertical hot wire cutting machine with an adjustable table. A ply template is cut to the side view of the float and this is pinned to one side of the block of polystyrene. Adjust the cutting table to give a cut of 10° out of vertical, to allow for the V-d bottom of the float. When this cut has been made, the process is repeated for the opposite side of the block. Accurate cutting is required to obtain an even centre line of the V-d bottom. A further ply template is cut to the plan view of the top of the float and Sellotaped to the top of the blocks at the end of the template. The sides of the float are then cut, again using a 10° angle, the template being in direct contact with the cutting table. Always leave a 'lead in' on the ply template to allow for the speed of cutting to be corrected before the actual area of the float is reached. Contact adhesive (not Evo-Stik type) such as 'Copydex' should be used

for adding the veneer or plywood, but before covering is commenced, the hardwood mounting blocks must be installed. PVA glue may be used for this purpose as it is not in contact with the water. The two sides of the float are covered first and trimmed with scissors and sanded accurately flush with the top and bottom edges. Note that the bottom surface must be covered in two parts, fore and aft of the step, and in the forward part it is necessary to cut a narrow V in the centre to follow the curvature towards the nose. Use 1/16 in. plywood to seal the rear of the float, and at the step, and hard balsa block for the front (or should it be bow?). Joints of the veneer are best reinforced with heavyweight tissue, or the whole of the float can be covered. Keep the bottom corners of the floats as sharp as possible; this also helps the floats to rise on to their steps.

Commercial floats, of the moulded foam, veneered foam and built-up types, are available and adaptable to most models. For larger models it is certainly worthwhile going to the extra effort of skinning the whole of the floats with glass cloth and resin; it makes for a tough, resilient and waterproof finish that will take the occasional knock from a semi-submerged branch or whatever. The need to make the airframe as watertight as possible cannot be over emphasised. Be sure that if there is even a pinhole below water level the water will find its way through. If the model is built in the first place with waterplane work in mind, more

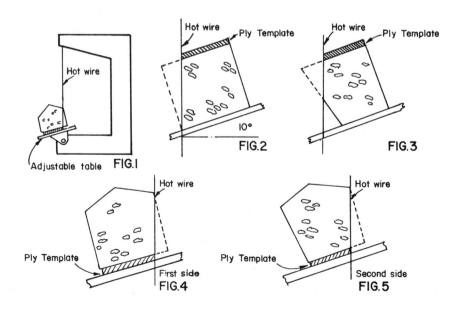

FIG.1 Adjustable table

FIG.2 Hot wire Ply Template 10°

FIG.3 Hot wire Ply Template

FIG.4 Hot wire Ply Template First side

FIG.5 Hot wire Ply Template Second side

can be done to reduce the effects of water ingress and to reduce the possibility of it happening. Obviously, we want to avoid openings in the fuselage and wings for linkages to exit. Standard pushrods, with metal rod ends, are not good for floatplane work, it is better to use a close fitting snake system where the outer tube can be thoroughly sealed where it breaks through the airframe. It will be necessary to operate the on/off switch from outside the fuselage, but the switch itself can be mounted internally. Actuation of the switch is by a metal pushrod sleeved where it passes through the structure and waterproofed with a smear of petroleum jelly.

Access will be required to the radio-control equipment, including any servos fitted in the wings and waterproof hatches should be fitted to these areas. Silicone rubber, applied as a bead and flattened by the hatch is a good bedding for a screwed on hatch and when used in conjunction with silicone grease as the final seal, gives a good waterproof joint. Silicone rubber self-adhesive tape is another way of producing a seal. All around the engine bay — and fuel-tank bay if that is accessible — should be thoroughly fuel-proofed. If during construction, there are any internal areas that you think may be vulnerable, then by all means dope and proof these areas.

Film coverings are not ideal for waterplane work — the fully amalgamated and fused finishes of nylon and dope are better. If heat-shrink film or fabrics are used the overlapping joints should be fuel-proofed carefully so that water cannot enter the through the seams.

Finally, a few general notes about the model and flying. The weight of the floats as illustrated, including all struts, dural U/C, etc. is just about one pound, and with this extra weight, drag and the effort in rising off the water, a larger engine than normal is required. Make sure that the model is well and truly fuel-proofed and the open areas sealed off to prevent the ingress of water. An extra coat of dope on nylon covering is a good investment for floatplanes, as the damp conditions have a habit of slackening off the covering rather rapidly. Always launch the model directly into the prevailing wind. With high wing models in particular, the wind can easily get under a wing and tip the model up. Steering initially, without water rudders, is fairly sluggish, and for that reason first

flights should be made with the model released at about two-thirds throttle to obtain a rapid acceleration. Once the model rises on to the step, control becomes much more positive and directional corrections can be made precisely. Lift-off should be accomplished without the application of very much up elevator. If any excessive degree of up elevator is required to haul the model off, it points to incorrect trimming. My first test flights are often undertaken over grass, just to prove that the model is correctly trimmed before undertaking water take-offs, and the model is put down very well on the longish grass.

What happens if models tip up in the water? Well, fortunately, they do not sink immediately; usually they finish in an attitude of a diving duck with the tail stuck in the air and the nose under the water. Even if they tip right over the wings are sufficiently buoyant to hold the model afloat without the water getting into the cabin area. After a dousing, do remember to run the engine again as soon afterwards as possible, and if you are not going to use it again for some time, inject a little oil.

One thing I can promise you with floatplane flying — is excitement. The excitement of the model pushing up a bow wave before rising on to the step and breaking the surface tension to lift into the air and the satisfaction of 'greasing' back on to the water takes some beating. Splash and gos are equally exciting, and either take the form of a single bounce on the water and round again, or you can touch down, let the model sink down on the floats and then open up the engine and take-off again. Either way it adds up to a lot of fun.

FLYING BOATS

Flying boats follow similar design principles to floats but, as there is only one main supporting body the wings also have to be restrained with tip floats or fuselage sponsons.

It is possible, with small and lightly loaded flying boats, to use a flat bottom hull and obtain good take-off and landing results. For any sizeable model, though, it is important to keep friction, drag and overall weight to a minimum and we must strive to obtain maximum efficiency both on the water and in the air. A single step 'V' bottomed hull with a long planing section works

The versatile Mighty Barnstormer *makes an ideal model for conversion to a floatplane.*

well with models and is as sophisticated as we need to go – unless a scale model dictates otherwise. Design requirements are, as stated, similar to those of floats, but let us take a look at some of the reasons for these design criteria.

1. The 'V' bottom to the hull, or floats, assists in allowing it to 'cut' through the water in its initial acceleration stage, pushing the water to either side as it goes. It is probable that the 'V' formation also assists in keeping the model in a straight line during the planing period.

2. The sloping longitudinal rise to the fore end of the hull prevents the aircraft from 'digging in' during the take-off up to the point of planing.

3. The sloping longitudinal rise at the rear is to allow the aircraft to rotate, as a tricycle undercarriage aircraft will rotate just prior to take-off. Without this rise the model would simply not get airborne from the planing position.

   To achieve lift-off the wing must be at a reasonable angle of attack to obtain maximum lift. If the rise at the rear of the hull underside is insufficiently steep it will not be possible to reach that desired angle of attack.

4. The step performs a number of functions. Without the addition of a step, plus the rear longitudinal rise, a satisfactory rotation would still not be able to take place. Most important of the functions of the step, however, is to cause a reduction of water friction, or suction. It does this by breaking up the smooth (laminar) flow of the bottom of the hull and a turbulent

stream occurs immediately behind the step. By causing this turbulation the surface tension is substantially reduced, allowing the planing phase, i.e. riding on the step area, to be reached more quickly. This separation can be further increased by introducing air, via tubes, to assist in the turbulation.

5. Step position to rear of C of G. When the aircraft has reached the planing stage the model is continuing to rise until it is planing on the last part of the underside forward hull, i.e. just forward of the step. With the step further forward there would be a tendency for the

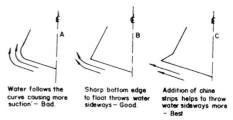

Float or hull sections.

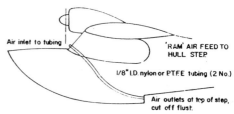

Arrangement of 'Ram' air feed tube to hull step.

model to 'tip' rearwards and achieve a premature take-off.

6. A wide front end of the hull is equally necessary because the majority of take-offs rely on the forward area of the hull. The rear end can, fortunately for aesthetic reasons, taper in gradually towards the tail.

TIP FLOATS AND SPONSONS

Because the 'flying boat' has only one, central supporting and planing surface, it is necessary to stabilise the model on water until the point of take-off. To do this we can use either tip floats or sponsons. If we are not using ailerons it is important to use tip floats and to have them fitted as near to the tip as possible. Frequently, during take-off we are going to have the condition of one wing tending to drop; with rudder only control, we have to try to pick this wing up by 'skidding' the model towards the 'high' wing. This may, or may not, be successful in 'picking up' the wing — it will also have the undesired effect of changing direction of the aircraft. By fitting the wing-tip floats as far outboard as possible, the wings are prevented, as far as possible, from dropping. With ailerons fitted we are able to raise a wing with aileron control without recourse to rudder control. In these circumstances it is possible to fit the floats further inboard — up to half span apart, or to use sponsons. Sponson areas need to be about 16–20% of the total wing area, set at 3°–5°, positive incidence, with the trailing edge touching the water at rest. A rigid fixing, built in with the hull, is needed for the sponsons but tip floats should have some form of positive shearing, achieved with tightly wound rubber bands or balsa shear pegs.

Many configurations of floatplanes can be tried, tractors, pushers, twins, biplanes (scale and non-scale), the full-size flying boats should give you plenty of ideas.

WATER RUDDERS

For shoulder and high-wing models it is possible to steer the aircraft in water without the use of water rudders; response will, however, be sluggish and it is only when the model has built up speed on the water that the air rudder becomes really effective. It is simple with a flying boat to fit a water rudder as an extension of the air rudder but a little more ingenuity is required for fitting them to floats and arranging the linkages. Tricycle undercarriaged models lend themselves easiest to fitting the linkage to the rudder as this can be taken direct from the steerable nose wheel position — with nose leg removed of course. For 'tail dragger' models the linkage is rather more complicated and must be taken from horns fitted to the air rudder or a separate connection from the rudder servo linkage.

SKIS

One of the problems with seasonal activities, such as fitting a model with skis, is that one is very rarely prepared for it. The intentions are usually good and you fully intend to try it out, but the tendency is to leave the preparation until the last minute. Do make your skis in good time for that first covering of snow. With our climate you are never sure when this is going to happen, and it is most frustrating to commence building skis when the snow falls only to find, on completion, that the snow has completely disappeared.

I have fitted many different models with skis of varying types and with varying degrees of success. Some models (notably the smaller ones) would not take-off with the normal engine power and some had a tendency to dig the nose of the skis into the snow and tip over if the engine was opened up too quickly. The power required in getting the model airborne safely is usually no more than that required for normal flying. The average sports high wing model does tend to be a little underpowered and the problem with ski take-offs is not only a matter of building up sufficient speed to take-off but also in keeping the model straight until a reasonable speed has been attained and the rudder becomes effective. Remember, there are no steerable nose or tail wheels with ski aircraft. If you are satisfied with hand launches and just use the skis for landing, then normal power requirements will be sufficient, but you will miss all the fun of the long, s-m-o-o-t-h take-off.

A number of materials have been tested for the skis themselves and the conclusions I have arrived at are that ⅛in. thick Perspex is ideal for models up to about 50in. span, and over that size plywood is a more suitable material. Perspex has the ad-

Scale, semi-scale, sports, twins and unorthodox models...

vantage of being easy to cut and very easy to form. To produce the forward curvature of the ski, it is only necessary to heat the Perspex, in boiling water or over a stove, until it is pliable and moulds to the shape required. This can be done over a wooden former or, with a little practice, in the hands. A theoretical disadvantage with Perspex is that it will become brittle in freezing conditions, but, in practice, no difficulties have been encountered with ski fracturing. Plywood skis can be formed in two different ways. One method is to build up layers of thin plywood (1/16 in. maximum for large skis) over a wooden former; in this way the individual layers of plywood will bend sufficiently without resorting to steaming or wetting.

The number of layers of plywood required will depend on the thickness of ply and the size of the ski, but for large models (60in. and above) three layers of 1/16 in. ply should be alright, and for small models of about 50in. span two layers of 1mm ply and a centre core of 1/16 in. ply gives a ski of sufficient strength. As an alternative to building up layers of plywood a single thickness of plywood can be used.

Cut out the shape of the skis from 5–6mm (3/16 – 1/4 in.) birch plywood, it should not be of less than 5 laminations. Mark out the positions of holes for the screws, drill and countersink. To obtain the forward curvature of the ski it is neces-

...all meet the challenge of flying from water.

sary to boil the tips of the skis for an hour or two until the plywood is pliable. You will probably find that, unless you are using an exterior grade plywood, that it will tend to delaminate, and glue should then be squeezed between the laminations

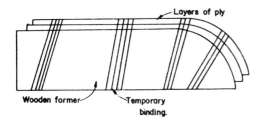

before the curvature is formed. Bend the tips by fixing the lower halves into the vice and attaching strong thread to the end of the tips; pull on the thread until the correct curvature is obtained. Secure the thread and leave to dry overnight; it may also be helpful to clamp any laminated plywood or bind it with Sellotape until dry. Trim and sandpaper the skis and give them three or four good coats of dope (very important if PVA glue has been used for laminations) and one coat of fuel proofer. Screw and glue in position the hardwood mounting blocks and fix the spring mounting bolts, nuts, washers and tags. Drill two small

197

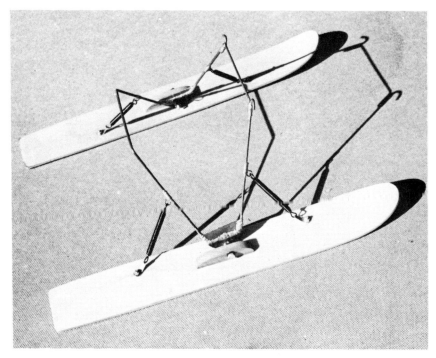

Skis constructed from wood (above) and Perspex (below).

holes in the dural U/C to take the other end of the springs. The skis are mounted to the dural U/C with bolts, high tensile by preference, with locking nuts, washers and a friction washer between the mounting block and dural. Make sure the springs are strong enough to prevent the skis from floating about during flight, otherwise large trim changes can occur to the model, particularly when one ski stays horizontal and the other assumes a vertical position. Additional 'stiffness' can be achieved by tightening up the friction washer although not to the extent of overcoming the power

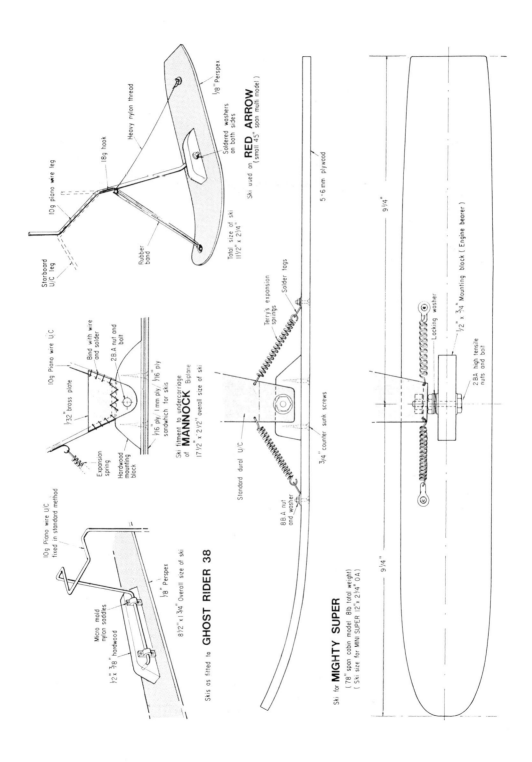

1/8" Perspex

Soldered washers
on both sides

Heavy nylon thread

18g hook

10g piano wire leg

RED ARROW
(small 45" span multi model)

Starboard
U/C leg

Rubber
band

Total size of ski
11 1/2" x 2 1/4"

Ski used on

5 - 6 mm plywood

10g Piano wire U/C

Bind with wire
and solder

2 B.A nut and
bolt

1/32" brass plate

1/16 ply, 1 mm ply, 1/16 ply
sandwhich for skis

Ski fitment to undercarriage
of **MANNOCK** Biplane
17 1/2" x 2 1/2" overall size of ski

Expansion
spring

Hardwood
mounting
block

Terry's expansion
springs

Solder tags

Standard dural U/C

3/4" counter sunk screws

8 B.A nut
and washer

9 1/4"

1/2" x 3/4" Mounting block (Engine bearer)

Locking washer

2 BA high tensile
nuts and bolt

9 1/4"

10g Piano wire U/C
fixed in standard method

1/8" Perspex

8 1/2" x 1 3/4" Overall size of ski

GHOST RIDER 38

Micro mold
nylon saddles

1/2" x 3/8" hardwood

Skis as fitted to

Ski for **MIGHTY SUPER**
(78" span cabin model 8lb total weight)
(Ski size for MINI SUPER 12" x 2 1/4" O.A.)

Scale model of Sopwith Baby *in flight — complete with floats.*

of the springs. The prototype skis had a noticeable 'toe in' on the wheeled version but this had no adverse effects, it may even have improved tracking.

The skis fitted to my *Mannock* biplane were similar in principle to those used on the 'Mighty Super' but used a piano wire U/C with brass inserts where the mounting blocks are fitted. As with all skis the hinge point is slightly forward of the centre position of the ski, i.e. the rear of the ski is slightly longer than the front.

Skis fitted to the 'Red Arrow' were connected to single piano wire U/C legs and expansion springs were dispensed with. In place of the springs I fitted rubber bands from the front end of the ski to the top of the U/C leg and used strong nylon thread from the rear of the ski to the top of the U/C leg. This allowed the ski to pivot when the rear of the skis hit first on landing, but held the

ski horizontal during normal flight. The system worked extremely well and is equally suitable for larger models.

Do not be afraid to experiment with new forms of skis, the snow is very forgiving to take-offs and landings that go astray.

I have seen many materials and methods used for skis, including floats, which work very well. One of the strangest form of skis, but highly effective, was a car number plate, with rounded edges, cut in half and the fronts bent up slightly. It is true to say that the larger models looked better than small ones when fitted with skis but virtually any model will provide you with an exciting new experience when the skies are blue overhead, the snow is crisp underfoot and your pride and joy comes 'hissing' in to a perfect landing.

CHAPTER 21

Ducted Fans and Gas Turbine Models

Two areas where modellers in the past have found practical difficulties in achieving their 'dream' models, have been in the spheres of scale models of jet powered prototypes and ultra large models. Over recent years developments in engines have made both of these aims reachable by proficient R/C modellers. Increases of power from two stroke engines (in excess of 2hp from 7.5cc capacity motors) and good engineering standards on the fan unit, cleared the way for many scale jet projects to be modelled.

Once the propulsion system had been proven as practical and reliable the commercial aspects of scale ducted fan units and models went from strength to strength. Larger capacity engines, up to '90' (15cc) were developed, with rear exhaust outlets for the fitting of tuned pipes and very high speeds and output efficiencies reached. Parallel

developments were made to produce more efficient ducted fan units and the combinations have resulted in a revolution in scale model jets. From a time when the models were under powered and unconvincing the 'jets' have progressed to, if anything, being too fast for true scale speeds. Kits are available for a wide range of subjects and although there will always be plenty of examples of BAe 'Hawks' and other trainer models, there will also be 'Starfighters', 'Blackbirds', 'Stealth fighters' and other exotica to get the heart pounding.

DUCTED FAN DESIGNS

Ducted fan systems do not operate on the principles of genuine jet engines or rockets, they can be compared to the standard propeller arrangement. To avoid the unsightly engine and propeller stuck

Most of the early jet types, and many modern aircraft, can be effectively modelled using ducted fan power units and powerful glow motors. Scale finishes on some of these models are exquisite. (This page and page 201.)

on the front, or rear, of the model the engine/fan unit is buried within the structure of the fuselage. Keeping the model within manageable dimensions, and allowing it to fly at a convincing scale speed, precludes the use of a standard propeller and this is substituted by a multiblade fan fixed to the front of the engine. With the smaller fan diameter the engine must be capable of turning faster than propeller equipped equivalents, hence the development of high speed, Schneurle ported engines with pressure pumps. Fans are less efficient than propellers, even with the close fitted shroud around the fan, and the drag from the air inlet and exhaust ducts adds to the power loss of ducted fan installations. We therefore have a situation where we must use the available power as efficiently as possible by careful airframe design, well proportioned and contoured air ducts and well engineered fan units. In its simplest form the ducted fan power unit

consists of the engine, fan, shroud and stators, the latter component being fitted behind the fan assembly to straighten out the airflow before it enters the exhaust duct. Tractor or pusher arrangements can be used, although the former installation is the most popular as it avoids disturbing the incoming air to the fan through passing over the engine.

Ducted fan models have been flown since the 1950s, when they were popularised in free flight form by P. E. Norman and Phil Smith of Veron. The models were lightly constructed and although they flew well enough as free flight designs they were not suitable for conversion to R/C operation − the additional load of the proportional radio equipment gave unacceptable flight performances. It was only when the 'hot 40' motors, developed for pylon racers, became available that ducted fan R/C designs started to become a practical reality.

Through the investigations of J. J. Scozzi and Bob Kress in the USA and P. E. Norman's son Marcus in the UK the fan units were developed to the stage where sufficient thrust was obtainable to sensibly power scale R/C models. Commercial fan units and engines are now available to allow an experienced modeller to use this 'out-of-the-box' technology to good effect and open up a whole avenue of new scale model projects. The term 'experienced modeller' is used advisedly as models must be accurately built, keeping a close check on weight limitations, and the engine/fan unit must be operated at maximum performance. With a conventionally powered model you will probably get away with a slightly 'sick' motor, or an unbalanced propeller, not so with a ducted fan unit. Good preparation is even more important with these designs and it is only advisable to fly when you are *certain* that everything is operating at 100% efficiency. Acceleration of a DF model is much slower than a propeller driven type and a good take-off area is necessary (models may be fitted with retracting wheels or take-off from a 'dolly' – fixed undercarriages are just not in keeping with fast jets!) Once airborne, the models will accelerate to very convincing speeds and some have been timed at 150mph plus. It is possible to construct your own fan unit from nylon sheet and plywood, Marcus Norman did it for many years, but the effort would barely seem worthwhile when there are excellent commercial products available. Consideration should be given to the fact that these fans are turning at speeds in excess of 20,000rpm and the breaking of a fan blade at full throttle can have disastrous consequences.

Not all jet prototypes are suitable for modelling as R/C ducted fan designs. Indeed, on looking through a selection of three-view drawings the initial impression is that very few will be suited to scale ducted fan work. Essential for any ducted fan model are reasonably sized air intakes and exhausts and many jet aircraft do not have these features. How can we overcome this limitation to widen the scope of aircraft selection? Exhaust duct sizes may only require a small degree of 'cheating' and should be acceptable to all but the most fastidious of scale modellers. Intake sizes may also be judiciously increased without offending the eye but it may be necessary to augment the intake areas in other ways. Where retracting

undercarriages are to be fitted it may be possible to use the noseleg wheel bay as an air scoop, necessary for the initial acceleration but not vital once the model has built up speed – and the undercarriage doors are closed. The simplest and most straightforward answer, one used by a number of American kit manufacturers, is to position a slot or hole on the underside of the model in front of the fan unit. This may seem to be a rather crude answer but these openings are not noticeable with the model at any distance. Units designed for '45'–'60' engines are the most popular but '20' and '90' sized DF units are also available, and one commercial kit is designed around the Cox .049cu.in. engine.

Installation of the R/C equipment may also pose a few problems with models of the 'straight through' duct types, i.e. Mig 15, 'Sabre'. The full length of the fuselage is taken up with the ducts and engine/fan unit/fuel tank and room for the R/C gear must be found elsewhere. Ingenuity is called for and the wings, fin and cockpit area have to be adapted to house the batteries, receiver and servos. Provision also has to be made for starting the engine, either by electric starter and belt drive, or through the air duct by direct contact to the spinner. Pre-planning the installation of the DF unit and radio equipment is, of course, totally essential; even the commercial packages of airframe/DF unit should be carefully checked against the plan for fitting of the engine and radio equipment.

Perhaps this all sounds too fraught with problems and dangers! If you have little time to spend on modelling and preparation and prefer to spend your time at the flying field, flick a propeller and get up into the air – ducted fan models are not for you. Alternatively, if your mind substitutes the words 'problems and dangers' to 'challenges and excitement' then building and flying jet type models offer new delights in R/C modelling.

REAL 'SUCK AND BLOW' ENGINES

For many years now Joe Koullen, from Holland, has been giving immaculate demonstrations with flying wing models powered by pulse jet engines. His displays are always professional, consistent, noisy and, for the public at large, thrilling. The popular commentator, Dave Bishop, is wont to state that the model, when airborne at altitude, can be heard six miles away! Perhaps a slight exaggeration, but certainly putting out more decibels than would be acceptable at a club flying field. Other teams, including one from Italy, have shown that pulse jets can be a welcome addition to a public display where noise, speed − even flames from the rear of the engine − all contribute to the excitement. For practical purposes, including trying to house the engines inside a scale model, the pulse jet is extremely limited. The potential for speed control of the engine is almost nil, the firing is working on a fixed pulse length, the engine case heat is sufficient to have it glowing red hot, the fuel supply needs metering and when petrol is used as the fuel the fire risk is not inconsiderable. Perhaps the pulse jet should have been left where

it originally started − on top of a V1

Where the future undoubtedly lies is with the miniature gas turbine engine. For many years it was doubted whether this form of propulsion would ever be practical. There were a number of magazine articles in which modellers claimed that they had successfully built and operated gas turbine engines but, when it came to the crunch, they were conspicuous by their absence. Not until the early 1990s did the commercial gas turbine engine become a reality, when the French company JPX introduced their T240 unit. Here at last was a true 'jet' engine which started well, could be operated by a team of two sensible operators and, carefully used, would give good service. It has to be said that the JPX was not the first model gas turbine model to be successfully operated, flying in a

Gas turbine power plants are going to be with us increasingly in the future. Costs are high but the thrill of flying a model with an engine turning 100K plus rpm has to be experienced to be believed.

model — that honour probably goes to Gerry Jackman. At least, he was the first to stand up and be counted and was prepared, many years prior to the JPX, to display it to the model press and public. Unfortunately, it was one thing to make a prototype but another to put it into limited production and maintain the required standards.

There were two limitations to the JPX model gas turbine engine. The first was that it operated on propane — and some of the modelling authorities considered that this was an unacceptable fire risk — and the second was the cost, well out of the range of many modellers. The power to weight ratios of the early units were adequate, without being sparkling and no doubt these figures will improve as development continues. Regrettably, most of the modellers who purchased these units had but one aim in mind — SPEED! Why this should be so is difficult to understand because the whole reason for wanting the model gas turbine engine in the first place was to emulate the prototype jets. As the present engines have characteristics similar to the early range of gas turbine engines it would seem logical to fit them into some of this era of jet aircraft models. To an old

'Vampire' jet jockey the sound of the JPX 'spooling' up and down is evocative music to the ears. If speed is the only requirement you might just as well put a conventional IC engine and propeller in the front of the model — just as effective and a heck of a lot cheaper.

The cost aspect is, in some ways, a blessing. Operating a model gas turbine engine is a responsible undertaking, with jet pipe temperatures high enough to burn the skin off your fingers we do not want every Tom, Dick and Dirty Harry coming up to the flying field and operating them. Even when they are run on kerosene (paraffin) there are still potential dangers and fire risks — they need to be treated with considerable respect. Prices will come down although, because of the extremely close tolerances of the machining, the costly metals and bearings included, they will never be inexpensive. They do offer a genuine scale power-plant for the jet aeroplane and we have to accept that we are, in real terms, in the jet age. Providing operators are sensible, no one is stupid or wilfully negligent, the model gas turbine engine offers real progress, although only as a form of propulsion for scale jet models.

The Dutch Flying Jet Team use futuristic looking delta models fitted with true pulse jet engines. Fast, noisy and very impressive.

CHAPTER 22

Mini-Models

As well as the large models perform there remains a fascination with the truly small model. In the days of single channel radio it was possible to produce a genuinely small model with non-proportional control on rudder only, but we always dreamed of the day that we could fly a model under full control, possibly indoors. Canon Industries in the USA were the first to produce small proportional radio control where the airborne weight of a four-function outfit was only four ounces or so. Unfortunately, this equipment was only available on the US frequencies and was not legal in the UK. We had to wait for other R/C manufacturers to take an interest in miniature equipment before it became generally available at an affordable price.

Now, all the major manufacturers feature a micro servo in their catalogues and the sub-micro is beginning to appear also. In weight terms micro can be taken as around 12g, anything less than this can be considered as sub-micro. Receivers down to this weight are not common, but are available and can be further lightened if you are prepared to dispense with the case. The availability of small capacity (and size and weight) rechargeable nicad batteries is one of the main reasons why we can have lightweight airborne packs. Whereas a 500mAh battery pack was the norm and 250mAh considered as small we can now use 50mAh for our small equipment. With two servos we can still expect to get three or four flights of five minutes' operation from a fully charged battery – but we must be cautious not to discharge it too far and use time checks. Switches also come in micro sizes, or a shorting-cum-charging miniature jack plug and socket can be used in place of the switch. It is also possible to dispense with plugs and sockets and direct wire the servos and battery to the receiver. This is quite acceptable for the servos, although it will reduce the flexibility of installation of the system and it is not advisable in the case of the battery. There is the risk of 'black wire corrosion' if batteries are left connected over long periods and it is advisable to make provision for disconnecting them. This is true for all R/C equipment, not just the micro versions, and batteries should be unplugged in airborne equipment and transmitters when they are not being used for a number of months.

You may ask why we should want to build small models when the 'standard' size models fly perfectly well and are probably more practical. It's that old menace 'challenge' again. How small can we get? What is the minimum size that we can build, and sensibly fly, a full-house aerobatic model? Perhaps, even, is our eyesight good enough and our reactions fast enough to cope with a tiny hot-rod? These challenges apart, there are two genuine reasons for building and flying small models.

Imagine a warm, calm summer's evening when there is an hour or so to go before the sun sets. This can be a magic time for flying, but not with a fast hairy aerobatic model. This is the time for a small model, powered by a little R/C diesel – or electric (or, sometime in the future when further miniaturisation is achieved, CO_2 powered). The model is small enough to keep in one piece, it doesn't take up much space in the boot of your car and you won't need a whole lot of equipment to lug around to operate the model. In the case of the diesel powered model all you will need is the transmitter, a small can of fuel and a piece of rag. For this type of work we are not talking about the ultra small model, perhaps a 30in. span biplane with a .55cc or .80cc diesel, mini servos, a 150mAh battery and operating rudder, elevator and throttle. Fill the tank, flick the propeller, adjust the compression, launch the model and away we go. The gentle purr of the diesel and the model in the soft evening light and all is well with the world – the aggravation of the day's work fading away. It isn't essential to have a throttle control, but it is nice to

be able to throttle the engine back and fly slowly past at low level. It isn't even essential to use miniature R/C gear, but the lower the wing loading the slower the model will fly and the more relaxing the flying will be.

The second legitimate reason for using micro R/C equipment is for indoor flying. Now this *is* something relatively new and started principally because one of the main halls became available for flying during the Model Engineer Exhibition organised by Nexus Exhibitions. Here was a challenge, not only to be able to fly an R/C model within the confines of the hall, but also to participate in a competition for scale models of Handley Page prototypes. Disregarding the scale contest there was challenge enough to fly any type of R/C model within the walls of the hall. It may look a reasonable size area when initially viewed, once the model is launched the walls seem to come inwards at a rapid rate! One of the problems is that you have to concentrate 100% on the model, not taking your eyes off it for a minute and then it's difficult to keep good orientation. The background of columns, balconies and windows whirr around at an alarming rate − unless you happen to be young with super reactions. To fly a model in this situation is not bad going but, to add a further dimension, they also organise pylon racing for Cox TD .020 engines, with three models flying around a two pylon course. It is all very adrenalin producing and hectic, but great fun and really appreciated by the spectators.

If you want to have a go at indoor R/C flying

Radio-control equipment is becoming ever smaller and lighter (note postage stamp). Indoor flying is now practical in exhibition and sports halls and it will not be too long before it is feasible in your lounge.

This mini-fun flyer is powered by an '049' (008 cc) engine and weighs around a half pound, including radio equipment.

I would suggest that you should choose between two types of models. The first would be a slow flying relatively large model with high lift wing section and producing plenty of drag. It could be IC or electric powered with rudder and elevator control, something in the vintage model style. The second type would be for the more adventurous and rely on its manoeuvrability by flying a little faster and including the use of ailerons and elevator (with throttle and rudder being optional). A fully symmetrical wing section can be used but the wing loading still has to remain low. With such a model it is possible to perform loops and rolls and, if rudder and throttle is fitted, stall turns. Going from one end of the hall to the other, throttling back and stall turning to change direction can look very neat.

Construction of these models, whether the slower or faster flying, does have to be as light as possible and selection of wood, cutting lightening holes and saving fractions of grammes at all times is important. Without doubt the best covering material for the indoor lightweight model is one of the heat-shrink, iron-on (but not self-adhesive) films, such as Litespan or Airspan. Use closed-loop control for rudder, with lightweight nylon monofilament cables direct from the servos to a 0.8mm plywood rudder horn. If it is feasible, use the same system for elevator control – it is low weight and has practically no inertia. The transmitter trims should be sufficient to cope with any small trim adjustments, certainly the standard clevises are out of place in this type of model. If a closed-loop system cannot be connected to the

All types of R/C models are subjects for miniaturisation, whether they are ducted fan jets or scale biplanes.

elevator use a ⅛in. diameter pushrod with 22swg or 24swg piano wire connectors on the end.

Before attempting to fly the model indoors it is prudent to test fly on a calm day outdoors − if you have time. It will give you a chance to check out the turning ability of the model and the general flying characteristics of the model. You can fly the model within an imaginary hall, if necessary mark it out on the ground. I crashed a small Gipsy Moth model in the Olympia contests because, although I had test flown it outside for one flight, I hadn't realised that the turn to the right was sluggish. To the left, with torque, she turned fine but I got myself into a position where I needed to turn right

and, bang, a cast iron column came up and smote the poor little Gipsy.

We have a long way to go yet with miniaturis-ation of radio control equipment. When scientists are talking about producing systems weighing a few grammes it is only a matter of time − and ex-pediency − before the same 'shrinking' is applied to our modelling equipment. Rather than technical limitations, it will probably be dictated by com-mercial considerations on how soon and how small our R/C equipment becomes. If the manufacturers are convinced that there is a market for the equip-ment, they will manufacture the product.

CHAPTER 23

Large Models

Defining a 'large model' is not simple, a nine foot wing span sailplane is large in terms of wing span but, with a high aspect ratio wing and short fuselage, it does not appear to be all that big. Conversely, a nine foot wing span powered Delta shaped model *is* large, with a wing area of over 2,500sq.in., and needing a large engine, probably around 80cc. The Civil Aviation Authority (CAA) define a model in relation to its all up weight and anything over that limit is classed as a light air-craft – even though it is not a man carrying aircraft. To legally fly an overweight model it is necessary to obtain an exemption to the Air Navigation Order (ANO) and this must be obtained *before* test flying of the aircraft is commenced. As previously stated, the maximum weight limitation for a model aircraft is being negotiated and the rules may be modified as experience is gained. It would be prudent to check whether your proposed model will require a dispensation from the ANO. The address to write to is: Civil Aviation Authority, General Aviation Section, Aviation House, South Area, Gatwick Airport, West Sussex RH6 0YR. Should your R/C aircraft come within their juris-diction they will list the information that must be furnished to them for a dispensation to be issued – allow 28 days for the approval.

Why should we wish to build these extra large models? Anyone having seen large scale or sports models flying will, I am sure, agree that they are very impressive to watch. Not only do they have a majestic appearance in the air but they fly in a very scale like manner. It is easier to achieve scale flying speed with large models, wing loadings need not be greater (and are often lighter) than smaller models. Flying a ⅛th scale model of a 'Piper Cub' (with a cruise speed of 90mph) would require a model air speed of 15mph – difficult to achieve. A one third scale replica can fly at a scale speed of 30mph, and this should be within the speed range of a very large, lightly loaded, model.

More detail can be included in large scale models and the take-offs and landings are reminiscent of their full-size counterparts – small models tend to 'leap' into the air, large ones fly themselves off the ground. In the final analysis, however, it is merely that some modellers are fascinated by large models in the same way that others will find their pleasure in going to the other extreme, with tiny R/C models.

No one should embark on the building or flying of large models without realising the full implica-tions of such action. Weights and, in many cases, speeds are appreciably increased and the potential damage the model can inflict may also increase. Safety must be the foremost consideration in operating these aircraft and the responsibility to the hobby as a whole is not to be underestimated. At a more practical level you should think about a few other possible disadvantages before you get started on a ten foot wing span 'monster'. Having built it (you do have a large enough building board?) where are you going to store it? Large scale 'modelitis' is quite a virulent disease and it does not take too long before you have filled the house with airframes. Transportation might also present difficulties, a six foot long fuselage doesn't fit into a 'Mini', so use your tape measure on the car as well as the model. Costs of building very large models are not inconsiderable, a built-up open structure may not break the bank but it does have to be covered. Use one of the 'exotic' iron-on fabric materials and you can run away with most of your pocket money! Running costs, with a petrol engine fitted, are more than reasonable; wooden propellers cost a few extra pounds (and you may break one or two initially) but there are tough moulded varieties, in most sizes, available. If you fly with your local club it is a matter of courtesy to check whether they will take kindly to large models being flown, not all club fields are suitable due to the size of the flying site or surrounding hazards. Most modellers' insurances do cover large models but ensure that this is the situation, or obtain separate cover on your own behalf.

Designing large models is not just a question of doubling up the size of materials used in a model only half as big. The larger the model the greater the structural integrity that is required; it may not entail a complete set of structural calculations (as for full size aircraft) but the design should be left to experienced designers. Similarly, you should have built quite a few normal size models before contemplating the skills needed for the larger designs. Construction of these 'super' models

follows similar practices to smaller versions, i.e. built-up structures or GRP and foam techniques but with refined detailing. Hardwood and ply-wood reinforcing is used in the built-up structures to strengthen high stress areas and large components (wing ribs and fuselage formers) are also of composite construction. GRP fuselages must be cautiously moulded to avoid excessive weight, particularly at the tail end, and local reinforcement strengthening, plus the use of carbon fibre, help to realise this aim. Expanded polystyrene wing cores may need hollowing out and the addition of hardwood spars to obtain a suitable strength/weight ratio. Obtaining sheets of obechi veneer in

Designing large models requires new understandings of structures and materials and should not be undertaken lightly.

sizes to suit the wings may be impossible, .4mm plywood may be used although this is a heavier material. For biplanes and braced monoplanes, the rigging should be structural, this will allow the construction of a lighter wing framework − the rigging takes most of the flying and landing loads. The same applies to struts, they should fulfil their original functions. Undercarriage assemblies do not have to be assembled from excessively large sections of piano wire, providing the design incorporates good springing. With large scale model design, the best advice is if in doubt, copy the original method.

Loads on the control surfaces will inevitably be greater in flight than with a smaller model − the areas are larger and the model may be flying faster. Our servos must be capable of operating the control surface under the optimum conditions, i.e. maximum speed and maximum deflection. Special, high power, servos are available for our purposes and it is commonsense to buy a servo type that is reliable and gives us a good reserve of power. Keep the lengths of the linkages to a minimum (unless direct closed loop systems are used) − with large models it is often possible to mount the servo adjacent to the control surface i.e. in the fin, and to use extension leads to the receiver. Separate servos may be used for individual ailerons and, for exceptionally large models, separate servos for each elevator. Control horns and clevises must also be of sufficient strength, there is no point in their being many times stronger than the power of the servos − standard mouldings will frequently take more than any load that can be supplied from 'mammoth' servos. Where additional servos are being used, and because the additional weight may not be a critical factor, a battery of increased capacity can be used for the airborne radio equipment, e.g. a 1.2mA pack. Finally, if you do require a CAA dispensation, you will need to fit a fail-safe device. In the words of the ANO exemption it should be 'equipped with a mechanism that will cause the said aircraft to land in the event of a failure of its control systems, including the radio link, and such mechanism is in working order before the said aircraft commences flight'. Short of duplicating *all* of the R/C equipment *and* linkages it is virtually impossible to comply with this condition ''to the letter''. What is generally accepted is a fail-safe which will cut

the engine. The fail-safe design should allow for regaining radio control if the loss of signal is only temporary.

It must always be remembered, however, that fail-safes are there not to protect the model, but to protect persons and property. Although it may be hard to accept, if we have fail-safe on all of the primary functions the safest set-up is for the engine to be totally cut, full up elevator and full left aileron and rudder control i.e. to 'crash' the model within the minimum possible distance travelled. If we regain control before the model hits the ground and we can glide into a safe landing, fine, but the controls should not be set in the hopes that control will be regained. Obviously, we arrange for the motor to cut − as opposed to going to idle − because a whirling propeller is potentially dangerous. It would be nice to have the engine go to a safe idle so that, if we did regain control, we could fly the model normally again, but the risk is too great, unless it is combined with an auto-pilot system.

The use of fail-safes will for ever be controversial and many modellers will complain that the systems have caused more crashes than they have ever saved. I happen to believe that this is true, but also that this is a fault of the equipment and not the principle. I can see no point in having a fail-safe system inherent on the equipment and then switching it out before flying. Not only is it illegal − with a large model − but it is self defeating in that there is no point in buying the equipment with this facility in the first place.

There are no radio systems sold specifically for large models because, the manufacturers tell us, all you have to do is to buy the more powerful servos and larger batteries and you have a system for large models! It is not quite as simple as that because we need such items as battery backers (a back-up battery system), long servo connector leads with diode protection and there are many items that could and should be available in a large model R/C system. In an ideal world we should be using, for the very largest, heaviest − and most expensive − scale models a radio system which operates on dual frequencies. With such a system the frequencies would be well separated, say the 35MHz and 72MHz bands and the change over from the principal to the back-up frequency would happen automatically if any interference was present on the primary frequency.

We are still very much on the learning curve with large models, aerodynamically, structurally and equipment wise. We can learn from one another and there is every reason to join the LMA (Large Model Association) to both learn from other members and to contribute from our own experiences.

Engines for the 'biggies' are either glo motors or spark-ignition (petrol) types. Multi-cylinder two and four stroke glow engines offer smooth running with a capability to swinging large propellers but they are expensive to buy and in fuel costs. The sound of a multi-cylinder four stroke engine is as near to scale as you are likely to get and the five, seven and nine cylinder types are beautiful pieces of engineering and remain practical – providing you do not mind risking a few hundred pounds worth of metal on the front of the model. A cheaper method of obtaining more suitable results from a standard two stroke single cylinder glow engine is by using a reducer unit. By reducing the engine crankshaft speed to about one third of the normal speed, larger diameter propellers can be used – these are more suited to

Spark ignition engines for large models are mostly converted chain saw style motors, although purpose manufactured model engines are coming onto the market in larger capacities.

larger, heavier models and are more efficient.

Petrol engines, in the larger capacities, offered the stimulus for creating larger models and make use of their ability to produce good torque at slower speeds. No longer do we have the original disadvantages of separate batteries, coils etc., for the ignition systems, the petrol engines are totally self-contained. Pressure carburettors, fitted to the modified industrial engines, ensure a positive supply of fuel with the fuel tank situated anywhere in the airframe. The petroil mixture used in the engines (as used in lawn mowers) is inexpensive compared with methanol based fuels and the petrol engine has a significantly lower fuel consumption than comparable glow engines. Effective fuel costs are at a ratio of around 3 to 1 in favour of petrol engines, a substantial saving considering that a gallon of fuel may be used during a flying session with large two stroke glow motors.

Starting these petrol 'beasties' is not unduly difficult once the techniques are learned – they can be hand started in the normal way, with a starter cord and pulley or from the specially uprated electric starters. If you want to create a bit of 'one upmanship' it is possible to fit an internal, electric powered, self starter. To place the model on the ground, stand back and flick a switch on the transmitter to start the engine will always provoke gasps of astonishment from the by-standers. Some radio interference problems have been experienced with certain engine/radio combinations but this is relatively rare and can normally be cured by plug lead screening, suppressors, bulkhead screening and positioning the receiver well away from the engine. Vibration levels tend to be higher with large single cylinder engines and more thought must be given to insulated engine mounts or to using a twin cylinder version. Cleanliness of operation with petrol engines – the oil content is low and the type of oil used is less 'clinging' than castor oils – is a further bonus. Most paint finishes are sufficiently fuel resistant to petrol without the need for further fuel-proofing. Petrol engines do offer benefits unobtainable with glow motors and further development of purpose designed units, plus comprehensively modified industrial examples, may be expected.

If you decide to join the growing band of 'outsize' modellers do remember your responsibilities – build and fly safely.

Large models are more impressive and fly better than the smaller types — they certainly entertain the public at displays.

CHAPTER 24

Helicopters and Autogyros

For many years the field of rotary wing model aircraft was relatively unexplored. Slight incursions were made mostly in the free flight and control line departments, but not resulting in any major breakthrough. As so often happens the breakthrough, when it did come, involved both helicopters and autogyros. Not that either were achieved without a tremendous amount of hard work, research and many failures before the success. Helicopters are now very much an established branch of our radio control hobby, and deservedly so, as they will appeal to a wide variety of modellers but especially those that cannot resist a challenge requiring very considerable flying skills. To many the thought of flying a helicopter was the dream of sitting on a deck chair in one's own garden and flying the model around the apple tree to land back at one's feet. The reality is far from the dream; to fly a helicopter at all − never mind in the confines of a garden − calls for skill, perseverance and practice. It is an expensive branch of the hobby − a helicopter kit contains a high degree of quality metal fabrications − but, to see the model performing in an identical fashion to the real thing is most rewarding.

Autogyros are something of an enigma. There are fewer problems than with a helicopter (because it is a simpler concept) but those problems can be more difficult to resolve. The basic difference between the two is that the helicopter motor is used to drive the main rotor and the tail rotor; by varying the pitch of the rotors, the tilt of the main rotor and the speed of the motor, it is possible to achieve forward, rearwards and sideways flight.

With an autogyro the motor is mounted on the front of the fuselage with a propeller, in the conventional power model arrangement, and the rotor blades are freely revolving. No tail rotor is fitted. A tailplane, fin and rudder are used, and this presents us with one of the problems; there is no device at the tail end to counteract the torque of

the main rotors. It is, theoretically, possible to design the rotors of an autogyro to hinge or flap or allow them to 'trail' during the forward movement of the blade. It is also theoretically possible to design the rotor blades to hinge or 'flap' but these innovations have yet to prove themselves in a number of successful designs − it will be done in time and, as with the first commercially available helicopter, one will wonder why it hadn't been done before.

AUTOGYROS

We are fortunate that some modellers are prepared to put a lot of time and effort into researching and experimenting with new modelling ideas. Frequently these modellers have no thought of monetary reward, or even recognition, but their efforts often contribute towards considerable advances in modelling. One such experimenter is Bob Brown who has been busy finding some of the answers to the 'problems' of model autogyros. Bob has tried out a whole series of models to test the efficiency and suitability of different rotor systems, some of the free flight types of autogyros include:-

1. Twin bladed single rotor with teeter head.
2. Four bladed single rotor with teeter head.
3. Four bladed single rotor (fixed) with stub wings.
4. Twin, two bladed, coaxial contra rotating rotors.
5. Tri rotored (side by side main rotors and one rotor replacing the tailplane) model.

But it was when he started development work with the side by side configuration of twin rotored autogyros that consistent success came and the suitability for adaptation to radio control. The theory of autogyro rotors is most interesting and Bob Brown's explanation is as follows: A conventional wing, if constrained at a certain incidence angle and allowed to move forward through the

Two helicopters constructed from commercial kits. The one below is the Bell Jet Ranger.

air, will descend in a more or less flat glide at a low rate of sink, dependent of course on the load it has to support. This forward motion can, however, under certain circumstances (e.g. a small landing area surrounded by obstacles) be an embarrassment!

However, imagine a series of such 'wings' each joined at one tip to a common rotating hub and spaced out like the spokes of a wheel. The forward motion now becomes a circular one, and the common central hub now sinks at a controlled rate without the need for horizontal movement.

Further, if the plane of rotation of the 'wings' or rotor blades is inclined and driven horizontally through the air (e.g. by using an airscrew) with its leading edge uppermost, it will not sink but rise, due to the extra velocity of the air passing through the disc, increasing the lift of the rotor blades.

Thus we have a 'wing substitute' which when driven through the air by a motor, will maintain height or climb but when deprived of a motive force will sink gently and vertically. Apparently, the ideal vertical landing flying machine.

Unfortunately, there are, as always, problems to be overcome. They are:

1. Because the rotor blades are travelling faster through the air when they are moving in the direction of flight than they are on the other side of the rotor disc, they produce more lift on one side of the disc than the other which tends to roll the whole disc (and thus the aircraft) on to its back.

2. In vertical descent, because of the friction of the rotor bearing, and because the fin has no 'steerage way', the whole aircraft tends to rotate in the same direction as the rotor.

3. Because of gyroscopic forces, if the rotor disc is disturbed (i.e. in pitch or roll) there is a reaction at right angles to the disturbing force, leading to instability. There would appear to be a number of solutions to these problems, as follows:

   (a) Allow the rotor blades to flap up and down, thus shedding the excess lift of the advancing blade and the gyroscopic forces (solves problems 1 and 3).

   (b) Allow the rotor blades to 'lag' in the plane of the rotor disc, thus slowing the advancing blade and accelerating the retreating blade (solves problem 1).

   (c) Incline the rotor head towards the side of the advancing blade to produce a sideslip which in turn causes the fin to exert a turning, and therefore rolling, force to counteract advancing-blade lift (solves problem 1 for steady flight conditions only).

   (d) Fit small auxiliary wings with sharply dihedralled tips (partly solves problems 1 and 3).

   (e) Fit two identical rotors rotating in opposite directions (solves problems 1, 2 and 3).

The angle of incidence of the individual rotor blades in relation to the plane of their rotation is best determined by experiment. The true angle of attack at any point along a blade depends on the horizontal velocity of the air relative to the blade due to its rotational velocity and the vertical velocity of air relative to the rotor disc, due to the descent of the autogyro through the air. (This is further complicated by the aircraft's forward motion when not descending vertically.) If the blade aerofoil has a very good lift/drag ratio, it can be a small positive angle. However, in model sizes the blades are so inefficient that a flat plate appears to be as good as anything and much easier to repair; they should then be rigged at a small negative angle to achieve autorotation (the writer uses a $-5°$).

Rotors normally require their blades to be higher at the tips than at the hubs; an upward slope (coning angle) of about 5° has proved adequate. The effect of this is analogous to dihedral on a normal wing. In order to ensure an adequate vertical component of airflow through the rotor disc when the autogyro is travelling forward under power, the axis of rotation should be given a backward tilt of 5°–7°.

Performance of the side by side twin rotor autogyro is extremely good and viceless. Models with this arrangement are not at all difficult to fly, certainly no more difficult than the average sports model, and they require little extra in the way of learning to fly them. They can be flown very much as a conventional model but with the bonus of the added ability to fly almost vertically up and down. Vertical flight, relative to the air, can, in fact be achieved, but with no forward speed directional control is lost due to a lack of air flow over the tail surfaces. With an engine failure in flight it is possible to land the autogyro in one of two ways. One is to quickly feed in down elevator to build up forward speed, keep the model descending into wind and then round out at the last minute and three-point the model on to the ground – a similar practice to that used with full-size helicopters. Alternatively the autogyro may be brought down vertically by holding up elevation. If the rotors are well balanced, and there is some wind blowing, the model will descend, maintaining its heading and touch down at a reasonable vertical rate. Hand launches or take-offs are possible and 'conventional' landings at normal forward speeds can be made. Basic aerobatic manoeuvres, loops, stall turns and rolls are part of the repertoire but inverted flight is very difficult to achieve. The reason inverted flight is a problem is that, on reaching the inverted position, the rotors must stop and then reverse the rotation to achieve 'opposite' lift. Even during rolls, and steep negative 'G' dives, the rotors will stop momentarily – quite a

Flying a twin rotor autogyro is no more difficult than flying a conventional sports model. The model below is flying inverted.

heartstopping moment, too, when it first happens. Three function radio is required (rudder, elevator and throttle) there being no equivalent to ailerons on these, fixed blade autogyros. Although it is very beneficial to have a reliable motor, capable of throttling consistently, it is not as critical as with a helicopter. An engine failure with a helicopter usually results in disaster.

Single rotor autogyros have been developed commercially by applying some of the technology from helicopters. A fully articulated and controlled rotor head certainly overcomes many of the torque problems associated with autogyros but you then have the disadvantage of needing a considerable take-off run before the rotors develop enough lift to become safely airborne. This problem, too, can be overcome by having a spin-up, by connecting, via a clutch, a drive from the engine to the rotor. By the time you have engineered the rotor head mechanism, the spin-up (for a jump start) drive and the clutch, you are approaching the complexities and costs of a true helicopter. As the limitations of the autogyros are greater than the helicopter, although it is easier to fly, it barely seems worth the trouble to opt for a single rotor autogyro. Keep to the more simple fixed pitch twin rotor autogyros.

HELICOPTERS

Technical breakthroughs, as stated previously, are indeed rare in the R/C model sphere but the award for the major breakthrough of recent years must go to the helicopter. Pioneers, as a breed, tend to be thoughtful, analytical, persistent and, above all, have the desire to overcome one problem after another until they reach their goal. All of these attributes were certainly required to produce the first practically successful radio controlled helicopter. Free flight helicopter designs had met with limited success, by ignoring some of the complexities of the aerodynamic problems and relying on the model flying to its own flight pattern. As soon as complete control of the model helicopter was required the problems became as great as, if not greater than, the problems associated with a full-size helicopter. The same number and type of controls are needed with the model but with less space for the engineering complexities and with no pilot to sit in the aircraft to relate to

the constant movements around the three axes; rotation around the yaw axis is, of course, much greater with a helicopter than with a fixed wing aircraft to the extent of 360° torque turns. Many modellers throughout the world had been applying their brains and technical skills in an attempt to solve the difficulties of achieving consistent and reliable helicopter flight, and it was the German, Dieter Schlüter, who first obtained the commercial breakthrough. After many years of study, and practical experiment, he produced semi-scale models of the Bell Huey Cobra, that not only flew well but were commercially viable in engineering terms and were 'repeatable' in their flying ability. Once the 'barrier' had been broken further individuals and manufacturers began to achieve similar successes and the R/C helicopter became a practical proposition – an expensive and challenging one – to the average modeller.

Most of the original helicopter models were large, weighing in excess of 10lb and it was left to the British designer, Peter Valentine, to extend the scope of R/C model helicopters by miniaturisation and making the 20cu.in. engine-powered model a feasible and workable proposition. Peter has, for his own sense of satisfaction, built helicopter models powered by much smaller engines (down to .020cu.in.) but this is for the purpose of experiment and is unlikely to become commercially available. Although not a pioneer in the design sense, a modeller responsible for a lot of 'spade' work in improving the standards of reliability and flying accuracy with helicopters is Dave Nieman. He was the first model helicopter pilot to fly the

Special wide 'trainee' undercarriage and floats assist the novice helicopter pilot to survive the first few flight trials without damaging too many rotor blades.

Scale subjects are quite popular with helicopter enthusiasts, but the majority of the models are of the sports variety and, at the best, semi-scale.

'Pod and boom' helicopters are used by the aerobatic helicopter flyers. This model is capable of advanced 3D manoeuvres.

model from a full-size helicopter and he was involved in the classic first cross-channel flight with a model helicopter. The subject is too complex to cover here in detail, but I would like to include some of his general comments to give a broader picture of the R/C helicopter branch of the hobby.

To build and fly a helicopter successfully, you don't need to be an expert in aerodynamics or have a degree in engineering or even have flown an R/C model before. In some respects it is an asset to be a newcomer to R/C modelling because some of the bad habits picked up in one's fixed-wing flying are often very hard to break. Some of the things you can get away with on a fixed-wing model could result in a crash with a helicopter. On the other hand, the benefits of having flown before are obvious, i.e. orientation, anticipation, familiarity with radio equipment, etc., etc.

The flying of R/C helicopters calls for a whole new set of rules and standards of building; after all we are calling for the same reliability in the model as is applied to its full-size counterpart.

Before rushing out and buying a kit, consider carefully your choice of model. They could be grouped into three categories:

Small — 19–25 power
Medium — 35–40 power
Large — 60–61 power and above

There are pros and cons for all three groups so forgive me for generalising, as it is difficult to analyse each individual model.

Small 19–25 power

Let's take the smallest group at the cheaper end of the price scale. They are fairly quick and simple to build, take a relatively inexpensive motor and can usually be transported even fully rigged in a small car. This is an important point because a model helicopter can sustain a fair amount of damage in transit. The main point in their favour is that they are pretty durable in the hands of a novice and crash damage is inexpensive and rapidly repaired.

On the debit side, they are not quite as easy to fly as the larger models, particularly under calm weather conditions. They tend to be rather sensitive on the tail rotor and sometimes marginal on power. Their small size can also be a problem when flying circuits, as it is easy to become disorientated at a distance. Nevertheless, a good introduction to R/C 'choppers'.

Medium 35–40 power

Still fairly economical, offering a much better power-to-weight ratio and there's not too much building. Both these and the smaller models are usually of the open frame or bubble and boom construction, but scale bodies may be available. A practical size — a little easier to see.

Large 60–61 power and above

Top end of the price range.

This being the most popular size, there is a

wider selection to choose from. Unlike the smaller models, most of this group employ a moulded or glass-fibre fuselage of semi-scale appearance. With this type and size of structure a bit more time and effort is needed to finish it, but the end result, when flying, could well be taken for full size. Depending on the motor used they generally have a good reserve of power.

Damage during the early stages of learning is usually confined to rotor blades, shafts, and superficial digs and scrapes, but a crash from any height could mean a time-consuming and more expensive repair with the larger model.

The trend with all models is to use collective pitch on the main rotors. A word of explanation for the uninitiated. Fixed pitch helicopters have the main rotor blades set at a pre-determined angle of attack. In order to gain lift, the speed of the rotors must be increased. However, there is an inevitable control lag with this system because the motor must first accelerate all the moving parts of the transmission and rotor head, etc., before the rotors produce more lift. Get rid of this delay and that's one less headache for the novice to overcome. Collective pitch has the pitch control of the main blades coupled with the throttle. As power is increased, so too is the pitch. This gives a much faster response to height adjustments as lift is gained or lost instantaneously.

The delay with fixed pitch calls for quite a lot of anticipation when hovering in gust conditions. Also when landing in a strong wind, very little power is required. The resultant low rotor speed slows response and things can get rather untidy. Collective pitch virtually eliminates this problem because the rotor speed remains fairly constant, giving good response even at low throttle settings. When landed, all lift can be dumped by closing the throttle with no danger of the model being blown over. There is a bit more work involved with collective, but careful setting up can produce a model which is a lot easier to fly.

THE MOTOR

Having decided on a particular model, one must now choose a suitable motor; as this is the heart of an R/C helicopter.

The large brown lump that you chiselled out of the front of your fixed-wing model won't do even

though it may have dragged your 'Super Swooper' around the sky at a great rate of knots. We are not looking for the motor that will turn a prop a couple of hundred rpm more than the next, for in a helicopter, the motor spends most of its time at between half and two-thirds throttle and full power is only used for aerobatics and stunt flying. What is required of a motor is good throttling characteristics, especially where the motor opening up cleanly can save a lot of hard landings. Other essentials are easy start, cool running and above all, reliability. I would personally trade a little power for a motor that throttles well, is reliable and not continually seizing up. Most of the modern Schnuerle ported motors fit the bill admirably; they are manufactured in a version specifically for helicopters.

RADIO EQUIPMENT

Although you can use a standard four or five-function radio outfit for controlling a helicopter it is more usual to purchase one of the sets specifically designed for helicopter use. Without getting into the technicalities, there are features for helicopter control (such as throttle-hold, pitch curves etc.) that are not to be found on standard, fixed-wing model, transmitters. For accurate, precise flying of helicopters you require rapid reaction time not only from the pilot but also from the equipment. This is an area where it pays to buy the best radio control system, if you are serious about flying this type of model. You are going to pay quite a lot of money for the helicopter kit, the engine and ancillary equipment − it would be illogical to skimp on the radio. A PCM computer combo (transmitter and receiver) will offer more options and automatic controls than a standard FM set will provide. The servos should be of the ball-raced, high-speed and torque types, with as little deadband as possible. A gyro is a virtual must for helicopters these days. This is used in conjunction with the tail rotor pitch control and helps to compensate for torque reactions due to engine throttle changes. As previously stated, learning to fly a helicopter is not, for the average person, easy but you might as well have as many advantages as possible. This is not a branch of the hobby where it is wise to 'do-it-on-the-cheap', I would think very hard before deciding to buy a second-hand helicopter and equipment and would certainly want to see it demonstrated before purchase. All too many 'would-be' helicopter flyers are seduced into the glamour of this form of flying, only to find that the reality does not quite meet the dream and it isn't a case of 'instant success'. As a result, there are quite a few second-hand helicopters and radios for sale. They may have had some pretty rough and ignorant usage and what may appear to be a bargain, can turn out to be an expensive mistake. If, however, the purchaser lost interest in the idea before even getting to the construction and flying stages, there may indeed be a bargain going. Your first action, in any case, should be to buy a specialist book on the subject of helicopter models (such as *Radio Controlled Helicopters* by Nick Papillon published by Nexus Special Interests 1996) − this can give far more information on the subject than it is possible to include in this chapter.

PUTTING IT ALL TOGETHER

Building your helicopter can give as much pleasure as flying it. Many flyers treat building as a necessary evil but if you take your time and don't be too impatient to see it fly, the result will be a far nicer model.

Before starting any building, read the instructions carefully. Study the plan to identify the components now as it will save mistakes later on. Most instructions have some reference to the theory of helicopter flight; read this also as it will help you to know the function of each part before assembly. Follow the building sequence and don't be tempted to take shortcuts.

Having completed the building and ground checking of your helicopter you will, naturally, be very keen to rush down to the field and put to test all the warnings of how difficult is the whole concept of flying model helicopters. However, as with fixed-wing aircraft, there are sensible and idiotic ways of approaching the business of learning to fly a helicopter.

From here on, let's assume that you have not been able to enlist the help of an experienced helicopter pilot. Something worth mentioning at this point is that not all good pilots are good teachers. Your club's resident prima-donna is not necessarily your best choice of instructor.

The last and most important item on the list is a good assistant. Ideally he should be someone who is keen but not too pushy, to lend a hand, give moral support and encouragement. Although difficult to find, such a person can be a real asset to help you through the initial stages. Also very useful to carry the heavy gear!

SAFETY

Dave Nieman, one of the first British helicopter pilots to conquer the vagaries of flying rotorwing aircraft − models and full-size − had this to say about learning to fly and the proper respect one should have for the process. Although it was written some time ago the advice remains relevant today.

Before venturing out to the field, stop and think for a moment. The machine you have created offers a real challenge, a great deal of satisfaction, opening up new horizons and adding a whole new dimension to your flying. But these rewards don't come without a certain number of potential dangers, all of which can be minimised with a little commonsense and patience. Don't be frightened of the model, but treat it with a healthy respect. Do not underestimate the forces involved in all those rotating parts. As you would not dream of poking under a motor whilst it was running, likewise keep a safe distance from your helicopter when it is doing its thing. Should you become a little blasé about the dangers, something to bear in mind is that in some cases, the tip speed of the main rotor blades can reach over 250mph and centrifugal forces acting on the blades can exceed 250lb. If the rotors were to hit you on the head, you'd know all about it; then again − you probably wouldn't. If you have any reason at all to doubt the reliability of the model or the radio then DON'T fly it. Avoid flying near obstructions such as buildings, trees, cars, etc. as apart from the obvious dangers, the turbulent conditions created by these in even the slightest breeze will make flying very difficult. DO NOT FLY near or over spectators or other flyers, at any time. 11lb of whirling and thrashing machinery dropping in unexpectedly will do little to enhance relations with fellow man.

OFF TO THE FIELD

You will probably be very proud of your model

and eager to show it off to the rest of the lads. This is only natural. But you can do without an audience on the first outing as you will be pretty busy and any distractions at this critical stage could mean costly mistakes. Therefore, it is better to find a quiet spot away from it all to carry out the initial adjustments. Model helicopters are still a novelty and consequently they attract a lot of attention, so on your first trip to the local flying field BEWARE!

Don't leave your model unattended, because the 'How's it work' and 'What's this for' brigade are everywhere. They are usually well meaning but notorious for blade tweaking and tail rotor kicking, which, if passed unnoticed, can be extremely dangerous. When all the questions have been answered and all curiosity satisfied, at the risk of appearing unsociable it is best to move away from the main group, ensuring of course that there are no frequency clashes. Set up at a safe distance where you can still be seen, but out of the path of other models. For some unknown reason there are a few unenlightened fixed-wing flyers who have a real aversion to helicopters. Happily they are a very small minority. During training the model spends most of its time on or near the ground and you can be droning your way through a tank for up to half an hour or more, so even the most amiable of your fellow club members may get a little disenchanted with you once the novelty has worn off. This is another reason for keeping your distance.

Once you are set up, carry out the prescribed range check for your particular radio gear. Although this first outing may be only to carry out adjustments, it is as well to get into the habit of doing a pre-flight check. Something along these lines:

Check for damage in transit.
Radio charged and operating properly.
Rotor head correctly fitted.
Main and tail rotor blades secure and undamaged.
All ball links secure and in good condition.
Tank fuel, and pressure lines secure and undamaged.

All these are quite easily checked, but the more involved items such as all nuts, bolts, couplings, drive shafts, push-rods, servos, etc., should be inspected as part of your routine maintenance and not left to be done on the field.

Only when you are completely satisfied that all is in order should you attempt to start the motor.

Most model helicopter kits contain adequate flying instructions but there are a few aspects that may assist the learner to avoid some of the more common pitfalls encountered by newcomers to helicopters. Flying a model helicopter, or any other radio controlled aircraft, is not something which can be mastered simply by reading a book. Like any other skill, proficiency only comes with patience and a lot of practice, for which there is no literary substitute. Although many of the kit helicopters are sufficiently responsive for the *proficient* helicopter pilot they may be slightly lacking in this respect due to the slowness of response of *you*, the pilot.

Initially your reactions are a lot slower than the model's until you gain experience and learn to anticipate its movements. Flying a helicopter is not the same as flying something like a pylon racer, where you have instant response to a given control input. Something which will give you an idea of the feel of a helicopter is a home-made simulator/game. This consists of a table approximately 18in.sq., supported underneath by a ball joint on which it can pivot. Attached to two adjacent sides are push rods from servos mounted on a baseboard. These represent the cyclic controls, roll and pitch. The servos are connected to a receiver and operated by the transmitter in the normal way. A steel ball is placed in the centre of the table and to simulate a steady hover, you have to keep it there. This is not too difficult with small corrective movements, but as soon as the ball moves any distance from the centre, it really accelerates and you can get into a real pickle trying to stop it − just like the real thing. Remember that you are not having to cope with any wind and the table is maintaining a constant heading, not swinging about its vertical axis, as would be the case if it were a model. By the way, when the ball reaches the edge of the table you have crashed!

This may sound like just a silly game, but in fact it is quite a useful preparation. It costs virtually noting in time and materials to build. The table must be perfectly flat, if necessary top it with a piece of glass. The pivot can be just a countersunk hole in the table into which you can fit a piece of dowel with a rounded end. A better method is to steal a top from a roll-on deodorant bottle, screw the ball to the underside of the table and epoxy the socket to a short length cut from a broom

Model helicopters have flown the English Channel but it is no easy matter to control the model from the confines of a full-size helicopter.

handle. Result − a perfect ball joint with no friction and capable of being snapped apart for storage. The only problem with this project is that if the family get their hands on it, you may have to buy another set of radio gear for the model!

The most exacting phase of helicopter flight is the hover, and it is this that you must learn first. On no account should the model be tethered or restrained in any way, as this would upset its natural stability and you would learn nothing by doing so except maybe how to repair crash damage.

One point I must stress is aimed at the competent fixed-wing pilot who is about to fly his first helicopter. Don't be tempted to fly round straight away, for no matter how good you think you are, there is little chance of surviving a flight without the model sustaining some damage. Really, the easiest way to learn is to start at the beginning. There is far less loss of face by exercising a little restraint than confidently hurtling around the sky for a few brief moments, only to end up by ploughing the model into the ground. Flying around is relatively easy, it is on the approach and landing where most people come unstuck. In forward flight a model helicopter behaves in much the same way as a fixed-wing model. It is the type of flying that is peculiar to helicopters that the fixed-wing pilot has to learn, i.e. hover, vertical, lateral and backwards flight. As most take-offs and landings employ at least one of the aforementioned,

you can see the folly in premature circuits.

Training flights should be made on the smoothest level ground you can find, clear of any obstructions and with plenty of space upwind. When flying from a rough uneven surface it is virtually impossible to predict the direction in which the model will travel when you lift it off. Even a slight depression or the smallest tuft of grass is sufficient to trip the model over as it will be skating around quite a bit at first. For this reason, the best all-round form of training undercarriage has proved to be inflatable floats. They are very durable and relieve the airframe of much of the punishment found in training, but more important, they allow the model to slide around and reduce the risk of it tripping over. Also, the model does not have to be at a complete standstill before touching down, a manoeuvre which takes quite a long time to perfect. It is not true that helicopters can be flown only under ideal weather conditions. Some of the Navy's Air−Sea Rescue operations put the lie to that rumour. Admittedly these are full size, but when scaled down you can still be having fun with a model helicopter in conditions where flying some fixed-wing models is just hard work. Avoid flying in strong winds during training, particularly gusty conditions, as such conditions call for quick reactions and good throttle response, especially near the ground. On the other hand a dead calm hot summer's day is not much use to the beginner

225

Non-scale helicopters can sometimes be converted to scale with an optional scale 'add-on' kit. This Hughes helicopter model is powered by a Laser four-stroke engine.

either. With high temperatures and no wind at all, there is a noticeable lack of lift which requires more power and increases the chances of the motor overheating.

No doubt development of helicopter design will continue and advancements of mechanics, automatic stability devices and engine reliability will be made, but it is unlikely that the model R/C helicopter will ever become an easy aircraft to master. In the early days of helicopter flying it was thought that the majority of fixed-wing type aerobatic manoeuvres would never be a possibility for helicopters, stall turns and torque turns (rotating on its own rotor shaft axis) were the limits of the repertoire. Now, loops and rolls are commonplace, indeed, the R/C model helicopter is capable of a flight pattern not attempted by the full-size versions − that of continuous inverted flight. It may seem, to the purist, totally incongruous to see

a helicopter with the rotor blade a few inches above the grass and the fuselage sticking up above but, this is often used as a party piece for the expert model helicopter pilot. Free style 3D aerobatics now include remarkable combinations of tumbles, rolls and tight radius manoeuvres all carried out at very low level and in close proximity to the pilot. At the opposite end of the spectrum, scale model helicopters are becoming far more scale authentic (using the correct number of rotor blades and dispensing with fly-bars) and the training models *are* becoming easier to fly. The complexities of control (all four functions are used for *most* of the time compared with the two or three of the fixed-wing aircraft) plus the problems of orientation are sufficient to ensure that the helicopter remains one of the 'challenges' of radio control model flying and building.

CHAPTER 25

Maintenance

In the Royal Air Force over 90% of all flying accidents are attributed to pilot error. This may look, on the surface, as if the standard of flying must be pretty awful but this is not the case. The reason for the high percentage is that the maintenance, as with all aircraft, is absolutely thorough and nothing is left to chance. With an aircraft, maybe carrying hundreds of people flying over the sea and built-up areas, it is imperative that the aircraft and equipment is operating to 100% efficiency. The art, if that is the correct word, of maintenance is to detect the fault and carry out the remedial action *before* the trouble happens. I will not say that maintaining a model and its equipment is quite as essential as the maintenance on a Jumbo Jet aircraft but just ask yourself this question. Would you like to have your children, or for that matter yourself, standing near to where a model is flying at speeds up to 100mph knowing that at any moment the model may be uncontrollable? Poor maintenance can result in just such conditions. Remember that a pennyworth of prevention is worth . . .

We can learn a lot about maintenance and checking models and equipment from procedures carried out on full-size aircraft and by pilots. Most procedures are laid down, must be strictly observed and are often learnt off by heart − frequently by the use of a mnemonic. A typical example would be, for pre-take off checks on a light aircraft T.T.M.F.F.A.O. − Trim, throttle, mixture, flaps, fuel on and sufficient, altimeter and oil pressure. In addition to pre, post and in flight checks there are also daily inspections of the aircraft, before flying, and more rigorous quarterly checks, annual inspections and others related to the number of hours flown. We all know that even with the most rigorous checks and maintenance of our model equipment things can still go wrong. Radio equipment is only as strong as its weakest link and if a transistor fails, out of the many components used in the outfit we may have real problems on our hands. It is the least we can do to keep all risks to an absolute minimum by good maintenance. Let us take a look at the drill for checking and maintenance, based on full-size aircraft procedures.

I remember an Australian model flyer, who also happened to be a Boeing 747 captain, who had three check lists, all typed out, for his R/C Sea Fury model. One he used before leaving for the field, the second for assembling and preparing the model and the third he used before each flight. He would religiously follow the check procedures and, as standby pilot for a major display in Sydney, he never failed to become airborne with a minimum of fuss and a maximum of safety. If regular checks are good enough for a 'Jumbo' pilot, surely they are good enough for us. Why not write out your own check lists.

DAILY INSPECTION

Perhaps not daily but at least every time we go out flying.

1. Check radio equipment installation. Receiver and batteries properly packed in foam. Receiver aerial not strained or frayed. All plugs secure including battery plug, aileron plug inserted in socket (where fitted). Servos secure in their mountings but not over-tight. Switch operating cleanly. Transmitter fitted with aerial.
2. Check linkages and hinges. Full and free movement of hinges and no damage to hinges. Pushrod keepers in place. Horns and clevises connected − retainers in position.
3. Engine not loose on its mounting. Servo linkage free. Propeller inspected for cracks, stress marks and nicks in leading and trailing edge. Prop nut tight.
4. Wheels secure, free-running and correctly aligned.

5. Wings properly secure, rubber bands not deteriorated and sufficient used. Check bolts and anchors when this type of fixing is used. Tail surfaces securely in place.
6. No warps in wing and tail surfaces (warps that have been 'cured' can tend to creep back in).
7. Batteries fully charged, including starter battery.

Assuming that all of these checks are completed satisfactorily, should any one item not be correct it must be put right before you proceed to the flying field, complete with field box and ancillary equipment, and on to the next series of checks,

STARTING CHECKS

1. Sufficient fuel in the fuel tank and flow to the engine clear.
2. Battery lead and clip connected to glow plug clip.
3. Engine primed, either by finger choking or a prime in the exhaust port.
4. Glow clip connected to glow plug.
5. Engine started by hand or with electric starter. Keep clear of the propeller arc.
6. Remove glow clip from head.
7. Wipe your hands with paper towel. Greasy oily hands and transmitter cases and sticks are not compatible.

8. Check thoroughly that no-one else is using the same frequency − this should be done at all stages of testing − and use the frequency peg if this system is being operated. Check that you have the correct frequency flag on your transmitter and that it is clearly displayed. With synthesised frequency and changeable crystal outfits check that the transmitter and receiver are matched.
9. Carry out range check, with aerial retracted or in accordance with manufacturers' instructions, before the first flight of each session This can be carried out at home if you have a suitable garden.
10. Ensure that the aerial is then fully extended.

PRE-TAKE OFF CHECKS

1. Engine is running smoothly and in the correct direction (it has been known for models to be launched with the engine backwards, just check that the 'wash' from the propeller is being blown towards the tail).
2. That the full range of engine speed is available, the idle is low enough and that the 'pick up' on opening the throttle is quick and progressive. Hold the model with the nose nearly vertical to see that the engine does not lean out too much.

Check the operation of all controls before giving the OK for the launch − when hundreds of hours have been spent designing and making a model, those final checks are all the more imperative.

Fingers and head as far from the propeller as possible.

3. That all control surfaces are operating fast and smoothly − no binding causing the servos to 'labour' − and that the surfaces are moving in the correct directions, i.e. left rudder on the transmitter stick is giving left rudder on the model etc.

4. There are no vibratory effects on the airborne radio equipment. No glitches or sudden twitches of the control surfaces or engine throttle.

5. That no-one is coming in to land or is taking off, and that no-one is trying to attract your attention. With the engine going it is very easy to miss someone who is calling to you, from a distance, to warn you that something is wrong.

6. All these checks should be carried out standing clear of the actual take-off and landing or pits area. If you are standing too close to the runway, you are likely to impede, or be hit by a model landing. Landing is the most difficult and dangerous period of flying and even experts can slip up sometimes.

It may seem to you that all of these checks are going to take up most of your flying session but, once you have a little experience, you will find that it will probably take less time to carry them out than it will to read them here. With all systems 'go' you are now ready to take-off and carry out your flight and landing. This is covered in Chapter 13, 'First Flights'. Should you, at any time during the flight, be unsure of your equipment, your model or yourself, land immediately.

POST-LANDING CHECKS

1. Switch off the receiver, then the transmitter − always in that order. In some radio equipment the servos will all 'move up to one end' of their travel if the transmitter is switched off before the receiver and this does not improve them or the linkages. There is also the danger that, with the transmitter off and receiver on, someone else, on an adjacent frequency, could take 'command' of your model accidentally. The results, quite clearly, could be both dangerous and damaging. If you have landed some way away from the landing area, and your helper is kindly fetching the model for you, brief him to switch off the receiver as soon as he reaches the model and to give a hand signal to that effect. This will enable you to then switch off the transmitter also and allow another modeller to carry on flying on that frequency.

2. Return the frequency peg to the control area.

3. Park the model neatly − where it will not be in the way of other modellers and where it will not be trodden on or knocked.

4. Wipe the model clean of excess exhaust oil ready for the next flight.

5. If you have been assisted during the flight by another flyer make a point of thanking him − it is always nice to know your efforts are appreciated.

6. After the last flight of the day empty the fuel tank and clean the model down with detergent and water, making a point of cleaning the rubber bands as well. Fuel will affect the rubber bands and they, too, need maintenance.

7. When you return home check quickly through the radio equipment and linkages etc. again. This is particularly important if you have had a crash or hard landing or have had some suspected radio trouble. Clean the transmitter case.

8. Recharge the batteries. If you are going to be flying within a week the batteries should hold their charge over this period. For longer periods you should still recharge the batteries immediately and then give them a boost of four or five hours the day before you intend to fly.

9. Put the model away. Use large polythene bags for storing the model in, when they are to be kept in a dusty atmosphere.

DE-BRIEF

All service pilots of full-size aircraft and such people as motor cycle and racing car drivers etc., know the importance of debriefing after a flight or a race. The function of debriefing is to ascertain, at the earliest convenient moment after the event, i.e. before it is forgotten, what faults or mistakes occurred and how to rectify them. Your aim after each flying session should be to mentally analyse your flights, to remember what went wrong and to rectify these faults. This may all sound rather technical and unnecessary, but, in fact, it is simple and most important. Let us imagine how our mental debriefing may go: 'Arrived at the field OK, noticed the farmer had chopped some hedges and trees down exposing the ditch, and also exposing some dumped empty cans of fuel − must mention this at next club meeting. Assembled model − nearly used up all large rubber bands, must buy some more. "Fuelled up" model and started engine; engine tended to "cut"; problem eventually traced to dirt in the fuel − must be sure to filter all fuel before using. Also noticed that one of the leads to the accumulator is nearly severed

from its tag − must resolder to tag and support the solder joint properly. Flew model for three of four flights, all tended to be over elevated − must make provision on the model for easier elevator trimming on the field. Remember, on thinking back, that I was doing nearly all my turns and all my circuits to the left − must practise doing more right-hand turns and circuits on next flying session, it may come in handy one day'.

Well, those are the type of thoughts you may have after a flying session, so make a written note of them (no, you will not remember them otherwise!) and act upon them at the earliest opportunity.

QUARTERLY CHECKS

The actual frequency of these checks will vary with the amount of flying you are doing over a certain period. In the summer, with a lot of flying activity it may be necessary to carry them out every month but, at other less busy times, every two or three months will be sufficient.

1. Check engine cylinder head bolts for tightness.

2. Check fuel tank for split or deteriorating fuel tubing. Check for leaks and clean out tank interior if necessary. This can be carried out by thoroughly flushing out with alcohol (methanol).

3. Remove filter and replace or dismantle and clean out.

4. Remove silencer and clean out.

5. Check the airframe for any stress cracks, fuel seepage or weakening joints.

6. Clean out the engine and fuel tank bays thoroughly, re fuel-proofing if necessary.

7. Clean out the interior of the model, in the radio compartment, removing radio equipment only if absolutely required. It is preferable to disturb the radio equipment, once it is installed and functioning correctly, as little as possible.

8. Check the undercarriage for sound solder joints or excessive play of undercarriage bolts.

WINTER SERVICING

Perhaps you will be the type of radio control flyer that will like to fly the whole of the year round, taking the cold and wet with the hot and fine. I hope so, because there can be the same exhilaration and satisfaction in flying on a cold winter's after-

Two unscheduled arrivals. Tarmac runways can be very hard on models — grass would have been kinder.

noon, albeit less comfortable, as on a warm summer's day. There must be a period, however, that must be set aside for major overhauling when engines and radio equipment can be returned to the manufacturers for servicing, airframes refurbished and, of course, new models built. It should always be your aim to have at least one reserve airframe in stock to avoid the frustration of having some beautiful flying weather and nothing to fly.

An engine that is going to be out of commission

for a number of months should never be left installed in a model, collecting dirt and dust, until it is next flown. Clean out the interior by flushing it out completely with methanol or petrol. The exterior, especially the burnt on fuel residues on the top of the cylinder head, can be cleaned with some types of oven cleaners. Experiment with household cleaners and find out which does the job most efficiently but do not allow any of the cleaner to enter the interior workings of the engine in case it contains elements of a corrosive nature. When the exterior is thoroughly clean, wash off with methanol or petrol. Protect the inside of the engine during storage with a few drops of gun oil dropped into the exhaust ports and air-intake and turn the engine over once or twice. Put the engine in a polythene bag and wind a rubber band around the neck of the bag.

Fuel oil seepage is always a problem with powered models and with a new model; particular note should be made of any places showing signs of oil infiltration. Remedial action may consist of further coats of fuel-proofer, or the use of one of the wing seating vinyl tapes for sealing the gap between the wings and fuselage. The important thing to remember is wherever the oil is getting in it must be stopped to prevent deterioration. For this reason also, the model should be cleaned down after each session. The method of cleaning down will depend a lot on the type of finish on the model. Methylated spirit is excellent for models covered in heat-shrink film. It is also suitable for models finished with hot fuel-proofer, but may gradually take a little of the surface off after repeated cleaning, the model will then require reproofing.

After a season's hard flying you may find that the radio equipment is performing as well as ever − I hope you do. Despite this there is bound to be some wear and tear on the moving parts of the equipment and the deterioration so gradual that you may not have noticed it. It is advisable to return the equipment to the manufacturers, or the servicing agents, for a routine check over. They have the electronic equipment to find any small faults and, with them rectified at this stage, may save you from an expensive crash at a later date. Do not leave it until just before the beginning of the next flying season before getting the outfit serviced; if everyone does this somebody is going to be disappointed when the equipment cannot be returned in time.

Whether or not you decide to return the equipment to the servicing agent you should at least check the servo and switch leads for any damage and, most importantly, the lead from the battery switch to ensure that there is no 'black wire corrosion'. This occurs only on the negative − normally black-sleeved − wire and will be obvious by the discolouring at the soldered joints and, if the covering is stripped off the wire, the dirty dull appearance of the wire, not bright and shiny as it should be. Replacement of the wire and possibly the plug and socket and switch is essential if this corrosion is found.

REPAIRS

Repairs to the model will certainly, sooner or later, be required. The important point is to carry out the repair at the earliest possible time. Try not to be tempted to carry on flying when obvious damage is apparent; it could be dangerous if there is the risk of structural failure and, at the best, it could make the eventual repair more difficult. Oil on the structure is one of the biggest problems to effecting a sound repair. Most adhesives will not stick to it nor will covering materials. It is possible to remove a lot of the oil by treating it with dope thinners and wiping the oil affected area with paper towels. When the structure is badly contaminated with fuel there is no alternative to cutting the area away and replacing it with new wood.

When a major repair is contemplated you must first make the decision whether to repair or whether it may be more sensible to rebuild that particular structural item. There are no hard and fast rules that can be given in this respect; it is more a question of common sense. If repairing will result in a weakened, or considerably heavier, structure then the decision must be to rebuild. I know modellers who find a fascination and challenge in making repairs and most crashed models are capable of being repaired. I detest repairing models and am far more likely to rebuild a model − or build a new one completely. Whether you find you like or dislike repairing do attempt to make the best job possible of it. A bad repair can seriously affect the flying characteristics of the model and make flying a lot more difficult. After a number of repairs have been made to a model you

Helicopters require a thorough blade balance and tracking check before flight. An assistant requires a cool nerve to hold the aircraft down.

will certainly find that the model is a lot heavier than it was originally, and, if it is also getting tricky to fly, it is time to retire it before you start to put the radio equipment to unnecessary risk.

Radio equipment repairs are strictly for the experts. Definitely no fiddling and attempts at home repairs here whatsoever. Damage to the equipment, or failure of it to function correctly, and the outfit should be immediately returned to the manufacturers or service agents. Assuming that you are unable to take the set personally for repair or servicing it will have to be posted off, a fairly terrifying thought for delicate electronic equipment but not too bad if the equipment is really well packed. The best box for use when packing the outfit is the original box that it was packed in. That box was almost certainly designed to be capable of being sent through the post originally. It will also have the foam packing specifically designed for all of the components. Without the original box all of the equipment must be carefully wrapped in foam using scrap polystyrene foam to fill the gaps.

Radio control equipment manufacturers try to give the best repair and servicing facilities they can. How long your outfit is with them will depend on a lot of factors. Perhaps they have a batch of new sets to finish off or perhaps they are awaiting delivery of a certain component before they can complete your repair. It is very difficult not to be impatient for the return of *your* equip-

ment but do allow a *reasonable* length of time before writing irate letters to the manufacturers. The chances are that your letter, if it only criticises and complains, will only have the opposite effect to that intended. Here is a suggested list of the action to be taken when a radio control set is returned.

1. Return the *complete* system even if you suspect only one part is at fault.
2. Completely separate the system from your installation. Do not send the receiver taped in foam, servos mounted on trays etc.
3. If plugs have been changed, or other modifications made which interfere with standard servicing procedures, you are likely to be charged more for the factory returning the equipment to its original condition for testing. Any unauthorised repairs and modifications will almost certainly involve the factory in additional work and therefore cost you more.
4. Disconnect the receiver battery pack and be sure the transmitter switch is off and cannot be accidentally knocked on.
5. Pack carefully and be generous with the amount of packing material.
6. Write a brief but thorough explanation of the problems encountered and the service required. Enclose this in an envelope and tape it onto the back of your transmitter. Label the servos to show their function at the time of the trouble.
7. Be certain to include your name, address and

Preparing P51 for R.O.G. and the moment of truth!

postal code number with the outfit, preferably with some self-addressed adhesive labels for returning the parcel.

8. Include a packing list of all of the items returned, making sure they match the list and keeping a copy for yourself.

9. Insure the parcel, or send it registered post.

10. Do not be tempted to explain to the manufacturers that the equipment failed in mid-air when the damage was really the result of a 'pilot error' crash. You may mislead the manufacturers and will cause them to take longer over the repair. Also, they are not fools and will eventually be able to discern the reason for the damage.

CHAPTER 26

Onwards and Upwards

So at last we have mastered those first nervous and tense moments of the first flights and are well on our way to becoming proficient pilots. We have certainly experienced one of the biggest thrills that we shall encounter in radio control model flying — the first solo — but there are many more exciting and exhilarating moments to come. What does the future hold in store for us? Well it is literally a case of the sky is the limit. In common with many other hobbies and sports you will get as much from it as you are prepared to put into it. Whatever your prime interest is — the building of the model, the flying only — radio control model aircraft have enough interest and challenge to keep you involved until you are in your dotage. Should anyone, referring to radio control model aircraft, moan to you that he is bored because he has 'done it all', don't believe him — it is impossible. It will be the modeller that is 'boring' and not the hobby. There are so many branches of the hobby and types of aircraft that one lifetime could never be sufficient to try all aspects to them; even in a fleeting fashion. Let us consider some of the other possibilities not covered in depth in the remainder of the book.

1. AEROBATIC COMPETITIONS

In the top competition field an aerobatic flyer must concentrate 100% on this form of flying if he hopes to succeed. This will entail practice week in and week out and still further practice until he knows the aerobatic schedules and sequences inside out. His dedication is of the style that makes great athletes, great tennis players, great singers and, in fact, all people that want to rise to the top of their particular tree. There is no easy way to become *the* top aerobatic flyer in the country or the world. Do not be fooled into thinking that, by buying the same radio outfit, same engine and building the same model, you will become as good as the

champion. You *may* be able to but it depends how willing you are to spend the hours of devotion necessary to improve your skills.

All of us do not want to become world beaters at aerobatics but that certainly does not preclude us from enjoying flying aerobatic manoeuvres, or from taking part in competitions at a lower level. As with a full-size pilot, you should be capable of putting the aircraft through every safe manoeuvre the aircraft is capable of performing — and recovering from it. Until you reach this stage of proficiency you are not the true master of the aircraft. Whether you opt for aerobatics for fun or for competition it will certainly enhance your enjoyment of flying.

2. SCALE MODELS

There are really two sorts of radio control scale modellers. One prefers the building of the model and the other enjoys more the flying. The former will go to the 'N'th' degree to produce a model that is as close in miniature as humanly possible to the original aircraft. No small details are omitted, from scratch marks on the wing roots where the pilot climbs into the cockpit to the miniature maps in the pilot's overalls. I confidently expect that the pilot in the model will, one of these days, be radio controlled himself and will unstrap himself, climb out of the cockpit and walk away. Many thousands of painstaking hours are spent on some of these 'super' scale models and, remember, that they must be test flown as any lesser model and that they are also at the same mercies of radio failure and interference. Little wonder that some of these miracles of workmanship are only flown once or twice a year in competitions.

The second type of scale model is much less sophisticated and is aimed at giving a scale appearance of the model when viewed from a few yards away and when it is in flight. The general outlines of the model faithfully follow the full-size counterpart although there may be a few deviations of tail surface areas, dihedral etc. to give a model with improved flight characteristics. This semi-scale approach (or Class 2 Scale) is popular because it produces a model that is practical, and can be flown at weekends, but can enter its own class of competition. When there was only one class of scale competition this type of modeller was put off from entering as he considered that he had no chance of winning against the super scale entries. Occasionally there were upsets, however, when weather conditions were bad many of the owners of the better finished models could not or would not fly. The reasons were either that the model had had insufficient trimming or flying or the pilot had insufficient practice. The results were that a modeller, with a 'second class' model, would come along and take first place by virtue of his better flying.

Now, standards of building and flying are so high at national and international scale competition levels that, to win, you must have a superbly finished and detailed model and to fly it with skill, accuracy and authority. So superb are the models that it is impossible for the aspiring scale modeller to produce a model to competition standards more than every few years, you have to be that dedicated. After all this is a *flying* scale branch of the hobby and unless the models will fly we might as well go back to building 'solid' models.

Should you have the opportunity of going along to the British National competitions, or other large scale competitions, I would heartily recommend that you take a look at the excellence of so many scale models. It should encourage you towards trying it yourself.

3. PYLON RACING

Imagine four models hurtling around a tight pylon course, at speeds well in excess of 100mph, locked in speed combat and this will give you some idea of the thrill, both participating and watching, of pylon racing. This is not an activity for the novice; the speeds involved and the reactions required for making the pylon turns, make it an event for the highly proficient flyer only. The dangers inherent in the race, not to mention the cost of damaged models and equipment, automatically

eliminates all but the experts and strong of heart. These .40cu.in. engined racers are generally based on formula 1, and other forms of full-size racing aircraft. Because it is a highly competitive sport, where maximum speed is essential, there is always the possibility of getting pylon models that are beginning to look like anything but the full-size aircraft – but still just manage to keep within the rules. This is one of the penalties of development from competitive flying and one that has to be reviewed from time to time. Again, in common with other competitive classes, much time is put in, on the model, on flying and particularly on the engine, by the modeller determined to be in the winners' circle. Pylon racing *is* only for the competitive modeller; there is little point in building a model and having no one to race with. Although they make fast aerobatic models there are many superior designs for this purpose.

The racing enthusiast who does not wish to spend the time or money on FA1 pylon racing is able to compete and enjoy all of the thrills, in a smaller class of pylon racing – Club 20. This class is for models using specific standard engines of .19 and .20cu.in. capacity and two functions – aileron and elevator with optional engine control. Models are built to minimum design sizes, must be 'scale-like' in appearance and with minimum/maximum weight limitations. Because it is a class designed so that the average club can organise a competition, the regulations are kept as simple as possible. It is unlikely, too, that clubs will have a flying field that is entirely suitable for small models to take-off and, therefore, models are hand launched.

Racing with these miniature models, at speeds of 100mph plus, can be every bit as exciting as with the larger models but it is still not a class for the novice flyer. For the novice racer, yes! It will give him a chance to take part in the excitement of pylon racing without breaking the bank.

There are other classes of pylon racing for those modellers not wishing to become involved in highly expensive engines, tuned pipes etc. Sport 40, as the name suggests is a class for '40' sized engines, but only front intake, side exhaust types of modest costs. In other respects the class is similar to FAE pylon racing with similar specifications for the airframes and the flying course. Quickie 500 is another '40' engined class, again with limits on the engines used and with an airframe that is definitely not scale or semi-scale. Attempts to popularise this latter class meet with spasmodic success.

4. DEMONSTRATION TEAMS

It is by way of a compliment to our hobby that many requests are received from organisers of fetes and rallies for demonstrations by radio control model aircraft. This is an excellent opportunity to improve public relations and to introduce new people to the hobby. Unfortunately many of these opportunities are wasted, or at least limited in their usefulness, by the lack of organisation by the organising club or group. When you put on a display before the public make it one worthy of the hobby and one that will show, to the best advantage, your skills. For large clubs or groups it is well worthwhile forming a permanent display group and working out set procedures and schedules for flying, varying according to the demands and limitations of the particular event. Flying a number of different aircraft in a random fashion may be fun to you but it will not mean very much to the average member of the public. Sort out a theme for the display; it may be a formation of three or four identical aircraft or it may be World War 1 types in mock attack, and work it up to a coherent and complete display. Try to incorporate the style of flying that will show the model off in the best way − a 'Stuka' will look no good at all trying to perform aerobatics at a high altitude; it must be carrying out a series of screaming dives at a ground target. Use ground 'props' to help you put on a more convincing show. Pyrotechnics will always enliven any demonstration and, perhaps most important of all, keep the public well informed with a first-rate commentary.

5. COMMERCIAL APPLICATIONS

It is not every modeller who wishes to make capital gain from his chosen hobby − or has the opportunity. I count myself most fortunate to have been in the position of augmenting my income by producing R/C model kits and plans, filming and writing about the subject in magazines and books. Far from making me disenchanted with my hobby, it has enhanced it and the challenges have added a greater dimension to my interests. Opportunities

to use R/C model aircraft for film and television work do not occur too regularly but you should not underestimate the potential in this field. If you do happen to have contacts with TV or film makers it will certainly do no harm to explain to them what R/C model aircraft are all about − you will find most of them ignorant of the advancements made over the years. Organise a demonstration of flying, prepare thoroughly, or make a video film for them to view.

Practically all of the firms advertising in the model magazines, trade and retail, were started by modellers − I cannot think of any that were started purely as a business venture by financiers. There *are* commercial openings in the modelling field providing you can produce what the modeller wants and sell it at a competitive price. Do not expect to make a fortune − very few have − but you may be able to make a living by doing something that interests you.

6. RECORD BREAKING

Even at club level breaking radio control records for height, duration, speed etc. can help to keep interest and development active in the hobby. National records, too, are always there for the breaking and you have just as much chance as the next person of obtaining a record − it is a matter of application. World records, however, are a different proposition. To equal or better most of these you must not only have a suitable aeroplane and pilot but may also require highly sophisticated radar tracking gear, or electronic timing devices, or even more daylight hours in the day than we can ever get in Great Britain.

7. COMPETITIONS

Competitions, in all forms, are essential for the betterment of any hobby or sport. It is only through competition, and the competitor insisting on the finest equipment, the most advanced models, the highest standard of engines etc., that all of these items improve. You will find that many manufacturers of radio equipment take part in competitions and this is always a healthy sign − if they want to win they have got to keep their equipment to the highest standards, and, with these improvements incorporated in their commercial equipment, you, the purchaser, benefit.

Never be scared of entering competitions, whether they are 'fun' competitions at the local flying field or more serious competitions. Don't take the attitude of 'they're all better than me and I don't stand a chance'. All of the competitors had to enter *their* first competition and it is only by taking part that you will improve. One word of warning — if you are a bad loser don't enter at all. There is a risk in most competitions of crashing a model, possibly not through your own fault, and if you can't take it you should not be in the competition at all.

For many of your chosen interests there will be specialist associations if not governing those aspects, at least there to organise competitions, meetings and events. They are there to help you, become a member and you will have access to like-minded modellers and the experience they have gained over the years.

There are also associations for general aeromodelling activities, including our governing body,

the British Model Flying Association. The Model Pilots Association also offers membership with full insurance, joining gifts, special deals on Nexus Plans and numerous other special offers. They have flying sites available for MPA members, organise visits to places of aeromodelling interest and supervise a residential MPA modelling week at each end of the flying season where modellers can go, with their families (they are at seaside leisure camps) and have instruction in building and flying.

A list of the various associations is given in the Appendix.

It may be that, through radio control flying, you may become interested in full-size flying — many modellers do. This, I always feel, is a tribute to radio control modelling and in many ways it is in the natural progression of things. Perhaps you may also go on to build your own full-size light aircraft, very much a case of constructing a very large model. This is also a logical step. Full-size aircraft pilots, though, seldom lose their interest

in radio control models and usually manage to combine both hobbies.

At all times, on the flying field and off, try to act as a good ambassador for our hobby. When someone complains that your flying disturbs them, whether it is a legitimate complaint or not, be diplomatic and try to see the other person's point of view. We do participate in a hobby that *can* give annoyance to other people and the last thing we want is to have any official action taken that will restrict our pursuance of it.

Finally, should you be lucky enough to get as much enjoyment and satisfaction from the hobby as I think you will, pass your enthusiasm on to other people. This can be followed up, when you are proficient, by helping the newcomer to overcome the first obstacles of radio control model building and flying. Think back occasionally to your own early days in radio control and remember the trials, frustrations and the times when you seriously doubted if you would ever be able to fly a model. With this in mind you will be more able to assist the 'new boy' in passing those first hurdles and going on to the richer rewards.

Useful Addresses

British Association of Radio Control Soarers
(BARCS)
c/o 51 Crutchfield Lane,
Walton-on-Thames,
Surrey KT12 2QY

British Electric Flight Association
c/o 1 Linwood Avenue,
Tolsburg, Middlesbrough,
Cleveland TS5 7RD

British Miniature Pylon Racing Association
(BMPRA)
c/o 6 Ullerwater Drive,
Spring Meadows, Gamston,
Nottingham.

British Model Flying Association (BMFA)
Chacksfield House,
31 St Andrews Road,
Leicester LE2 8RE

British Radio Control Helicopter Association
(BRCHA)
c/o 7 Kiln Way, Badger Drive,
Grays, Essex RM17 5JE

British Waterplane Association (BWA)
c/o The Hollies,
48 New Street, Kenilworth,
Warwickshire CV8 2EZ

Civil Aviation Authority (CAA)
General Aviation Section,
Aviation House, South Area,
Gatwick Airport, Gatwick,
West Sussex RH6 0YR

Club Twenty Association (CTA)
c/o 9 Shelley Gardens, Hinckley,
Leics LE10 1TA

Great Britain Radio Control Aerobatic
Association (GBRCA)
c/o 84 Hollymoor Road,
Hollymoorside, Chesterfield,
S42 7DX

Large Model Association
c/o 59 Ashdale Crescent,
Chapel House Estate,
Newcastle-upon-Tyne NE5 1AX

Model Pilots Association (MPA)
Nexus House, Boundary Way,
Hemel Hempstead,
Herts HP2 7ST

Northern Ireland Association of Aeromodellers
c/o 28 Colston Avenue, Holywood,
Co. Down, N. Ireland

Scottish Association of Aeromodellers
c/o 2 Forth Avenue, Kirkaldy,
Scotland KY2 5PN

Society of Antique Modellers (SAM35)
c/o 9 Queens Road, Wellington,
Somerset TA21 9AW

Sport Forty Association
c/o 82 Hermitage Road, St Johns,
Woking, Surrey
GU21 1TQ

Here's the route to successful model flying

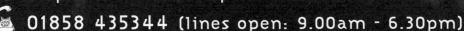